ADVANCES IN SPORTS AND ATHLETICS

VOLUME 1

ADVANCES IN SPORTS AND ATHLETICS

Additional books in this series can be found on Nova's website
under the Series tab.

Additional E-books in this series can be found on Nova's website
under the E-books tab.

ADVANCES IN SPORTS AND ATHLETICS

VOLUME 1

JAMES P. WALDORF
EDITOR

Nova Science Publishers, Inc.
New York

NOTICE TO THE READER

Library of Congress Cataloging-in-Publication Data

ISSN: 2158-0332

ISBN: 978-1-61122-824-3

Published by Nova Science Publishers, Inc. † New York

CONTENTS

PREFACE

This volume gathers important research from around the globe in the field of study including sport marketing; risk management strategies; fantasy sport participation; motivational profiles of sports fans; student-athletes' perceptions of homosexuality and identification with multiple sporting teams

Article 1- The prominence and popularity of American sporting events, encourages an examination of levels of safety. Because of their potential impact on the US economy and culture, American sporting event venues may be considered attractive targets of attack for several reasons. First, the large numbers of people attending sports contests provide potential foes with not only the potential of massive casualties but also increased media exposure. For example, Saturday afternoons during the fall season in the United States, are typified by large gatherings of people, some exceeding 100,000, attending intercollegiate football games. Because an enemy's choice of targets may include the high probability of mass casualties and infliction of economic loss, these factors may be considered rewards for an attack. Thus, an assault on a major sporting event such as an intercollegiate college football game could produce what a terrorist may seek: mass casualties and economic harm.

A second reason for concern of a terrorist attack at an athletic event is that sports venues are categorized as "soft targets". Soft targets are susceptible locations that are not well-protected, offer relatively easy access, great numbers of individuals who continually enter and exit a stadium or arena during a contest and the relative congestion that exists of those spectators in the facility. A third reason relates to previous incidents in which large numbers of individuals have previously been attacked by terrorists in the United States prior to September 11, 2001. An explosive device was detonated under New

York's World Trade Center in 1993, causing over $500 million in structural damage, killing six people and injuring more than 1000. Two years later, the Murrah Federal Office Building terrorist bomb blast occurred in Oklahoma City that ultimately took 168 lives, including 19 children. For all these reasons, it should come as no surprise that terrorists have shown a desire to attack major sporting events such as the Super Bowl or World Series.

Article 2- Negligent marketing assumes that promoters should not engage in strategies that increase the risk that patrons may injure either themselves or others.

Marketing campaigns portraying a product being consumed in a negligent manner that leads to the development of an unsafe environment may put the service provider at risk. If a defendant can establish the marketing campaign influenced how the product was consumed, service providers could be found liable. Sport organizations allowing companies to deliver such marketing campaigns or that are associated with products that promote dangerous or reckless behavior may also be liable. Sport organizations should be careful not to create the impression that negligent consumption of a product is part of a consumers experience. Sport marketers must evaluate situations to identify potentially dangerous actions or behaviors.

On a crisp autumn afternoon, Christine Bearman and her husband caUSlly strolled through the parking lot towards their car. Following an afternoon of college football, the Bearmans decided to leave the event a little early to avoid possible traffic delays on the way home. As the Bearmans made their way through the Notre Dame parking lot, an intoxicated "tailgater" knocked Christina to the ground. Ms Bearman suffered a broken leg in the incident and required medical attention. No security or event management staff was in the vicinity when the incident occurred.

Article 3- This project examined fantasy sport participation among the college student population and compared it to previously completed work. Specifically, 155 college students were surveyed from a large midwestern university. The study supports most college student fantasy participants are male and nearly a third of these males participated in paid leagues. Interestingly, most respondents (73.3%) indicated they felt fantasy participation was not gambling. The investigation also revealed 29.9% of students generally read more and 23.5% watched more about a sport when they participate in fantasy leagues. In addition, 77.6% felt the success of their fantasy team did not determine how much they watch sports and another 91.8% of respondents declared the elimination of their fantasy team from playoffs or postseason competition failed to eliminate their desire to watch sports. Similar to other studies, NFL, MLB, and NBA leagues, in that order, emerged as the most popular fantasy leagues. Finally, this study's college student fantasy league participants come from various backgrounds. For example, many different academic backgrounds/majors were present in the sample population and nearly 91% of fantasy players played high school level athletics or higher.

Article 4- This paper discusses student-athletes compensation issues. The author expresses his concern over the unwillingness of the National Collegiate Athletic Association (NCAA) to fairly compensate these athletes. Since the main concerns according to the N.C.A.A. over such a system are workman's compensation and academic reform the authors will look into both of those issues as well. A historical perspective will be applied to these issues. The authors will look into the possibility of some of the main athletic conferences breaking away from the N.C.A.A. and starting a new classification of student-athlete. The advantages and disadvantages of such a move will be looked at as well. The leadership structures of both higher education and the N.C.A.A. will be discussed.

Article 5- While a number of studies have examined motives sport fans have for attending different sports, few have examined motives for attending different levels of the same sport. The present study was designed to examine motives for attending five different levels of baseball games—T-Ball, Little League, High School, College, and Minor League. Participants were 224 adult fans who attended a game at one of the five levels. They completed measures of sport fandom, team identification, and motivation for attending the game. Different motivational patterns were evident among the different levels. Implications for the findings are discussed.

Article 6- The push for student-athletes to graduate college has never been greater. Student-athletes are under more pressure to not only complete their degree but, to do it in a timely manner under NCAA guidelines. The intent of this study was to determine if men's football and men's basketball coaches at the university or college level utilize an assessment instrument when recruiting and evaluating potential student-athletes. Specifically studied through interviews were the characteristics that these coaches look for in successful and unsuccessful student-athletes, how they currently collect information during the recruitment period and whether collecting data on student-athletes is of importance or not. The population for this study consisted of current Division IA men's football and men's basketball coaches in the Big 12 Conference. The study helps to define through research and development an assessment instrument to more effectively define the needs of student-athletes prior to entering universities.

Article 7- Alternative dispute resolution (ADR) is an integral part of the sport industry. It allows leagues, teams, and players to resolve disputes that arise without using litigation. It is essential for people who work within sports to understand the value of ADR. The purpose of this article is to provide an extensive overview of ADR as it relates to sport. This article takes a conceptual approach in addressing the many aspects of ADR. The two major applications of ADR, arbitration and mediation, are discussed, with a focus towards arbitration. In order to properly utilize ADR one must understand the relevant statutes and cases. Therefore, federal and international laws, along with cases that define ADR are discussed. Additionally, this article will examine the benefits of ADR, what distinguishes mediation from arbitration, the arbitration process, how ADR is applied to amateur sports, how the Olympics and international sport community employ ADR, how US professional sports utilize ADR, and how new emerging hybrid forms of ADR are applied to sport-related disputes. In order to illustrate these concepts, recent sport examples are presented.

Article 8- NCAA certification guidelines now stipulate that member institutions must have policies, support opportunities, and educational programs in place to ensure a safe environment for student-athletes with diverse sexual orientations. This research measures student-athletes' general level of homophobia. The results indicate that student-athletes are comfortable with other people being gay or lesbian, but they would not be comfortable if they found themselves attracted to someone of the same-sex, or if someone of the same sex was attracted to them. If coaches and athletic administrators are aware of how student-athletes perceive sexual orientation, they can be more intentional in choosing educational programming to meet specific needs of each team.

Article 9- Psychophysiology is the study of psychological processes through the measurement and interpretation of physiological responses. The realisation of the relationship between the so-called "mind" and "body" has encouraged the application of psychophysiology in various areas of psychology, including sport psychology. Unfortunately, methodological problems have limited the application of psychophysiological techniques to the study of sport. The gross body movements in most sports cause considerable degradation in the quality of the physiological recordings. The obtrusiveness of the electrode attachments and the wiring of the electrodes to a data acquisition system can also severely impede the athlete's mobility and performance. It is perhaps not surprising that most psychophysiological research has been concerned with sports that involve minimal movements, such as pistol shooting. However, a range of new technological advances are giving encouragement for future applications of psychophysiological methodology in sport.

Article 10- The current study examined the identification with multiple sport teams by sport fans, as a potential means to maintain these positive benefits of identification by switching identification to another sports team. Sport fans were predicted to report following fewer teams closely compared to moderately, and fewer teams moderately compared to casually. Additionally, sport fans were predicted to be higher identified with teams they followed closely compared to those teams moderately followed, and more identified with moderately followed teams compared to teams they followed casually. The first hypothesis was not supported, as participants reported following more teams closely compared to moderately and casually. The second hypothesis was supported, as participants reported being more identified with the teams they closely follow compared to the moderately and casually followed teams. Implications of these findings for sport researchers and sport marketers are discussed.

Article 11- The purposes of this study were to (a) explore motives of international student-athletes who come to the United States to participate in intercollegiate athletics, and (b) examine differences in motives of international student-athletes based on selected socio-demographic attributes (e.g., gender, types of scholarship received, types of sports participation and region of the world). An exploratory factor analysis revealed four motivation factors: intercollegiate athletics attractiveness, school attractiveness, desire for independency, and environmental attractiveness. Data analysis indicated differences in motivation factors based on types of sports participation and region of the world. The study will help coaches and athletic administrators understand international student-athletes' motivational factors, which play a critical role in recruiting these international student-athletes. Knowing why an international student-athlete wants to participate in intercollegiate athletics in the United States will aid coaches in developing specific recruiting plans to attract these athletes. This information will also assist coaches in satisfying those needs once the student-athlete is competing in intercollegiate athletics.

Article 12- Intercollegiate athletics is recognized as a dynamic industry that places high demands on the time and energy of personnel regardless of the competitive division or size of the institution. Personal sacrifices in time and energy for the sake of the program are equated with contributing to high levels of work-life conflict. The purpose of this study was to analyze the perceptions towards work and life conflict among senior woman administrators and athletic directors at NCAA Division I, II, and III institutions regarding the work-life climate within the athletic department and the existence of workplace benefits offered at their institution. The impact of the presence of children on the perception of work-life climate within the athletic department was also examined. There were significant differences noted in the availability of benefits between DI and DII / DIII, but no significant differences in the perceptions of availability of benefits between ADs and SWAs.

Article 13- Interpersonal power involves the extent to which an individual has the ability to influence or change the attitudes and behaviors of others. French and Raven (1959) suggested that there were five common forms of interpersonal power: reward, coercive, referent, legitimate, and expert. The current investigation examined the extent to which teammates possess differential levels of these five power bases. Based on the theoretical framework offered by Whetten and Cameron (1984), it was hypothesized that players occupying positions that were central, critical, flexible, visible, and relevant would be perceived as possessing greater levels of power than teammates playing positions that lacked these characteristics. To test this prediction, college intramural flag football players were asked to rate the power possessed by their team's best quarterback (a highly central, critical, flexible, visible, and relevant position) and best offensive lineman. The data indicated that the quarterbacks were viewed as possessing greater amounts of reward, expert, and legitimate power. Quarterbacks and offensive linemen were not perceived as possessing differential levels of coercive and referent power.

Versions of these chapters were also published in *Journal of Contemporary Athletics,* Volume 3, Numbers 1-4, Volume 4, published by Nova Science Publishers, Inc. They were submitted for appropriate modifications in an effort to encourage wider dissemination of research.

In: Advances in Sports and Athletics, Volume 1   ISBN: 978-1-61122-824-3
Editor: James P. Waldorf   ©2012 Nova Science Publishers, Inc.

RISK MANAGEMENT STRATEGIES AT DIVISION I INTERCOLLEGIATE FOOTBALL STADIUMS: DO SPECTATORS PERCEIVE THEY ARE PROTECTED AGAINST TERRORISM?

John Miller, Andy Gillentine and Frank Veltri

The prominence and popularity of American sporting events, encourages an examination of levels of safety. Because of their potential impact on the US economy and culture, American sporting event venues may be considered attractive targets of attack for several reasons. First, the large numbers of people attending sports contests provide potential foes with not only the potential of massive casualties but also increased media exposure (Wade, 2000). For example, Saturday afternoons during the fall season in the United States, are typified by large gatherings of people, some exceeding 100,000, attending intercollegiate football games. Because an enemy's choice of targets may include the high probability of mass casualties and infliction of economic loss, these factors may be considered rewards for an attack (Schneider, 2002). Thus, an assault on a major sporting event such as an intercollegiate college football game could produce what a terrorist may seek: mass casualties and economic harm.

A second reason for concern of a terrorist attack at an athletic event is that sports venues are categorized as "soft targets" (Levitin, 1998). Soft targets are susceptible locations that are not well-protected, offer relatively easy access, great numbers of individuals who continually enter and exit a stadium or arena during a contest and the relative congestion that exists of those spectators in the facility (Clonan, 2002; Picarello, 2005). A third reason relates to previous incidents in which large numbers of individuals have previously been attacked by terrorists in the United States prior to September 11, 2001. An explosive device was detonated under New York's World Trade Center in 1993, causing over $500 million in structural damage, killing six people and injuring more than 1000 (Fischbach, 2001). Two years later, the Murrah Federal Office Building terrorist bomb blast occurred in Oklahoma City that ultimately took 168 lives, including 19 children (Rosenblatt, 2000). For all these reasons, it should come as no surprise that terrorists have shown a desire to attack major sporting events such as the Super Bowl or World Series (Fallon, 2003).

FORESEEABILITY

The potential for a terrorist assault at a sporting event is an issue for the foreseeable future (Hurst, Zoubek, and Pratsinakis, 2002). Thus, it is becoming more foreseeable that even in a free democracy the best available security may not impede a terrorist assault. Bethune (2002) summed up this concept by stating:

> Today's reasonable man is not the same man he was before September, 11th.
> What the public - the community that is the reasonable man - considers foreseeable with respect to terrorism and what it regards as reasonable steps to prevent terrorist attacks have been fundamentally altered (p. 24).

The foreseeable danger of terrorism conveys potential implications for those who own or operate sport stadiums. Previous court rulings have stated that a facility manager has a duty to act on threats of violence as if they had actually occurred (*Bishop v. Fair Lanes*, 1986). According to *Isaacs* v. *Huntington Memorial Hospital* (1985), "… authorities who know of threats of violence that they believe are well-founded may not refrain from taking reasonable preventive measures simply because violence has yet to occur" (pp. 125-126).

Foreseeability may be regarded as the most significant consideration in determining the extent to which a person is owed a duty of reasonable care (Dobbs, 2000). Reasonable security measures are viewed in light of any specific warnings given to the venue indicating that an attack was foreseeable. To assist in alerting potentially foreseeable terrorist actions, the Department of Homeland Security has enacted a multi-level color-coding ranking system that identifies potential security threats to the public. The five levels and their accompanying colors are: low (green); guarded (blue); elevated (yellow); high (orange); and severe (red). Each level and color identifies the potential threat of an attack and a set of recommended procedures for federal departments and agencies (Homeland Security Advisory System, 2004). If a risk is perceived to be high or severe, an attack may be extremely foreseeable during that time (Barkett, 2003).

Concept of Risk

To understand how to manage it, the concept of risk must be addressed. Some have recognized risk as the potential harm of valuable items resulting from an individual's actions (Kates and Kasperson, 1983). Slovic and Peters (2006) delineated risk into two categories: risk as feelings and risk as analysis. Risk as feelings relates to a person's innate reaction to a harmful situation. Risk as analysis incorporates items such as logic, reason, and scientific forethought to determine how to handle a dangerous situation. Klinke and Renn (2002) referred to risk as:

> ... the experience of something that people fear or regard as negative. It is also clear that this fear is extended to an event or situation that has not yet occurred but could occur in the future (p. 1076).

Moreover, risk can include such items as uncertainty, catastrophic potential, and controllability (Slovic, 2000). Certainly the catastrophic potential of a terrorist assault may be perceived as immeasurable in regards to loss of life and economic considerations. This immeasurability strongly relates to the concept uncertainty (Nohria and Stewart, 2006). It is through uncertainty that fear arises (Lerner, Gonzalez, Small, and Fischhoff, 2003; Lerner, and Keltner, 2000). To the extent that an attack is thought to be unique or isolated, the immediate impact may be limited and fleeting (Liesch, Steen, Knight, and Czinkota, 2006). This may result in uncertainty and accompanying fear to be contained at a lesser level. If on the other hand, attacks are perceived by fans to be directed to more vulnerable or 'soft targets' such as the sport stadium, the more insidious the uncertainty would be thereby increasing the level of fear among the people (Ip, 2004).

Risk Management Components

While intercollegiate stadiums have not been victimized by a terrorist attack, other researchers have indicated that the potential for one exists (Baker and Connaughton, 2005; Miller, Veltri, and Phillips, 2007). Moreover, previous research has indicated that security personnel seldom possess sufficient anti-terrorist training (Goss, Jubenville, and MacBeth, 2003). Because sport events generally have large numbers of individuals in a heightened state of excitement continually moving in, out and throughout a facility that is hard to supervise it is imperative that organizations are adequately prepared for emergencies. According to Decker (2001), the most accepted approach that can guide an organization's effort in preparing against attacks is through the appropriate development and enforcement of risk management policies.

Risk management is concerned with addressing potential, foreseeable risks that are tied to the prospect of injury or loss through a blend of several distinct approaches such as threat, vulnerability, and criticality assessments. A threat assessment may be used as a decision support tool to assist in creating and prioritizing security-program requirements, planning, and resource allocations (Decker, 2001). When an organization embarks on a threat assessment effort, it is primarily searching for potential sources of concern and determine its' credibility.

Since not every threat might be identified or threat information may be incomplete, vulnerability assessments are essential to better prepare against threats. A vulnerability assessment estimates the susceptibility of a potential attack by those desiring to create physical or psychological harm to an organization's infrastructure, including employees or patrons (Hall, 2004). Thus, a vulnerability assessment assists in the identification of weaknesses that may be exploited and suggests options to eliminate or address those weaknesses (Decker, 2001).

The third component of managing risks is determining which assets, structures, or functions are the most critical to protect. Identifying the criticality of these items provides the sport facility manager to better direction of resources to areas of highest priorities (Decker, 2001). Once the priorities have been developed the risk event manager would be able to identify potential targets and implement appropriate risk management measures.

Public Inclusion in Risk Management

Because the word "risk" has many connotations, problems in communications exist. Despite this confusion, probabilities and outcomes of adverse occurrences have usually been thought of as being quantifiable through the assessments of risk management. However, the social science analysis does not accept this concept by arguing that the objectivity of potential outcomes is lacking or false (Slovic and Weber, 2002).

According to Slovic and Weber (2002) it is the perceptions of both public and officials that have played a significant role in the ability of Americans to prepare and deal with the threat of terrorism. A key issue in deciding the most effective course to follow in managing a risk is the contribution of the public in delineating appropriate levels of risk and safety (Slovic and Peters, 2006). In theory, since it is the individuals who are most affected by a foreseeable harm, they should be allowed to participate with an organization in determining levels of acceptable safety (Webler, 1999). Slovic (2000) revealed that as the societies in industrialized countries have attempted to make lives healthier and safer, more people have become more concerned about risks. Slovic goes on to state that early investigations about risk perception exhibited the public apprehensions could not merely be placed on ignorance or irrationality. More precisely, people are now viewing themselves as being exposed to more severe risks than ever before and that the state of affairs in regards to facing significant risks is increasing.

PURPOSE OF THE STUDY

An important aspect for risk management research is to provide policy-makers with the information that they need to identify potential threats, determine vulnerabilities, and prioritize critical aspects to aid in the development and implementation of innovative risk management strategies through the insights of the general public (Slovic, 1987; Slovic and Weber, 2002). While previous reports have addressed risk management issues in intercollegiate sports (Fried and Metchick, 2005; Gillentine and Miller, 2006; Miller and Gillentine, 2006), research regarding risk management strategies of NCAA Division I affiliated universities from the general public, specifically, event spectator's viewpoint are non-existent. This investigation attempted to determine whether spectators attending games at selected NCAA Division I football stadiums perceived that risk management procedures were being effectively implemented to protect them against a terrorist-related attack.

METHOD

Instrument

The authors for this investigation developed a 1-5 Likert scale 20-item questionnaire. The Likert scale responses ranged from 1=strongly agree, 2=agree, 3=unsure, 4=disagree, and 5=strongly disagree. The questionnaire consisted of sections relating to the following areas: demographic information, overall perceptions of security at intercollegiate football games from previous experience, perceptions of security practices at intercollegiate football games, and perceptions of security personnel at intercollegiate football games.

In order to ensure the reliability of the questionnaire, a test-retest protocol was conducted with two present and three former sport event managers. Several changes regarding item inclusion and item wording were suggested and implemented on the questionnaire. The re-test was accomplished two weeks later with the same group of professionals and no additional modifications were recommended. To determine the validity of the instrument, a Pearson product-moment correlation coefficient (Pearson's r) was employed. The reliability coefficient was determined to be .82, which is well within the acceptable range for the interpretation of scores for individuals (Patten, 2000).

To ensure consistency, each investigator and their teams distributed the surveys at two pre-selected intercollegiate home football games at each institution. The investigative teams were made up of 3-4 sport management graduate students from each institution in addition to the authors. Since the questionnaires were distributed at multiple games, each investigative team member was instructed to ask each potential respondent if they had previously filled it out. While somewhat rudimentary, this process was utilized to prevent duplication of respondents. Confidentiality was assured in a short written statement given to the potential respondent as well as a verbal promise given by the respective team member.

A total of 1102 surveys were returned to the respective investigative teams, of this total 1048 surveys were deemed USble for the study. Reasons for not using a survey included incomplete answers, inappropriate responses, indecipherable responses and non-attendance to an intercollegiate football contest at the selected site prior to September 11, 2001. Indecipherable answers occurred when the respondent circled the response so that it appeared to have included two different answers (e.g. the answer could have been agree or unsure). Rather than selecting what potentially could have been an incorrect response, the survey was discarded even if only one such response existed on the instrument. Additionally, due to the nature of the study if a respondent had not attended an intercollegiate football game prior to September 11, 2001 the survey was discarded.

RESULTS

Demographics

The first part of the survey asked the respondents to indicate demographic information such as gender, age, and number of intercollegiate football games previously attended in the past two years. The results indicated that 629 (60%) were males and 418 (40%) were females. In descending order 409 (39%) were between 26-33 years of age, 325 (31%) were between the ages of 34-42, 199 (19%) were 18-25 years old, and 115 (11%) were over 42 years old. The respondents were asked how many intercollegiate football games they have averaged attending over the previous 2 years. The results revealed that 587 (56%) attended 4-5 home football contests, 398 (38%) were present at 2-3 games while 63 (6%) attended either 1 or no games in the previous years.

Since all of the respondents had attended games prior to September 11, 2001 they were asked to indicate their perceived level of safety while attending an intercollegiate football game within a year after the attacks as well as four years later. Whereas 817 (78%) believed that they were safe attending games from 2001-2002, 964 (92%) revealed they felt safe four years after the attacks. When asked whether they thought that an attack on a football stadium could occur, 985 (94%) felt that such an incidence was now improbable. However, 1027 (98%) believed that should an attack occur, a significantly negative and catastrophic impact would be felt.

Threat, Vulnerability, and Criticality Assessments

Seven hundred and sixty (69%) perceived that multiple targets, which may have been considered an additional threat for an attack, were present in the community. When asked about potential vulnerabilities 796 (76%) felt that security systems were given priority and attention to detail before, during, and after an intercollegiate football game. However, 629 (60%) agreed that avenues of ingress and egress to/from the facility were given significant attention prior to, during and after a contest. When asked if the distance from the facility to the parking lots are given significant attention prior to, during and after a contest, 597 (57%) agreed that enough attention was given to this potential vulnerability. Seven hundred and eighty-six (75%) agreed that intercollegiate football stadiums might be considered targets of symbolic significance. Finally, 639 (61%) agreed that intercollegiate sporting events were considered critical functions within their community.

Perceptions of Risk Management Practices

Over a period of time, risk management plan enforcement may become less stringent (Alston, 2003). The results of the survey supported this contention as 534 (51%) respondents agreed that risk management procedures were overly apparent at intercollegiate football games which may be the result of 943 (90%) had observed security presence either in the stadium or in areas immediately outside the stadium. However, 573 (52%) perceived that the enforcement of risk management procedures had become more lax since 9/11. Thus, it would appear that although safety personnel are present on the premises the enforcement of risk procedures were not stringent. Interestingly, 566 (54%) indicated that they would be willing to pay more for increased safety at sporting events.

Respondents were asked to identify their perception of the adequacy of risk management practices that were communicated through signage or verbal announcements. Four hundred and nineteen (40%) believed that risk management procedures had been adequately communicated through signage or announcements at intercollegiate football games previously attended.

DISCUSSION

The findings of this survey revealed a significant number of sports fans felt safer attending contests now than they did more immediately after the attacks of September 11th. However, American sporting events are subject to the real and present threat of a terrorist attack and must remain at a heightened state of alert. This is substantiated by a recent report in which the Department of Homeland Security (DHS) identified a dozen possible strikes it viewed most devastating, including a truck bombing of a sports arena (Lipton, 2005).

Since a sports venue operator has a legal duty to warn the invitees about reasonably foreseeable and credible threats (Dobbs, 2000; Mallen, 2001), it is disturbing that less than half of the respondents revealed that risk management practices through communication and announcements procedures had been followed. If a credible or foreseeable threat exists on a premises and it cannot be corrected an invitee must be warned of such a threat so they may avoid it (Montgomery and Nahrstadt, 2004). Signage and verbal communications can be used, in dire circumstances, for directional purposes. For example, identification of the most expeditious exit routes as well as manner of conduct can be explained by signage and verbal communication. This may result in not only minimizing confusion but also potential injuries among the spectators.

The results also indicated that while the probability of an attack was unlikely, the impact would likely be catastrophic. Risks may be regarded as the chance of something happening that will have a negative impact upon organizational objectives. These risks can be measured in terms of probability and impact. The amount of risk is produced by its impact (e.g., low, medium, high) and the probability of occurrence (e.g. never, sometime, and often). In the event that the risk producing harmful incidents is considered improbable, it may be perceived that the management of risks would be relatively unimportant. However, if the risks were considered severe enough in producing events that could negatively impact the organization, the ability to manage such a risk would be important.

Over half of the respondents perceived that risk management procedures had become more lax in the past five years. This may relate to the theory of the threshold of effective zerohood (Rescher, 1983), often referred to as the theory of probability which states that once the probability of an incident becomes small enough, the potential of the incident occurring may be viewed as outside the range of appropriate concern. In other words, if it hasn't ever occurred or hasn't happened in a long time the probability of it occurring may be negligible. Since no intercollegiate football stadiums have ever been attacked the perceived likelihood of an attack occurring is construed as zero. This could lead the event sport manager, the organization and potentially spectators to fall into the risk of complacency. After the first attack on the World Trade Center and the Oklahoma City bombing but prior to the 9/11 attacks, Gips (2000) warned:

While the World Trade Center and Oklahoma City bombings may be gradually receding into the collective subconscious, leading the public to become complacent, more recent events indicate that the terrorism threat remains and is a stark reminder that the physical protection of America's signature properties continues to be a critical issue. (p. 1)

If the probability of an incident occurring is considered to be close to zero, the perception may very well be to set aside the need for the assessment and management of risk. However, the assessment of whether a situation is considered a risk and the resulting management of those actions depend on the perception of the risk (Lyytinen, Mathiassen, and Ropponen, 1998). If the analysis of the impact were the primary concern, the scope of the risk would increase. In other words if the organization can foresee the realization of a threat occurring as well as negative impact that an attack could create, the level of the management of risks would be elevated. As such, when a plausible danger is multiplied by the potentially harmful impact, the level of risk increases (credible threat x potential negative impact = level of risk increases). If an organization possessed credible information indicating that an attack was foreseeable such as a red alert from the Department of Homeland Security, but did not respond to respond suitably, they may have breached their reasonable duty of care (Picarello, 2005).

Although all of the areas that could injure a spectator cannot be totally eliminated, they can be managed with the appropriate amount of attention, monitoring and intervention. A goal of risk management is to enable individuals and organizations to isolate risks and to recognize potential mitigation options. An acceptable method for alleviating possible risks is through the vigilant application of threat, vulnerability, and criticality assessment procedures and the resulting enforcement of risk management procedures.

A threat assessment allows the organization to recognize potentially foreseeable hazards and compare the probability of an injurious situation occurring (Alston, 2003). As such, threats are examined on the basis of the likelihood of occurrence relating to the impact of the threat. The results indicated that almost 70% of the respondents perceived that multiple targets, which may also be considered as a target for an attack, existed in the community. Although one of the locations where a survey was conducted was in a major metropolitan area, the other two schools were situated in much smaller markets. This may indicate that universities that support Division IA football may have additional attractions for an attack regardless of city size.

The information gleaned from a vulnerability assessment plan allows sport facility managers to decide which option would be most appropriate and act to either eliminate or minimize the risk. Among potential areas of weakness include closed-circuit security systems, avenues of entrance and exit, and potential distance of vehicles from the stadium. A prior investigation reported that avenues of ingress and egress to/from intercollegiate football stadiums as well as security systems were given sufficient attention prior to, during and after a contest (Miller, Veltri, and Phillips, 2007). This investigation supports that finding as a majority of the respondents in this study believed that these avenues were satisfactorily addressed by the organization. It is important that organizations provide detailed attention to this area as the lack of this risk management protocol could expose the organization to potential vulnerabilities as avenues of ingress and egress, or the distance from parking lots to important buildings as being so close that a car bomb detonation would damage or destroy the buildings and the people working in them (Decker, 2001).

The criticality assessment permits the organization decision-makers to prioritize the assets. Previous research has indicated that event managers of large intercollegiate football stadiums believe that the stadiums are considered to be of symbolic significance and intercollegiate sporting events are considered as critical functions within their community (Miller, Veltri, and Phillips, 2007). The results of this study supported that contention as three-quarters of the respondents in this investigation believed that intercollegiate football stadiums might be considered targets of symbolic significance and over half perceived intercollegiate contests as being critical functions within their community. Should organizational decision-makers overlook the perceived importance of the contests, lack risk awareness or simply ignore the need to develop, implement and enforce safeguards, it may be only a matter of time before an incident occurs (Alston, 2003).

Research Limitations

As with any research study, limitations exist. First, it can only be assumed that the subjects responded in a truthful and honest manner. Second, these findings may not be generalized to the greater population of NCAA Division I athletic departments that sponsor intercollegiate football. However, the information from this investigation should only be construed as the "tip of the iceberg". This will be addressed in the next section.

Future Research

Future investigations could be conducted regarding spectator perceptions of risk management procedures attending NCAA Division I intercollegiate football games at the majority of universities and colleges in the United States. Secondly, an investigation dealing with the university/college athletic department's familiarity and understanding of current risk assessment procedures as recommended by State and Federal agencies could be examined. Finally, future studies could be conducted to determine how university/college athletic departments develop, implement and assess event risk management policies and procedures.

CONCLUSION

Risk does not exist in a nebula as an autonomous aspect, waiting to be measured. While it is impossible to predict exactly where the next terrorist attack may occur, this study indicates that intercollegiate football venues appear to be managing potential risks well as perceived by the spectators attending. To further assist in preventing, limiting, detecting and responding to potential risks, the public should be involved in the risk management process. It has been reported that as efforts to make life safer have been developed, a large percentage of the general public has become increasingly concerned about risks (Slovic, 2002b). With this knowledge, innovative viewpoints and approaches to influence public perceptions may be required to manage risks efficiently by the sport venue operators.

Early investigations indicated that the public's perception of risk and subsequent concern cannot simply be blamed on ignorance or irrationality (Covello, Flamm, Rodricks, and Tardiff, 1983). However, recent reports have indicated that public perceptions of risk have been important in assisting the establishment of priorities and legislative agendas of regulatory bodies such as the Environmental Protection Agency (Slovic, 2002a). The involvement of more people recognizing and reporting potentially harmful situations or events increase the knowledge base about potential areas of concern. This in turn may create an opportunity for the decision-maker to gain greater amounts of insights and knowledge to efficiently apply or implement the best possible solutions to the problem area.

To meet these goals the effective development, implementation and enforcement of a risk management program should be foremost in the minds of sport event managers. Loewenstein, Weber, Hsee, and Welch (2001) have stated that the perceptions of risks are as much driven by affective processes as reasoned-based quantifiable processes. This is an important concept for sport facility managers to embrace. For example, while quantifiable assessments are important in some decision-making situations, relying on the affective process is often quicker and more efficient method of addressing potential risks (Slovic and Peters, 2006). If a sport facility manager can promote a risk management program to spectators attending intercollegiate football games to develop an attitude of taking a conscious approach to assessing potential threats and vulnerabilities and relaying them to the appropriate authority, the potential for creating a reasonably safe environment may increase significantly. This inclusionary process can then help move risk management from the domain of the accidental to the domain of the proactive.

REFERENCES

Alston, G. (2003). *How safe is safe enough?* Burlington, VT: Ashgate Publishing. Baker, T.A. and Connaughton, D.P. (2005). Terrorism: A foreseeable threat to US sport facility owners and operators. *Journal of Contemporary Athletics, 1*(2), 109-124.

Barkett, J. M. (2003). If terror reigns, will torts follow? *Widener Law Symposium Journal, 9*, 485-543.

Bethune, E. (February 4, 2002). What's expected now: The "reasonable man" standard for liability is much higher since Sept. 11. *Legal Times*, 24.

Bishop v. Fair Lanes Georgia Bowling, Inc., 803 F.2d 1548 (11th Cir. 1986).

Clonan, T. (October 26, 2002). Any time any place, *Irish Times*, W1.

Covello, V. T., Flamm, W.G., Rodricks, J. V., Tardiff, R. G. (1983). *The analysis of actual versus perceived risks*. New York: Plenum.

Decker, R. J. (October, 2001). *Homeland security: A risk management approach can guide preparedness efforts*. Retrieved on January 29, 2006 from http://www.gao.gov/cgi-bin/getrpt?GAO-03-102.

Dobbs, D. B. (2000). *The law of torts*. St. Paul, MN; West Group. Emergency Survival Program Home Page. (2001). *ESP Bulletin*. Retrieved on March 13, 2007 from www.cert-la.com/ESP/Terrorism2001.pdf.

Fallon, R. H. (2003). Legal issues in sports security. *Fordham Intellectual Property, Media, and Entertainment Law Journal, 13*, 349-401.

Fischbach, A. F. (2001). Towering security. *Electrical Construction and Maintenance, 100*(3), 46-56.

Fried, G. and Metchick, R. (Winter 2005). Camp Randall Memorial stadium case study: University of Wisconsin – October 1993. *Journal of Legal Aspects of Sport, 15*(1), 139-176.

Gillentine, A. and Miller, J. (2006). Legal issues associated with tailgating. *International Journal of Sport Management, 7*(1), 100-109.

Gips, M. (May, 2000). Building in terrorism's shadow. *Security Management [Online]*. Retrieved on February 2, 2007 from http://www. securitymanagement.com/.

Goss, B.D., Jubenville, C.B., and MacBeth, J.L. (2003). *Primary principles of post-9/11 stadium security in the United States: Transatlantic implications from British practices.* Retrieved on December 12, 2006 from www.iaam.org/CVMS/Post%20911%20Stadium%20Security.doc

Hall, T. (March, 2004). You've completed your vulnerability assessment...now what? *Public Works, 135*(3), 34-36.

Homeland Security Advisory System. (2004). Retrieved on February 17, 2006 from http://www.dhs.gov/dhspublic/display?theme=29.

Hurst, R. Zoubek, P. Pratsinakis, C. (2002). American sports as a target of terrorism. *Sport and the Law Journal, 10*(1), 134-139.

Ip, G. (March, 2004), "Terror in Madrid: the aftermath: after September 11, the US learned about its economic resilience; attacks shocked markets, but the overall impact was milder than expected", *The Wall Street Journal*, A15.

Isaacs v. Huntington Memorial Hospital, 695 P.2d 653 (Cal. 1985).

Kates, R. W. and Kaperson, J.X. (1983). Comparative risk analysis of technological hazards: A review. *National Academy of Sciences, 80*(22), 7027-7038.

Klinke, A. and Renn, O. (2002). A new approach to risk evaluation and management: Risk-based, precaution-based, and discourse-based strategies. *Risk Analysis, 22*(6), 1071-1094.

Lerner, J.S., Gonzalez, R. M., Small, D.A., and Bischoff, B. (March, 2003). Effects of fear and anger on perceived risks of terrorism: A national field experiment. *Psychology Science, 14*(2), 144-150.

Lerner, J. S., and Keltner, D. (2000). Beyond valence: Toward a model of emotion-specific influences on judgment and choice. *Cognition and Emotion, 14*(4), 473-493.

Levitin, H. (December, 1998). Preparing for terrorism: What every manager needs to know, *Public Management*, 4-6.

Lipton, E. (2005, March 16). US report lists possibilities for terrorist attacks and likely toll. *New York Times*, A1.

Liesch, P., Steen, J., Knight, G. and Czinkota, M.R. (2006). Problematizing the internationalization decision: Terrorism-induced risk. *Management Decision, 44*(6), 809-823.

Loewenstein, G. F., Weber, E. U., Hsee, C. K., Welch, E. (2001). Risk as feelings. Psychological Bulletin, *127*, 267-286.

Lyytinen, K., Mathiassen, L., and Ropponen, J. (1998). Attention shaping software risk- A categorical analysis of four classical risk management approaches. *Information Systems Research, 9*(3), 233-255.

Mallen, S.A. (2001). Touchdown! A victory for injured fans at sporting events? *Missouri Law Review, 66*(2), 487-505.

Miller, J. and Gillentine, A. (Summer 2006). An analysis of risk management policies for tailgating activities at selected NCAA Division I football games. *Journal of Legal Aspects of Sport, 16*, 197-215.

Miller, J. Veltri, F. and Phillips, D. (2007). Preparing against a terrorist attack: The application of risk management at intercollegiate football stadiums. *Journal of Contemporary Athletics.*

Montgomery, C. B. and Nahrstadt, B.C. (Spring, 2004). A primer for the entertainment community: Legal and practical issues about venue safety - what you should know. *Virginia Sports and Entertainment Law Journal, 3*, 257-283.

Norhia, N., Stewart, T.A. (February, 2006). Risk, uncertainty, and doubt. *Harvard Business Review, 84*(2), 35.

Patten, M. L. (2000). Understanding research methods: An overview of the essentials. Los Angeles: Pyrczak Publishing.

Rescher, N. (1983). *Risk: A philosophical introduction to the theory of risk evaluation and management.* Washington, D.C.: University Press of America.

Rosenblatt, R. (May 29, 2000). How we remember. *Time, 155*(22), 26-30.

Schneider, R. (2002, September). *American anti-terrorism planning and design strategies: Applications for Florida growth management, comprehensive planning and urban design.* Nelson Symposium on Growth Management Legislation, Fredric G. Levin College of Law, University of Florida.

Slovic, P. (1987). Perception of risk. *Science, 236*, 280-285.

Slovic, P. (2000). The perception of risk. London: Earthscan.

Slovic, P. (2002a). Terrorism as hazard: A new species of trouble. *Risk Analysis, 22*, 425-426.

Slovic, P. (2002b). The risk game. *Journal of hazardous materials,* 86(1), 17-25.

Slovic, P. and Peters, E. (December, 2006). Risk perception and affect. *Current Directions in Psychological Science, 15*(6), 322-325.

Slovic, P. and Weber, E.U. (April 11, 2002). *Perception of risk posed by extreme events.* Paper presented at the conference of Risk Management Strategies in an Uncertain World. Palisades, New York.

Wade, J. (December, 2002). Safeguarding the Meadowlands. *Risk Management*, 18.

Webler, T. (1999). The craft and theory of public participation: A dialectical process. *Journal of Risk Research, 2*(1), 55-71.

Advances in Sports and Athletics. Volume 1   ISBN: 978-1-61122-824-3
Editor: James P. Waldorf   ©2012 Nova Science Publishers, Inc.

NEGLIGENT MARKETING: "WHAT ALL SPORT MARKETERS SHOULD KNOW"

Andy Gillentine[*1], *John Miller*[2]
and Austin Stair Calhoun[3]
[1]University of Miami, Florida, US
[2]Texas Tech University, Texas, US
[3]Washington and Lee University, Virginia, US

ABSTRACT

Negligent marketing assumes that promoters should not engage in strategies that increase the risk that patrons may injure either themselves or others (Ausness, 2002).

Marketing campaigns portraying a product being consumed in a negligent manner that leads to the development of an unsafe environment may put the service provider at risk (Sebok, 2003). If a defendant can establish the marketing campaign influenced how the product was consumed, service providers could be found liable. Sport organizations allowing companies to deliver such marketing campaigns or that are associated with products that promote dangerous or reckless behavior may also be liable (Rabin, 1999). Sport organizations should be careful not to create the impression that negligent consumption of a product is part of a consumers experience. Sport marketers must evaluate situations to identify potentially dangerous actions or behaviors (Gillentine, 2003; Jackson and Polite, 2003; Gillentine and Miller, 2004).

---

[*] Contact Information: Andy Gillentine, Ph.D. Associate Dean, University of Miami, Dept. Exercise and Sport Sciences, P.O. Box 248065. Coral Gables, FL 33124. (O) 305-284-3102. (FAX) 305-284-5168. agillentine@miami.edu

On a crisp autumn afternoon, Christine Bearman and her husband casually strolled through the parking lot towards their car. Following an afternoon of college football, the Bearmans decided to leave the event a little early to avoid possible traffic delays on the way home. As the Bearmans made their way through the Notre Dame parking lot, an intoxicated "tailgater" knocked Christina to the ground. Ms Bearman suffered a broken leg in the incident and required medical attention. No security or event management staff was in the vicinity when the incident occurred.

Sport marketers are constantly challenged to find new and innovative ways of marketing their sport product or services to the consumer. Marketing strategies and campaigns are often designed to take advantage of the latest consumer trends in order to attract specific market segments. Often, these trends are influenced by current pop culture figures, events and symbols. The use of celebrities and popular music may help expose the sport product to a broader or specific group of consumers. The use of Kid Rock and "the Twins" in Coors Beer commercials and depictions of painted and costumed raucous groups simulating fans attending a "typical" sporting event are examples of these trendy marketing strategies. Sport marketers also often design an alternative version of the marketing campaign which targets a different demographic group. This portion of the marketing campaign frequently features images of athletic events including school mascots playing with children, families picnicking on university grounds and the promise of a Family Fun Zone or Family Friendly atmosphere, implying that the event is a safe, wholesome environment for the sport consumer. These dichotomously different representations can often cloud the issue of regarding products or services actually being promoted and sold. These mixed images fail to paint the complete picture for either segment, as to what type environment the consumer might actually find at the sporting event.

Tailgate parties have been acknowledged as an important component of intercollegiate as well as professional athletic events. Previous research examining motives for participating in tailgating events identified alcohol consumption as a primary motivating factor and also indicated that subjects had missed an event due to tailgating related activities (Gillentine, 2003). Additional research has indicated that drinking alcohol can increase an individual's violent tendencies, especially when placed in an emotionally charged atmosphere (Harford, Wechsler, and Muthen, 2003; Leonard, Quigley, and Collins, 2002; Graham, Larocque, Yetman, Ross, and Guistra, 1980). This research may be further exemplified by recent incidents where fatalities were attributed to drinking at tailgate parties (Romig, 2004). Sport organizations should understand and acknowledge that alcohol consumption will and does take place at their events. This relationship should alert university athletic officials about the potential for inappropriate and disruptive actions of participants, which may endanger themselves and/or others.

The principles of tort law specify that before a person or organization can be held liable for unlawful activity, that entity must breach an affirmative duty (Dobbs, 2000). Supporters attending an athletic event and/or its subsequent activities (i.e. tailgating) are considered business invitees. As such, the university has a duty to take reasonable measures to warn or protect the business invitees from foreseeable harmful or criminal acts committed by a third party (Miller, Gillentine, and Malhorn, 2006; Gillentine and Miller, 2006; Mallen, 2001; Dobbs, 2000). By issuing an invitation to attend these athletic activities (e.g. marketing campaigns; event promotions, etc), the sport organizations signifies that the premises and related activities to be safe (Wong, 2002). The failure to provide a safe environment for invitees through misleading marketing of the event may lead to their actions being regarded as negligent marketing.

NEGLIGENT MARKETING

The principle of negligent marketing assumes that promoters should not engage in strategies that increase the risk that patrons may injure either themselves or others (Ausness, 2002). Negligent marketing is typically categorized into three areas of identification: 1) product design, 2) inadequate supervision and 3) advertising and promotional activities (Ausness, 2002). While legal precedence in the area of negligent marketing has most frequently been cited in reference to the manufacturing and sale of firearms, it has also been applied to events in which patrons are invited to participate in an activity about which they have not been adequately informed (Merrill v. Navegar Inc., 2001).

Marketing campaigns that portray a product being consumed in a negligent manner that leads to the development of an unsafe or dangerous environment may put the service provider at risk of negligent marketing. If a defendant can establish that the marketing campaign influenced how the product was consumed, service providers could be charged with contributory negligence. Additionally, sport organizations that allow companies to deliver such marketing campaigns or that are associated with a product that promotes dangerous or reckless behavior may also be liable for negligent behavior of consumers (Rabin, 1999).

ENABLING TORTS

Sport organizations should be careful not to create the impression that negligent consumption of a product is part of a consumers experience when they consume the sport product. Sport marketers also need to ensure that they are not creating an unsafe environment that has potential impact on all sport consumers (Sebok, 2003). While sport marketers may maintain that they are not responsible for the inappropriate actions of consumers, they may be held accountable if the environment in which the sport product is offered and consumed is not safe from foreseeable harm. It is the responsibility of the sport marketer to evaluate situations to identify potentially dangerous actions or behaviors. Previous research has suggested that additional policies and regulations regarding the marketing and hosting of sport events need to be instituted (Miller, Gillentine, and Malhorn, 2006; Gillentine and Miller, 2006; Gillentine, 2003; Jackson, Polite, and Barber, 2003). The cavalier attitude that such matters are the responsibility of event management staff or security is simply unacceptable.

By providing an environment through which the sport product may inappropriately consumed, the sport marketer may have enabled the consumer to be at significantly higher risk of harm. This concept is referred to as an enabling tort (Rabin, 1999). An enabling tort is an emerging concept that provides a broader view of proximate cause. Sport marketers may find themselves in violation of this enabling tort concept if they have engaged in marketing activities that will increase the likelihood that their product will be purchased and/or consumed by customers who are more likely to injure either themselves or others (Ausness, 2002). Rabin (1999) further describes this evolving concept and its potential application to the sport industry,

> "...the erosion of the proximate cause limitation for intervening acts can be regarded as a temporal shift in moral sensibilities from a more individualistic era to one in which tort law...increasingly reflects more expansive notions of responsibility for the conduct of others" (p. 441-442.).

This concept further implies that no special relationship needs to exist in order to establish responsibility (Rabin, 1999). It does place great emphasis on the placement of the patron in a position posing a foreseeable risk of harm. This expands the level of expected responsibility of the sport marketer to be even more inclusive than the previously established designation of patrons as business invitees.

SOCIAL HOST LIABILITY

In addition, the creation of an environment in which unsupervised alcohol consumption is allowed and/or tolerated the sport organization may find itself in violation of social host expectations. Social host liability refers to statute or case law that imposes potential liability on social hosts as a result of their serving alcohol to obviously intoxicated persons or minors who subsequently are involved in crashes causing death or injury to third-parties. The expectation of the social host may be extended from the actual sale or serving of alcohol to the prevision of the environment for its consumption. Through this interpretation, sport organizations must develop and implement specific policies for those patrons attending athletic events and activities in order to demonstrate appropriate levels of control.

RECENT TAILGATE EVENT INCIDENTS

In October of 1999, Ronald and Fazila Verni, accompanied by their daughter Antonia, were driving back from selecting a pumpkin for Halloween when a truck driven by Daniel Lanzaro struck the Vernis. As a result Antonia, who was 2 years old at the time, was paralyzed from the neck down. Lanzaro, who had been attending New York Giants football game, was found to have a blood-alcohol content that was three times the legal limit. He was eventually sentenced to 5 years in prison.

Subsequently, the Verni's filed a lawsuit naming Lanzaro, the Giants, Aramark (the company in charge of concessions at Giants Stadium), and the National Football League. According to the attorney for the Vernis, Lanzaro gave a vendor a $10 tip so the vendor would sell him (Lanzaro) six beers at the same time. The vendor did so even though it violated the two beer maximum rule at the stadium. A jury awarded $75 million in punitive damages and $60 million in compensatory damages. The compensatory damages were assessed equally against Lanzaro and Aramark Corporation, the Giants Stadium concessionaire that sold beers to him at the game. The jury ruled that Aramark was liable for the additional $75 million. According to a research group that examines developments in personal injury lawsuits, the award was the largest alcohol liability award in the United States in at least 25 years (CourtTV.com, 2005).

The Verni's attorney stated that what the NFL is doing is promoting the idea that, "We're having a party, so park you car in our backyard, drink as much as you want, come into the stadium, get more wasted and then drive home." Additional evidence presented by the plaintiff's attorney revealed showed that vendors continually violated rules against selling more than two beers to a single patron at a time. There were hardly any occasions, in what the attorney referred to as "the culture of intoxication" at the stadium, in which drunken patrons were stopped from ordering more drinks. "The name of the game was to sell as much beer as possible," the attorney continued (Gottlieb, 2005).

Intercollegiate sports are not immune to these kinds of unfortunate events occurring as a result of tailgating. *Bearman v. Notre Dame* (1983) should serve as the benchmark ruling upon which sport marketers evaluate control issues involved in event development and promotion. The Bearman's filed suit against Notre Dame for damages resulting from that incident. In 1983, the Third District Indiana Court of Appeals ruled that,

> Notre Dame was aware that alcoholic beverages are consumed on the premises before and during football games. They also were aware that tailgate parties are held in the parking areas around the stadium. Thus, even though there was no showing that the University had reason to know of the particular danger posed by the drunk who injured Bearman, it had reason to know that some people will become intoxicated and pose a general threat to the safety of other patrons. Therefore, Notre Dame is under a duty to take reasonable precautions to protect those who attend its football games from injury caused by acts of third parties.

In *Bearman v. Notre Dame* (1983), the university acknowledged that individuals attending tailgating parties may become intoxicated, thus posing a threat to others on the premises. Yet, the university did not provide any warning or supervision for the patrons attending and participating in the pre-game activities. (Mellowitz, 1983). At a minimum, "…sponsored activities require some type of increased safety measures." (Wong, 2002, p. 125). Moreover, the Restatement of Torts (Second) (1965) comment f explicitly states

Since the possessor is not an insurer of the visitor's safety, he is ordinarily under no duty to exercise any care until he knows or has reason to know that the acts of the third person are occurring, or are about to occur. He may, however know or have reason to know, from past experience, that there is a likelihood of conduct on the part of third persons in general which is likely to endanger the safety of the visitor, even though he has no reason to expect it on the part of any particular individual.

A more recent incident occurred in 2004 when a North Carolina State University student and his brother were charged with the shooting deaths of two men at a tailgating party. In a split verdict, one of the defendants was recently found guilty of first-degree murder (Mason and Calloway, 2004).

Threat Matrix

Control of alcohol beverage use, limiting or supervising the practice of tailgating in pre-game and post-game situations, warning signs or providing an adequate number of trained security personnel to be present at tailgating events would minimize the likelihood of a harmful incident occurring (Miller, Gillentine, and Seidler, 2003). These control measures require specific acknowledgement on behalf of sport marketers when athletic events and activities are evaluated through the premises of a threat matrix. The threat matrix helps to identify foreseeably harmful incidents that may threaten an event or organization and places them into categories that help imply the frequency (often, average, seldom) and severity (high loss, moderate loss, low loss) of the potential threat. An example of a threat matrix that may be used by a sport marketer to identify potential harmful incidents is provided. It should be kept in mind that many other instances could occur and as such Table 1 supplies potential occurrences and should not be construed as an absolute example.

Through this matrix, a sport marketer can recognize the foreseeability of a specific threat and recommend actions to prepare or adjust for the threat. Additionally, the marketer may adjust the marketing plan for the event in order to minimize the likelihood of negligent marketing. Failure to identify foreseeable risks involved with an athletic event can lead to costly litigation for the sport organization.

Implications and Responsibilities for Sport Marketers

The application and recognition of potential legal pitfalls is an area of relatively new concern for sport marketers. Despite the newness of these concerns the sport marketer is nonetheless responsible for becoming educated regarding legal aspects of sport marketing and the development of effective and efficient plans for adhering to these legal concerns. Often a different advertisement will depict fans tailgating with alcoholic beverages; others painted from head to toe in school colors involved in raucous behavior or seas of the fans storming the field after a big win and tearing down the goal posts.

Table 1. Threat Matrix

		Risk of Occurrence		
		Likely	*Possible*	*Unlikely*
Seriousness of Injury or Damages	*Minor*	E	F	D
	Medium	B	A	I
	Significant	C	H	G

A- Fisticuffs are reported between tailgaters supporting opposing teams.
B- Patron has leg broken due to actions of an inebriated tailgater.
C-Grill is tipped over causing coals to spill under a car.
D- A tent is blown over scraping a vehicle.
E- A tailgater scrapes elbows on pavement playing "tag" football.
F-A patron receives cuts on leg from falling on broken glass.
G-Tailgater(s) shoot and kill other tailgaters
H-Patron becomes inebriated at tailgating party; kills/paralyzes another while driving home.
I-Tailgater becomes over-intoxicated, passes out and becomes comatose.

These images are in stark contrast to the aforementioned family fun zone depiction often offered and promoted. Each method of advertising is aimed at a different market segment, yet both are selling the same product. By confusing the public regarding the actual product being sold or the actual nature of the product, the marketer may be guilty of negligent marketing.

A primary concern to the sport marketer must be to ensure an appropriate environment for the athletic event is established. To facilitate the development of an appropriate environment, the sport marketer should incorporate the following seven action steps:

1) Develop a comprehensive marketing plan. This plan should be developed not only with the promotion of the specific event in mend but also with concern for the safety and well being of the patrons.

2) Play an active role in the development and promotion of specific policies for participation and attendance at athletic events (i.e. tailgating policies) to further minimize the risk to patrons, the marketer must

3) Coordinate marketing plans and the specific event policies with existing organizational policies. Policies that are not in concert with existing organizational policies will present additional legal concerns and will most likely be rendered inefficient and ineffective. Perhaps the only thing worse than none existent policies are contradictory ones.

4) Implement effective communication systems to promote adherence to plans and policies. This communication process should involve the education of event and marketing staff.

5) Gather feedback from patrons regarding the understanding and enforcement of the policies.

6) Educate the athletic staff and/or the event patron and relate the consequences for policy violations as well as promote the positive aspects of adhering to the policies.

7) Design an evaluation component to determine the effectiveness of the marketing and/or event plan. This must be done to ensure the effectiveness of the marketing and event plan as well as to ensure that the plans themselves are not promoting potentially harmful activities.

Good marketing and event management plans are adaptable and dynamic processes that should be frequently communicated and documented. As the number of potential risks associated with athletic events are never static, nor should the plans for promoting and administrating sporting events. When the presumption that previous success guarantees future achievement, the organization will eventually fail to provide the environment for a successful and safe consumer event. This failure can lead to consumers avoiding doing to sport venues based on the owners' lack of assurance that they are committed to safe and secure venues (Toohey, Taylor, and Ki-Lee, 2003).

CONCLUSION

Athletic events are often correctly marketed as an exciting and fan-friendly event appropriate for patrons of all ages. In order to ensure this, it is the duty of sport marketers to engage in the ethical marketing and planning of athletic events and activities. This demands that the marketer keep the safety and well being of the patron as the foremost concern for any plan or event. Regardless of outcome, litigation can take a tremendous financial toll on the sport organization and its product as well as negatively impacting its reputation. These damaging implications can potential affect the marketability of the sport organization and its product. Without this understanding, the near perfect opportunity for sport promotion may become a near perfect opportunity for litigation.

REFERENCES

Ausness, R.C. (2002) Will more aggressive marketing practices lead to greater liability for prescription drug manufacturers? *Wake Forrest Law Review,* 37(1), 97-139.

Bearman v. University of Notre Dame, 453 N.E.2d 1196 (Ind. Ct. App. 1983).

CourtTv.com. (2005). *Group: $135 million jury award a warning to vendors and teams.* Retrieved from http//: www.courttv.com/news/2005/0121/aramark_ap.html.

Dobbs, D. B. (2000). *The law of torts.* St. Paul, MN; West Group.

Gillentine, A. (2003). *Factors associated with participation in pre-game activities.* Paper presentation at Southern District AHPERD. Savannah, GA. Feb.

Gillentine, A. and Miller, J. (2006). The legal implications of tailgating at athletic events. *International Journal of Sport Management.* 7(1), 102-111.

Gillentine, A. and Miller, J. (2004). *Bearman vs. Notre Dame – Twenty years later:The implications for sport marketers.* Paper presentation at the North American Society for Sport Management Conference. Atlanta, GA.

Gottlieb, H. (2005). Jury duns stadium beer vendor $105 million for injuries caused by drunken fan. *New Jersey Law Journal.* Retrieved from http//: www.freerepublic.com/focus/f-news/1326439/posts

Graham, K., Larocque, L., Yetman, R., Ross, T.J. and Guistra, E. (1980). Aggression and barroom environments. *Journal of Studies on Alcohol, 41*, 277-292.

Harford, T.C., Wechsler, H. and Muthen, B.O. (2003). Alcohol-related aggression and drinking at off-campus parties and bars: a national study of current drinkers in college. *Journal of Studies on Alcohol, 64*(5), 704-711.

Jackson, N., Polite, F. and Barber, A. (2003). *Crossing the legal line: Issues involving tailgating.* Paper presentation at the Society for the Study of Legal Aspects of Sport and Physical Activity. Atlanta.

Leonard, K.E., Quigley, B.M, and Collins, R.L. (2002). Physical aggression in the lives of young adults: Prevalence, location, and severity among college and community samples. *Journal of Interpersonal Violence, 17*, 533-550.

Mallen, S.A. (2001). Touchdown! A victory for injured fans at sporting events? *Missouri Law Review, 66*(2), 487-505.

Mason, S. and Calloway, V. (2004, September 6). Brothers in custody following fatal shootings outside NCSU game. *WRAL.com*. Retrieved on September 23, 2005 from http://www.wral.com/news/3707350/detail.com.

Mellowitz, J. (October 10, 1983). Tailgate parties in jeopardy? Court remands injured fan's suit. *The National Law Journal*, p. 4.

Merrill v. Navegar, Inc., 28 P.3d 116, 119 (Cal. 2001).

Miller, J., Gillentine, A, and Malhorn, N. (2006). An investigation of tailgating policies at Division 1A Schools. *Journal of Legal Aspects of Spor, 16(2), 197-215..*

Miller, J., Gillentine, A. and. Seidler, T., (2003). *Is the National Football League responsible for injuries due to third party acts?.* Paper presentation at the Society for the Study of Legal Aspects of Sport and Physical Activity. Las Vegas, NV.

Rabin, R.L. (Winter 1999). Enabling torts. *DePaul Law Review, 49*, 435-453.

Restatement of Torts (Second) § 344 Comment F (1965).

Romig, J. (2004). Niles man sentenced in hit-and-run death. *South Bend Tribune (Indiana),* June 26, 4A.

Sebok, A.J. (Winter 2003). What's law got to do with it? Designing compensation schemes in the shadow of the tort system. *DePaul Law Review, 53*, 501-525

Toohey, K., Taylor, T., and Lee, C. K. (2003). The FIFA World Cup 2002: The effects of terrorism on sport tourists. *Journal of Sport Tourism, 8*(3), 167-185.

Wong, G. M. (2002). *Essentials of sports law.* 3rd Ed. Greenwood Publishing Group.

Advances in Sports and Athletics. Volume 1   ISBN: 978-1-61122-824-3
Editor: James P. Waldorf   © 2012 Nova Science Publishers, Inc.

INVESTIGATING FANTASY SPORT PARTICIPATION AMONG COLLEGE STUDENTS

Chad Seifried[*][1], *Corinne Farneti*[1], *Brian A. Turner*[1], *Martin Brett*[2] *and Jerry Davis*[1]

[1]The Ohio State University, Ohio, US
[2]DeSales University, Pennsylvania, US

ABSTRACT

This project examined fantasy sport participation among the college student population and compared it to previously completed work. Specifically, 155 college students were surveyed from a large midwestern university. The study supports most college student fantasy participants are male and nearly a third of these males participated in paid leagues. Interestingly, most respondents (73.3%) indicated they felt fantasy participation was not gambling. The investigation also revealed 29.9% of students generally read more and 23.5% watched more about a sport when they participate in fantasy leagues. In addition, 77.6% felt the success of their fantasy team did not determine how much they watch sports and another 91.8% of respondents declared the elimination of their fantasy team from playoffs or postseason competition failed to eliminate their desire to watch sports. Similar to other studies, NFL, MLB, and NBA leagues, in that order, emerged as the most popular fantasy leagues. Finally, this study's college student fantasy league participants come from various backgrounds. For example, many different academic

---

[*] Send Correspondence to: Dr. Chad Seifried, The Ohio State University, A248 PAES Building, 305 W. 17th Ave., Columbus, OH 43210, Phone: 614-247-8971, Fax: 614-688-3432, Email: seifried.5@osu.edu

backgrounds/majors were present in the sample population and nearly 91% of fantasy players played high school level athletics or higher.

Fantasy sports are games in which a people serve as coach, owner, and general manager of his or her own team by drafting and managing individual players from a professional or college organization (Felps, 2000; Hiltner & Walker, 1996; Standen, 2006; Williams, 2006). The fantasy sport player usually participates in a league and competes against other players' teams, based on the professional athletes' statistics. Each league creates its' own rules for play through its' league "commissioner" or agreement among participant members. The rules usually determine the point value assigned to each statistical category (Felps, 2000). Leagues can produce weekly winners or culminate with one award for winning the entire season. The rewards vary and in many cases depend on the entry fee (Miller, 2005). Fantasy sport competitions remain attractive to today's audiences because they utilize the actual performance of real players in real time (Hiltner & Walker, 1996; Williams, 2006).

The majority of completed research on fantasy sport(s) focuses on its' explosive popularity over the last decade and a half. For example, Schwarz (2004) and Ballard (2004) suggest fantasy sport accounts for roughly $1.5 billion in spending a year and approximately 15 million adults participate in at least one fantasy sport league annually. Similarly, a Fantasy Sports Trade Association survey in 2003 reported a total of $1.65 billion generated from fantasy sports. Included in these figures are league entry fees, advertising/branding deals, game-play web services, fantasy publications, and web tip/expert services (Ballard, 2004). Other recent data also demonstrates a huge participation rate. Specifically, according to Fanball.com, about 30 million fans worldwide played fantasy sports in 2000 (Felps, 2000). In 2002, 15% of Americans over 18 enjoyed participation in at least one fantasy sports league (Reilly, 2002). Interestingly, the portion of revenue surfacing from these media-driven sources appears substantial and likely to increase in future years. For instance, in 1996, CBS SportsLine employed three people to run its fantasy operation; as of 2004, 50 worked on the fantasy site (Ballard, 2004).

Fantasy leagues exist for the four "big" sports in the US (i.e. Major League Baseball, National Football League, National Basketball Association, National Hockey League) as well as for other sports such as NASCAR, golf, bass fishing, cricket, pro wrestling, soccer, and thoroughbred racing. The NFL and MLB enjoy the most popularity (Ballard, 2004). College Sports Telvision (CSTV) recently introduced college football fantasy leagues, but experienced problems in making it as popular as its pro counterpart. This likely occurs because attractive fantasy college athletes leave early for the professional ranks and the NCAA only allows the drafting of a school and a position, not the specific name of a student-athlete (Miller, 2005).

While very few academic studies exist on topics related to fantasy sport, plenty of information surfaces on the evolution and legality of fantasy participation in mainstream publications and media outlets. The purpose of this study aims to examine fantasy sport participation among the college student population and compare it to previously completed work. Appropriately, the investigation intends to determine the status of a variety of subtopics. Primarily, the questions sought to identify the sport(s), which enjoys the most participation, whether fantasy participation generated any money for them and if they thought paying to participate was gambling. Other questions sought to discover the level of effort respondents placed in organizing their team and if participation in fantasy sport influenced their interest in sport(s). Finally, this research project also asked students to indicate if they found following sport(s) more enjoyable because of fantasy league participation and if their level of interest in sport(s) was directly influenced by the success rate of the team they managed.

LITERATURE REVIEW

The introduction of fantasy sport appeared at least two decades ago. For example, Felps (2000) and others suggested fantasy contests started around the 1960s (Miller, 2004; Schwarz, 2004). Specifically, Schwarz (2004) pointed out Harvard professor William Gamson developed a baseball seminar in 1960, which prompted him and some of his colleagues to draft players onto a team and select a winner based on their end of the year statistics. Additionally, in 1963, Bill Wikenbach, a limited partner of the American Football League (AFL) Oakland Raiders, introduced his friends to a game he devised called fantasy football. Many other sources point to Daniel Okrent, editor of the New York Times, as the founding father of fantasy sports leagues, specifically fantasy baseball (Ballard, 2004; Horgan, 2005; Hruby, 2003, Schwarz, 2004). Reports indicate Okrent thought up the game while on a flight to Austin, Texas on November 17, 1979 (Ballard, 2004). Upon arrival back to his New York home, he called a meeting of his fellow members in the "Phillies Appreciation Society" to explain his new idea. Apparently, they liked what he said and the group met monthly at La Rotisserie Francaise Restaurant, for what they dubbed Okrent's "Rotisserie League." The Rotisserie League idea spread like wildfire across the country via the members' media connections. By 1983, major league baseball players acknowledged awareness of the game; and by the early 1990s, Rotisserie baseball led to similar football and basketball leagues (Ballard, 2004). In any event, none successfully patented the game, which remains so popular today (Ballard, 2004).

A major step in legitimizing and increasing the awareness fantasy sport occurred on August 1, 1998 at the Fantasy Insights '98 Fantasy Football Convention. During the convention, a group of five diverse media members joined together to discuss various issues in the fantasy sport industry. Most notably, they decided to establish a trade association called the Fantasy Sports Trade Association (FSTA). Appropriately, the twelve-member board and its elected officers developed the following mission to help the growth of fantasy sport:

> ...a non-profit trade organization, was founded for the betterment of the fantasy sports industry and to encourage participation in Fantasy Sports Leagues. The FSTA will look to protect the commercial and consumer rights of individual players and business owners, address government regulations and serve as the unified voice of the Fantasy Sports Industry. (Fantasy Sports Trade Association, 2006)

Interestingly, the FSTA holds bi-annual conferences to discuss issues in the industry, network, and of course, hold the seasonal draft. The FSTA also formed a Fantasy Sports Hall of Fame and gives out awards semi-annually to promote the awareness and attractiveness of fantasy sport participation (Fantasy Sports Trade Association, 2006).

Fantasy sport participations increased dramatically in recent years as media units multiplied, embraced athletics into their mediums, and ultimately changed the way they present sporting events (Razzano, 2006; Williams, 2006). For instance, the "sports ticker" provides more diverse statistics and resources directly aimed at the fantasy players (Horgan, 2005). Additionally, the media often dedicates an entire on-air segment to fantasy sports like ESPN News does for baseball (Hruby, 2003). Felps (2000) suggests the Internet and numerous other technology and communication mediums contributed towards much of this growth mentioned above.

Advancements in technology helped revolutionize fan interaction to change how we think about sport. Furthermore, better technology allowed fans instantaneous updates on teams and player statuses when in the past long and arduous calculations would prevent individuals from managing a fantasy team.

Essentially, communication technology and advanced sophisticated software packages facilitated the explosive growth of fantasy sport participation. Many fantasy team owners utilize some kind of service to manage their teams and leagues. Typically, these services developed software packages, which help fantasy league managers in a user-friendly format track statistics, injuries, trades, free agents, weather patterns, and other elements. In many cases, participants pay fees to these service organizations to enjoy access to their software. For example, CDM Sports, a fantasy league software manufacturer out of St. Louis, MO, uses its software to format actual player stats into a user-friendly league (Montagne, 2006).

Within the past two years, the NFL partnered with CBS Sportsline.com for fantasy games at NFL.com. Furthermore, they launched a $7.99 fantasy preview magazine and the first fantasy TV special on the NFL cable channel (Petrecca, 2005). ESPN followed suit by producing a $6.99 fantasy football guide and plans on launching fantasy TV program of its own. Fox Sports offers a weekly television show dedicated completely to fantasy sports, while Sirius Satellite Radio also regularly runs a three-hour fantasy football show. EchoStar's Dish Network offers fantasy racing and a football challenge on its interactive satellite-television channel (Vuong, 2005). This trend also extends to the print media because at least three times as many fantasy football preview magazines exist over actual football preview magazines (Ballard, 2004).

The boom in fantasy sport provided an opportunity for outside companies to profit as well. For example, Jostens now offers rings that fantasy leagues can award to their annual winners (Grimaldi, 2004). Electronic Arts appears as another company benefiting from fantasy sports because they designed fantasy-based video games and added special features to several games, like Madden NFL, which lets players track their fantasy teams while playing (Petrecca, 2005). The General Motors Company (GMC) emerged as one of the first non-sport corporations to latch onto fantasy sport websites. They began by sponsoring fantasy baseball on Yahoo! and now added football, basketball, and Mexican Soccer to their portfolio. Stoffer (2005) suggested the large number of visits to hosting sites provide corporations like GMC a great benefit through sponsorships (Stoffer, 2005). Overall, Petrecca (2005) posited these products not only bring in money from their sale but also serve to drive fantasy players to use their respective websites.

METHOD

While much appears written about the current controversy regarding fantasy sport participation, little prior research determined the current extent of the relationship between fantasy sport and college students. The researchers developed several items to examine college student fantasy sport participation. Respondents were asked questions regarding: (a) if they operated a fantasy team(s) and in what sport(s); (b) if they paid money to participate in a fantasy league(s), achieved financial success, and if they consider this gambling; (c) what sport(s) do they dedicate most of their time and effort organizing; (d) whether their participation in a fantasy league(s) influences their interest of sport(s); (e) if fantasy sport participation prompted individuals to watch and read more about their team(s); (f) if fantasy sport made following the sport(s) more enjoyable; and (g) if the success rate of a fantasy team impacted the participants' continued level of interest in sport(s). Questions related to D through G utilized a Likert Scale where respondents were asked to indicate their level of agreement.

The investigators provided questionnaires along with a cover letter explaining the purpose of the research to 155 college students in a class about spectator sports at a large midwestern university. All 155 responses were used in the analysis of data. Respondents ranged in age from 18 to 28 ($M = 20.63$; $SD = 1.63$). Males produced 121 of the responses (76.6%) while 30 females (19.0%) completed the rest (four individuals failed to specify their gender). The respondents were primarily Caucasians (86.1%) but African-Americans (8.6%), Asian-Americans (3.2%), Hispanics (0.6%) and Native American (0.6%) also completed the survey. The academic standing varied among the students but sophomore, junior, and senior totals accounted for 143 (90.4%) responses in the sample population. Interestingly, we found the sample group enrolled in several different colleges at the institution. They fell in this order: 1) College of Business (33.5%); 2) Arts and Sciences (18.1%); 3) Social Sciences (11.4%); 4) Food, Agricultural, and Environmental Science (7.0%); 5) Humanities (6.3%); 6) Engineering (5.7%); 7) Medicine and Education (3.2%); 8) Graduate School (1.3%); and 9) Social Work (0.6%). The sample population also showed 91 individuals (57.6%) enjoyed a cumulative grade point (GPA) average between 3.0 and 4.0 while another 47 (29.7%) reported a GPA between 2.5 and 2.99. Finally, when asked about the highest level of sport participation, 18 (11.4%) reported they participated on college varsity teams, 18 others indicated university club experience, 104 (65.8%) responded they partake in high school athletics, while 15 (9.5%) fulfilled only recreational competition.

Several works indicate purposive sampling appears suitable for exploratory research like this because it aims to generate new thoughts and perspectives on a phenomenon (Gratton & Jones; 2004; Salant & Dillman, 1994). Trochim (2001) and others also promoted the effectiveness of purposive sampling when the proportionality of a population appears as a minor concern because of the homogeneity of the group (Gratton & Jones, 2004; Kerlinger, 1986; Patton, 1990; Salant & Dillman, 1994). We feel the demographic information provided above in regard to race, G.P.A., college enrollment, and highest level of sport participation offer an adequate representation of college campus.

RESULTS

Nearly half (52.5%) of the respondents stated they operated no fantasy team. Over 20% (n=33) managed one team with another 17 (10.8%) and 11 (7.0%) directing two and three teams respectively. Expectedly, few individuals, only 8 (5.3%) led more than three teams (Table 1). Of those participating in fantasy leagues, 21 (30.4%) indicated they paid to compete against others for their league championship. Fourteen of these individuals stated they paid to participate in only one league. Four more managed teams in two leagues. When asked the question if they thought paid fantasy league participation was gambling 26.7% of respondents answered "yes" while the remaining 73.3% answered "no." Most respondents (89.4%) also indicated they received no money or return on their investment for their participation. Only 7.1 % agreed they obtained financial gain for their fantasy sport participation.

Professional sport enjoyed the most fantasy league participation from the sample population (Table 2). The National Football League (NFL) saw 51 (73.9%) fantasy participants utilize statistics for its leagues competitions. Nearly 30 (42.0%) individuals participated in Major League Baseball (MLB) fantasy leagues. About half that number (n= 14; 20.3%), emerged to utilize National Basketball Association (NBA) statistics. The National Hockey League (NHL) and NASCAR also prompted another five (7.2%) individuals to join fantasy leagues. The researchers also asked students to indicate whether they participated in fantasy sports with college players. A total of twelve responses (7 college football 5 college basketball) appeared to indicate they operated teams based on college performance. Predictably, fantasy league participants spent the most time and effort closely following and organizing leagues based on the NFL ($n= 28$; 37.3%) and MLB ($n= 19$; 25.3%) but many also they indicated they followed college football ($n= 19$; 25.3%) as well despite the low participation rate found here.

Most respondents felt their fantasy sport participation impacted little on their level of interest with a sport. For example, 86.9% fantasy sport participants stated they would still watch an activity if they failed to participate in a related fantasy league. Furthermore, more than two-thirds (68.3%) of respondents disagreed they would watch more games and read more about a sport because of their fantasy interests. Still, almost one-third indicated the opposite. Our sample population also generally defended a position they were not more concerned about their fantasy team then their favorite team. Specifically, 77.6% of respondents held this position. In a related question, 77.6% also disagreed their fantasy team's success determined how much they watched a sport. Additionally, 91.8% opposed the proposal that their interest in a sport would cease when an opponent eliminated their fantasy team from the playoffs.

Table 1. Number of Fantasy Teams Operated

# of Fantasy Teams	Frequency	Percent	Valid Percent	Cumulative Percent
0	83	52.5	54.6	54.6
1	33	20.9	21.7	76.3
2	17	10.8	11.2	87.5
3	11	7.0	7.2	94.7
4	2	1.3	1.3	96.1
5	3	1.9	2.0	98.0
6	1	.6	.7	98.7
7	1	.6	.7	99.3
10 or more	1	.6	.7	100.0
TOTAL	152	96.2	100.0	

Table 2. Self-Identification of Fantasy League Participation

Types of Fantasy Teams		Frequency	Percent of Fantasy Participants
1	NFL	51	73.9
2	MLB	29	42.0
3	NBA	14	20.3
4	College Football	7	10.1
5	NASCAR	5	7.2
5	NHL	5	7.2
5	College Basketball	5	7.2
8	Pro Golf	1	1.4
9	MLS	0	0
9	Other	0	0

Finally, when asked if participation in fantasy sport led to a greater level of enjoyment, nearly one-third (31.8%) suggested fantasy membership raised their delight. Not surprisingly, a similar number (34.1%) advocated fantasy sport participation made watching a sport more enjoyable. Furthermore, 41.2% felt fantasy sport membership provided them something to talk about during the day with their friends and peers.

DISCUSSION

The results produced by this survey generate a number of topics to discuss. First, while nearly 51% of males surveyed participated in a fantasy league only seven of the 30 females (23.3%) directed a fantasy team and none controlled more than one. This percentage of female participation is larger than previous studies. For example, Ballard (2004) stated 93% of all fantasy sport participants are male. We should acknowledge our sample population is likely more interested in sport and thus more prone to have female fantasy league participants because the survey population comes from a class that is an elective on spectator issues related to sport. Still, this work and others suggests fantasy league organizers or providers could do a better job in the future of marketing fantasy sport to females because they appear as a potential untapped market. Specific evidence comes from Wilner (2005) and others who found females constitute more than 40% of the fans for the NFL, NHL, and MLS (Hofacre, 1994; Meyers, 1997; Mihoces, 1998).

Significant monetary loss appears as a negative consequence of fantasy sport. Again, if a participant plays in more than one league, these fees and other costs like website subscriptions, long distance phone calls, and preview magazines add up (Hruby, 2003). A 2003 Harris poll indicated fantasy sports players spend $110 a year per sport (Hruby, 2003), and on average, those who participate in fantasy sport belong to more than two leagues (Yi, 2004). Expectantly, we discovered nearly a third of fantasy members participated in paid leagues; however, few participants paid for two or more teams. Surprisingly, one individual marked they paid to operate 20 teams. We found participation in paid fantasy leagues interesting because of the likely limited financial resources available to college students the fact that each knows they can expect little financial success. On average, the typical fantasy player tends to be 37 – 41 year-old professionals with a bachelor's degree and a household income over $80,000 and thus likely more able to participate in paid leagues (Petrecca, 2005; Stoffer, 2005). Expectantly, college individuals were more likely to be concerned about their team and sport and followed it closely on a regular basis when they paid to participate.

Some criticize the time invested in fantasy sports as wasted. In other words, participating in fantasy sports might not act as the best way to maximize your productivity or contribution to society (Ballard, 2004). This criticism appears especially noticeable and somewhat appropriate when it comes to work productivity. For instance, almost two-thirds of fantasy football players say they check their fantasy teams online during work hours (Petrecca, 2005). This practice shows little signs of slowing down. In 2002, players spent two hours, 45 minutes per week on their teams. In 2004, the number rose to two hours, 58 minutes. Overall, these respondents indicated they think about fantasy sports 38 minutes per day, on average (Petrecca, 2005). According to data based on only 10 minutes of fantasy research per day, employers lose $196.1 million in productivity (Vuong, 2005). Applying this figure to Petrecca's average, employers would lose approximately $600 million in productivity per year, a troubling figure. For the college student, fantasy sport could provide an unnecessary distraction away from their studies. This study discovered 29.9% of students generally read more and 23.5% watched more about a sport because of their fantasy participation. However, we do not feel the students surveyed demonstrated an unnecessary or detrimental amount of time on fantasy participation because most indicated little change in their behavior. Specifically, 87% of respondents stated the lack of a fantasy team would not affect their attention to sport and 77.6% felt the success of their fantasy team did not determine how much they watch sports. In addition, another 91.8% of respondents declared the elimination of their fantasy team from playoffs or postseason competition failed to eliminate their desire to watch sports.

Both researchers and government officials alike identified problems classifying fantasy sport. For example, some regard fantasy sport as similar to playing the stock market because financial risks are involved, research is very helpful, and unforeseen events can positively or negatively affect outcomes (Aamidor, 2005). Appropriately, debate persists on whether or not fantasy sport should be considered gambling. Some say fantasy sport seems addictive for the same reasons as gambling. Specifically, both foster a pathology of promise and a neurotic assurance victory can surface just around the corner (Hruby, 2003). When the topic of whether fantasy sport participation was gambling or not, most respondents (73.3%) indicated they felt it was not gambling. The reasoning behind this basically surrounds fantasy sports being considered games of skill, not chance. Thus, because of this philosophy, the Internet Gambling Prohibition Act of 1997 was amended in 1999. This new proposal exempted fantasy sports leagues from state gaming laws and thus likely influenced a generation of students, like the one from this sample, into believing fantasy sport participation was not gambling (Hruby, 2003).

To support the claims fantasy leagues were contests of skill and educationally valuable, companies and entrepreneurs worldwide now offer fantasy sports "camps" to the fantasy player for a hefty fee. These camps include chances to receive tips from sports legends and the option to try your skills at professional venues (Piore, Brooks, Flynn, & Sparks, 2004). The literature also notes fantasy sports serve as educational learning tools. For example, Gillentine and Schulz (2001) use simulation fantasy football to enhance marketing concepts, while Einolf (2001) utilizes it as a tool to teach economics of sports courses at Mount Saint Mary's College. In the future, we could see more opportunities for people to join fantasy sports camps based on its educational and entertainment value.

Fantasy sports leagues obviously encourage participants to be abreast of player statistics and injuries. Appropriately, it causes an increase in viewership and overall interest in sporting events. For example, fantasy participants watch two to three more hours of football than non-fantasy players (Snel, 2005). Participation also helps fans gain appreciation for the inner-workings of a sport. By acting as a coach and manager, they experience the day-to-day decisions that take place in a sports league (Ballard, 2004). Standen (2006) and others suggested some fantasy participants enjoy acting as the general manager as much as watching or playing the sport itself (Hiltner & Walker, 1996; Razzano, 2006). Clearly, professional teams at all levels should recognize the benefit of promoting fantasy sport in this manner. For instance, it is possible leagues or associations could improve merchandise sales through fantasy sport specific items, raise attendance figures through special fantasy player promotions, and improve game attendance satisfaction through incorporate more advanced personal seat technology (i.e. smart or choice seats) at their facilities. An interesting study from this perspective would focus on if fantasy sport participation effects brand loyalty.

Within this study, professional football (NFL) followed by MLB and the NBA emerged as the three most popular fantasy sports to play but college football replace the NBA as the third most sport they focus their time and efforts. Overall, the NFL, MLB, and college football grabbed the attention of 88% of respondents. This matches other findings offered by the literature. For example, one-third of fantasy players begin participating in a football league because it requires only a modest time commitment but move onto other sports such as baseball and basketball that conduct contests much more frequently (Hruby, 2003). Other sports, in this survey, like college basketball, professional hockey, golf and NASCAR, also enjoyed fantasy leaguer participation but again they remained far behind the NFL, MLB, and NBA. Obviously, these leagues could do more to catch the NFL and MLB. Perhaps making efforts to capture the female market would be a start.

Roberts (2006) reports 82% of fantasy players played sports in high school or beyond. This survey produced similar supportive results. Roughly 91% of fantasy players in this survey played high school, college club, or college varsity athletics. This dispels the myth "geeks" rule the fantasy sport realm (Ballard, 2004). This number also supports the proposition that communication networks established between league members can eventually lead to camaraderie among participants, which often turns into friendship, despite their lack of an introduction beforehand because participants/ competitors establish a sense of social support from friends made in their fantasy leagues (Ballard, 2004). Fantasy sport participants typically include individuals who want social opportunities with others. They are not traditionally the stereotypical "superfan" (Schwarz, 2004). Our research also supports the friendship concept as 41.1% of respondents declared they felt fantasy sport participation provided them something to talk about with others. Still, as Ballard (2004) pointed out, issues such as trade or rule disputes possess the possibility of ruining friendships for members of highly competitive leagues.

REFERENCES

Aamidor, A. (2005, June 14). National fantasy pastime: Millions draft imaginary squads to score virtual victories. *The Indianapolis Star.* Retrieved March 2, 2006, from http://www.indystar.com

Ballard, C. (2004, June 21). *Fantasy world:* These three play (Jennie Finch, Dan Marino and Michael J. Fox). Your neighbor plays. Your boss plays. Everybody plays. Once the secret preserve of stats geeks, *fantasy* sports are now a billion dollar business. *Sports Illustrated, 100*(25), 80-89.

Einolf, K.W. (2001). Turn fantasy into reality: Using fantasy football in an economics of sports course. In *Teaching Economics: Instruction and Classroom Based Research.* Irwin/McGraw Hill Publishers.

Felps, P. (2000, September 20). Fantasy sports players getting a big assist from the internet. *The Dallas Morning News.* Retrieved February 27, 2006, from http://www.dallasnews.com/

Fantasy Sports Trade Association. History. Retrieved March 3, 2006, from http://www.fsta.org/history.shtml

Gillentine, A. and Schulz, J. (2001). Marketing the fantasy football league: Utilization of simulation to enhance sport marketing concepts. *Journal of Marketing Education, 23*(3), 178-186.

Gratton, C. and Jones, I. (2004). *Research methods for sport studies.* New York: Routledge.

Grimaldi, P. (2004, September 9). Jostens hopes to score with fantasy football rings. *The Providence Journal.* Retrieved February 27, 2006, from http://www.projo.com

Hiltner, J.R. and Walker, J.R. (1996). Super frustration Sunday: The day's prodigy's fantasy baseball died; An analysis of the dynamics of electronic communication. *Journal of Popular Culture, 30* (3) 103-117.

Hofacre, S. (1994). The women's audience in professional indoor soccer. Sport Marketing Quarterly, 3, 25-27.

Horgan, S. (2005, December 17). The fantasy game: The man credited with starting it all. *Sun News.* Retrieved February, 27, 2006, from http://www.myrtlebeachonline.com/mld/myrtlebeachonline/.

Hruby, P. (2003, April 29). The case against fantasy sports. *The Washington Times.* Retrieved February 27, 2006, from http://www.washtimes.com

Kerlinger, F.N. (1986). *Foundations of behavioral research* (3rd. ed.). Fort Worth, TX: Holt, Rinehart, and Winston.

Meyers, B. *(1997, August 28). Feminine touches planned but blood and guts remain. US Today, pp. Al, A2.*

Mihoces, G. *(1998, May 7). Women checking in more as NHL fans. US Today, pp. C1, C2.*

Miller, S. (2005, December 12). The real revenue in fantasy sports: The statistics, players and profits are authentic; just the teams aren't. *Multichannel News*. Retrieved February 27, 2006, from http://www.multichannel.com/article/CA6290241.html?display=Special+Report

Patton, M. Q. (1990). *Qualitative evaluation and research methods* (2nd ed.). Newbury Park, CA: Sage Publications.

Petrecca, L. (2005, August 25). Marketers tackle participants in fantasy football. *US Today*. Retrieved February 27, 2006, from http://www.UStoday.com/

Piore, A, Brooks, A., Flynn, E., and Sparks, J.D. (2004). Play like pros. *Newsweek, 143* (16/17), 76-80.

Razzano, R.T. (2006). Intellectual property and baseball statistics: Can Major League Baseball take its fantasy ball and go home? *University of Cincinnati Law Review, 74*, 1157-88.

Reilly, R. (2002, April 22). Rotisserie roast. *Sports Illustrated, 96* (17), 92.

Roberts, B. (2006, January 13). Power Figures. *Sporting News, 230*(2), 32-33.

Salant, P. and Dillman, D.A. (1994). *How to conduct your own survey research.* New York: John Wiley and Sons, Inc.

Schwarz, A. (2004). *The numbers game: Baseball's lifelong fascination with statistics.* New York: Thomas Dunne Books.

Snel, A. (2005, September 13). Fantasy leagues make real cash. *Tampa Tribune*. Retrieved February 27, 2006, from http://www.tampatrib.com

Standen, J. (2006). The beauty of bets: Wagers as compensation for professional athletes. *Willamette Law Review, 42* (4), 639-668.

Stoffer, H. (2005, May 16). GMC makes a play for millions of fantasy sports fans. *Automotive News, 79* (6147), 38.

Trochim, W.M.K. (2001). *The Research Methods Knowledge Base.* (2nd ed.). Mason, OH: Atomic Dog Publishing.

Vuong, A. (2005, September 6). Fantasy football turns into big business. *The Denver Post*. Retrieved February 27, 2006, from http://www.denverpost.com/

Williams, J.F. (2006). The coming revenue revolution in sports. *Willamette Law Review, 42* (4), 669-709.

Wilner, B. (2005). Fueling the female fan base. *Sportbusiness International,*
101, 20-21.

Yi, M. (2004, June 17). EA takes a run at fantasy football: Firms' Madden
video game expected to drive interest. *San Francisco Chronicle*. Retrieved
February 27, 2006, from http://www.sfgate.com

Advances in Sports and Athletics. Volume 1   ISBN: 978-1-61122-824-3
Editor: James P. Waldorf   ©2012 Nova Science Publishers, Inc.

A Look at Academic Reform, Student Athlete Compensation and the Case for a New Classification of Student-Athlete

Frank Adrien Bouchet
Texas A and M University, Texas, US

Abstract

This paper discusses student-athletes compensation issues. The author expresses his concern over the unwillingness of the National Collegiate Athletic Association (NCAA) to fairly compensate these athletes. Since the main concerns according to the N.C.A.A. over such a system are workman's compensation and academic reform we will look into both of those issues as well. A historical perspective will be applied to these issues. We will look into the possibility of some of the main athletic conferences breaking away from the N.C.A.A. and starting a new classification of student-athlete. The advantages and disadvantages of such a move will be looked at as well. The leadership structures of both higher education and the N.C.A.A. will be discussed.

A Look at the History of Student-Athletes Compensation

The following paper will focus on student-athlete compensation in today's world of intercollegiate athletics. We will look at the higher education governance and leadership systems under both the university and the National Collegiate Athletic Association (N.C.A.A.) banner. The question Does the degree outweigh the dollar will be examined. Does learning, goal setting, and team work, all of which have been legs on which college athletics stood for still matter? Or have they been replaced by the quest for the dollar? Is the "new vision" of learning really how to make the dollar work for the university at the expense of student athletes? We will drill down on the decision making process as it relates to compensating student-athletes. We will also look into the reform movement at both the higher education and N.C.A.A. level as well as the various schools that make up the N.C.A.A. The Knight Foundation Commission on Higher Education report (1993) as well as the recently implemented Academic Progress Report will be examined. In the later part of the paper we will look at the student-athlete as a workforce and explore all the changes that have taken place over the last fifty years that have brought us to the place where examining the compensation structure of the current N.C.A.A. is a much needed exercise.

In 2002 the Association of American Colleges and Universities launched an initiative called Greater Expectations: The Commitment to Quality as a Nation Goes to College. This initiative brought to the forefront the need for meaningful reform in higher education. "The report calls for a dramatic reorganization of undergraduate education to ensure that all college aspirants receive not just access to college, but an education of lasting value"(National Panel Report, 2002, p1).

Like athletics, many people have different opinions about what exactly the college experience should entail.

Many students and parents see college as a springboard to employment; they want job related courses. Policy makers view college as a spur to regional economical growth, and they urge highly targeted workforce development. Business leaders seek graduates who can think analytically, communicate effectively, and solve problems in collaboration with diverse colleagues, clients, or customers. Faculty members want students to develop sophisticated intellectual skills and also to learn about science, society, the arts, and human culture. For the higher education community as a whole, college is a time when faculty and students can explore important issues in ways that respect a variety of viewpoints and deepen understanding (National Panel Report, 2002 p. 2).

As one can see from the above paragraph defining what needs a college should meet are as tough as defining the needs of the campus athletic department. One of the focuses of this paper will be the need to include the overhaul of college athletic departments in this topic. The last fifty years has brought drastic changes to the university and its central mission. Perhaps no other department in a university has seen its overall mission changed as much as the campus athletic department. Like the university as a whole, today's athletic department differs drastically from the one started in the early 1900's. As the university has battled increasing responsibilities in areas such as affordability, access, and relevant education, the athletic department is facing such issues as commercialism, spiraling cost and academic reform. To add to these responsibilities there is growing concern among college stakeholders that if a university is not going to educate their student-athletes than they need to compensate then in other forms.

HISTORY OF LEADERSHIP AND GOVERNANCE OF HIGHER EDUCATION

Although college athletics have only been around since the late 1800's universities have been in existence since the late 1600's when the legislature of the Massachusetts Bay Colony established Harvard. They subsequently established a committee of overseers including the state governor, treasurer as well as three magistrates and six ministers. This would later serve as the first governing board. The College of William and Mary was the second college to be formed. William and Mary took a slightly different route in their formation and that of their governing board. "Virginia was a royal colony dependant on officials from London, and the colony itself was dominated by plantation owners, many of whom did not rank public education as a high priority (Cohen, 1998 p.41).

In the early 1690's a group from the Anglican church in Virginia went to London to seek permission to charter a college. Their charter, which was authorized in England, included eighteen Virginia men to serve as "visitors" of the college. These visitors were authorized to charter a school and to set rules and regulations. The third college, Yale, was formed by a group of Connecticut Congregational ministers. They were authorized to manage the schools funds and to grant degrees without consent of the church. "The 1701 charter thus established a college operating without the direct participation of secular officials, even though the General Court promised to grant an annual sum to sustain the institution" (Cohen, 1998 p. 41). Brown University in Rhode Island was the next college formed although its board was predominantly composed of Baptists it also included many different denominations. The College of New Jersey, later renamed Princeton, was the first school formed that advocated religious freedom specifically requiring that all religious parties be accepted. Although graduates of these institutions were free to pursue any career they wished many chose the clergy or public service. A good many of this first group of college graduates would go on to become leaders in their state legislature.

During the 1800's hundreds of college were formed as states started to take over from what had been predominantly church financed colleges. The federal government also rewarded state colleges by offering land as an incentive to the schools thus starting the land grant colleges. This record growth in the number of colleges also helped start intercollegiate athletic events between schools. The first athletic competition of record was a crew event between Harvard and Yale in 1852. Over the next thirty years almost all colleges were competing in some form of intercollegiate athletics. It's interesting to note that the universities in Europe experienced almost a similar growth in athletics with one major difference. "Athletics were part of the collegiate experience in English and German universities as well, but they were different in the United States because of commerzation" (Cohen, 1998 p. 122).

HISTORY OF THE NCAA

The origins of the modern National Collegiate Athletic Association (NCAA) began with President Teddy Roosevelt comments "No student shall represent a college or university in any intercollegiate game or contest....who has at any time received, either directly or indirectly, money or any other consideration" (Byers, 1995). These comments were made in the year 1907 after athletic representatives had been summoned to the White House because of a Presidential inquiry into the deaths of several players. Thanks to Teddy Roosevelt and the fledgling N.C.A.A., deaths among football players became rare, and academic cheating and pay-for-play were kept sufficiently under control for the games to go on.

One of the country's most prestigious organizations, the Carnegie Foundation commissioned a report in 1929 on the state of college athletics in particular football. The report was a scathing indictment on the way universities ran their football programs. The report called for a de-emphasis of football because of an attitude of win at all cost coaches, increased commercialization and illegal players. In the early 1940's University of

Chicago President Robert Maynard Hutchins noted: "Education is primarily concerned with training of the mind, and athletics and social life, though they may contribute to it are not the heart of it and cannot be permitted to interfere with it... An educational institution can make one unique contribution, one denied to a fraternal order or a bodybuilding institute: It can educate. It is by its successes in making this unique contribution that it must be judged." (Byars, 1995) Perhaps President Hutchins foresaw the anti academic pressures on student-athletes better than most, as the University of Chicago withdrew from the Big Ten athletic conference in 1946. Such statements document the fact that today's student-athlete compensation issues have been in discussion since the beginning of intercollegiate sports. "Although the N.C.A.A. was promoted as the guardian of amateur principles and integrity in sports, since it was dominated by coaches and athletic directors, its primary purpose increasingly became that of defending college sports against true reform" (Duderstadt, 2000, p.72). This would become more of a problem in the coming years as television began to exert its control over the college sports essentially turning what was a regional sport into a national one. "Television networks found that by promoting and marketing college sports much as they would other commercial – generating great media hype, hiring sensationalistic broadcasters, urging colleges to arrange even more spectacular events – they could build major nationwide audiences" (Duderstadt, 2000 p.73). It would not be until the next century that college president's would take back control of the N.C.A.A.

Like there forefathers today's college presidents show little inclination toward compensating student-athletes. There argument is that the student-athlete is compensated by receiving a college education in exchange for his/her athletic talents (Duderstadt, 2002, p.75). This argument only has merit if the student-athlete is in reality receiving an education. While it is true that the academic success of most athletic department mirrors closely the student body as a whole the situation in the main revenue sports of football and basketball is much different. The average academic achievement of student-athletes in football and basketball programs ranks below that of the student body in general (Duderstadt, 2000, p.199). The numbers decrease even further when you take out the football statistics. Only 41 percent of all student-athletes graduate and the graduation of black basketball players have dropped to 33 percent, the lowest level in 15 years (Duderstadt, 2002, p.199). It is obvious from these numbers that universities are not graduating student-athletes at an acceptable rate.

Academic Reform within the N.C.A.A.

"It has been difficult of late for an academician to read an issue of the *Chronicle of Higher Education* without concluding that the most interesting collegiate sports news is no longer made on the fields of play" (Porto,1985). While that comment was first made in 1985 little has changed in the last twenty years to change how an academician views college athletics. This section will focus on the leadership systems in place at the college level and how their actions affect student-athletes. The N.C.A.A. recently passed an academic reform package designed to address the troubling issue of graduation rates at member schools (N.C.A.A., 2004). While on the surface it would appear that academic reform has little to do with the compensation of student-athletes if one looks deeper into the problem you will see that the two issues are intertwined.

One of the main arguments against the so called "pay for play" is that student-athletes are receiving a free education. It is only after looking at the dismal graduation rates that the conversation about student-athlete compensation gets more serious. Another of N.C.A.A. President Myles Brand major initiatives is the Academic Progress Rate (APR).

The A.P.R. is a real time assessment of a particular team's academic performance. The scoring system consists of two points for each term a student-athlete meets academic eligibility requirements and who remains . enrolled at the institution. A particular team's A.P.R. is earned by the team at a given time divided by the total points possible. The N.C.A.A. has set a rate of 925 as the score with which teams must achieve. This number takes into account an expected graduation rate of 50 percent of all student-athletes competing for the university. If teams fail to score 925 points contemporaneous penalty are assessed.

These contemporaneous penalties might include the loss of a scholarship for an academic year. The next level of penalties is the historically based penalties. These penalties are assessed to teams that have repeatedly been penalized for academic deficiencies. These penalties might result in additional scholarship reductions, recruiting restrictions, lack of access to postseason competition and loss of N.C.A.A. membership.

The recently passed academic reform package also show that the current structure within the N.C.A.A. is one in which the university presidents have clearly taken control. Prior to the presidents taking control of the N.C.A.A. during the 1996 convention the organization had been controlled by athletic directors and coaches. It was obvious to all that these parties cared much more about their own empire building than about student-athletes. Under the new reform package, schools that have student-athletes who do not meet specific academic standards would lose athletic scholarships, recruiting opportunities, and post season revenues. Schools that obtain repeat offender status could eventually risk losing post season invitations or N.C.A.A. membership rights. These reforms are important to college athletics for three main reasons. The first reason is that receiving a free education is often cited as one of the main reasons behind the universities not wanting to monetarily compensate student-athletes. The second reason is that they strengthen the chances of academic success and the third reason is that they hold institutions accountable for the academic success of their student athletes.

The measure, which passed last summer, has been in the works for the past three years is seen as a major victory in the agenda of N.C.A.A. President Myles Brand. The N.C.A.A. prior to 1996 was one in which voting on specific reforms was handled in a "town hall" type setting. In 1997 the voting was changed to a format with more presidential input. This change in voting was due in part on recommendations by the Knight Commission.

While these new academic standards are a key component to true academic reform, the jury remains out on their effectiveness in raising graduation rates of football and basketball student-athletes.

The Knight Commission was a high powered commission designed to study ways to bring academics back to the forefront of college athletics. One of the main focuses of the Commission was that university presidents needed to take back control and oversight of their college athletic departments. This sent an important message that university presidents who had long held the party line of no compensation for student- athletes were firmly in control.

The Knight Commission was formed in 1989 by the trustees of the John S. and James L. Knight Foundation. The trustees concern grew as abuses increased in college athletic departments. They believed the abuses and the greater number of infractions that were threatened the very integrity of higher education. In 1989 the foundation created a Commission on Intercollegiate Athletics with one main focus: propose an agenda designed to reform college athletics.

It should be noted that the Knight Foundations main goal was to reform the culture of college athletics, the commission did not partake in any study on the compensation of student-athletes (Knight, 1993). However, this report was an important step towards academic reform which serves as the main argument against monetary compensation for student-athletes. While the Commission had no formal governing rights over college athletics, it was clear from the start that it had the full support of the N.C.A.A. and its member institutions. To further illustrate this point it is worth noting that in 1993, a full four years after the Commission published its findings, nearly two thirds of its specific recommendations had been endorsed by the N.C.A.A. The commission appeared to go out of its way to stressing that it was not out to abolish intercollegiate athletics. James L. Knight, Chairman of the Foundation said "We have a lot of sports fans on our board, and we recognized that intercollegiate athletics have a legitimate and proper role to play in college and university life" (Knight, 1993). He added "Our interest is not to abolish that role but to preserve it by putting it back in perspective"(Knight) The climate concerning intercollegiate athletics in the late 1980's and early 1990's that the Knight Commission found was one of increasing violations. In the N.C.A.A.'s Division I 57 of the 106 member schools were cited with infractions between the years of 1980 through 1990. In addition to the constant barrage of infractions, 48 member institutions had graduation rates under 30% for their men's basketball and 19 universities had the same low rate for football players (N.C.A.A., 2004) With monetary incentives tied to ever increasing television-rights fees, universities are under constant pressure to perform. The Knight Commission noted: "The current practice of shared governance leads to gridlock. Whether the problem is with the presidents who lack the courage to lead an agenda for change, trustees who ignore an institutions goals in favor of the football team, or faculty members who loath to surrender the status quo, the fact is that each is an obstacle to progress" (Knight, 1993, p.11).

The Knight Foundation Commission on Intercollegiate Athletics met over the course of five years (1998 – 2003) and produced three reports. They found one of the main problems in the college ranks was one of university presidential neglect. Presidential oversight was also the main focus of reform for the Commission. The Commission recommended a "one-plus-three" model which consisted of presidential control directed toward academic integrity, financial integrity, and independent certification.

The key component of this new model required that university presidents be held accountable for their athletic departments. The first initiative after presidential control was academics. The key point in the academic integrity initiative was that students that participate in athletics deserved the same rights and responsibilities as all other students. Financial integrity was the second initiative discussed in the report. Regarding financial integrity the report stated: "The central point with regard to expenditures is the need to insist that athletic departments' budgets be subject to the same institutional oversight and direct control as other university departments" (Knight, 1993). Among the concerns were reducing football and basketball expenditures and aligning coaches compensation within the context of the academic institutions that employee them. The last of the main initiatives was independent certification. Independent certification of the athletic department would be accomplished through periodic assessments by an independent auditor. The audit would cover the entire range of academic and financial issues pertaining to intercollegiate athletics.

The report freely admitted that most presidents were historically uncomfortable with athletic department oversight and all to willing to turn over that responsibility to athletic directors. In order for these new reforms to work it was clear that presidents had to take back control of their athletic departments. The Commission stated: "the presidents goal must be nothing less than the restoration of athletics as healthy and integral part of the athletic enterprise" (Knight, 1993).

The Commission recognized that there was not a "magic pill" that would cure all the ills of intercollegiate athletics when they stated: "Reform is not a destination but a never ending process" (Knight Report, 1991). By publicly stating this they appeared to realize that these changes would have to be implemented over a long period of time.

A positive sign that the N.C.A.A. was taking a serious stance towards these reforms occurred in 1996 when the N.C.A.A. adopted a governance structure which placed all planning and policy activities including budgets with the college presidents instead of with athletic administrators.

After the final report was released the Commission was disbanded but not before agreeing to monitor the situation and meet periodically to review the progress being made. In 2001 the Commission did indeed meet to discuss the state of intercollegiate athletics. By stating that "Reform is not a destination but a never ending process" the general consensus was the committee gave themselves some leeway in determining whether or not the recommendations had been a success.

The selection of Indiana University President Myles Brand to lead the N.C.A.A. was seen as a step in the right direction. Prior to his appointment the N.C.A.A. had for the most part been led by former college athletic directors. The appointment of Myles Brand, a university president, sent notice to the college athletic community that reform was on its way and that critical issues regarding student-athletes and academics would be addressed.

As one might have determined this move has elicited response from people on both sides of the issue. While reformers such as Brand contend "In college athletics, the focus is on the individual athlete, he or she is a student-athlete first. Their primary reason for being in college or university is – or should be – to obtain an education." (N.C.A.A., 2004) Brand continued to say that "these are strong and well thought out reforms that are critically necessary to ensuring that college athletes are academically successful." (N.C.A.A., 2004).

Although the Presidents have exercised their power concerning academic reform there still remains a hierarchy with athletic directors on top followed by the coaches and then the student-athletes. Within the last ten years there has been a tremendous rise in the salaries of both athletic directors and coaches from revenue generating programs without an obvious increase in either extra duties or increased performance. Within the corporate ranks salary increases have usually been in line with superb performance or increased responsibilities. This is clearly not the case within an athletic department. Perhaps no other position has benefited from the rise in commercialization more so than the head coaches in both football and basketball. Over the past fifteen years the average salary for the respected head coaches in these sports has increased sizably. The one area that has not changes is the compensation structure for student-athletes.

STUDENT ATHLETES AS A WORKFORCE

In this section we will look at the student-athlete as a workforce. The one constant in college athletics is the monetary value of the student-athletes scholarship. While college athletic administrators and coaches salaries have continued to climb, the incentives for student-athletes have stayed the exact same. This has put an increased strain on the relationship between the student-athlete and the institutions in which they serve. Increasingly student-athlete's view themselves as an uncompensated workforce. In a country that relies on the court system to guide us on legal matters the courts are at an impasse on this issue. In an article for the *Journal of Sport and Social Issues*, Porto (1985) writes:

> In raising the issue of whether or not a college scholarship was a contract of employment which entitled an injured athlete to worker's compensation, this case has produced two very different interpretations of the relationship which exists between scholarship athletes and the universities. Both constructions are seriously flawed: while one would create unnecessarily onerous financial, administrative, and educational implications for the

universities, the other ignores the close resemblance which participation in big-time intercollegiate sports bears to employment and the extent to which the integrity of university athletic programs has been compromised as a result (p. 20).

According to University of New Haven Professor Allen Sack (1985)

> The view that scholarships are quid pro quo contracts becomes more convincing when one examines factors often used in worker's compensation cases to determine whether there exists an expressed or implied contract for hire (Sack, p. 2)

The workman's compensation issue is cited primarily because it is one of the main arguments against monetarily compensating student-athletes.

The argument is not a new one in fact it's been discussed since colleges and universities started participating in athletics. It has been well documented that certain language has been deliberately omitted from the actual scholarship papers a student-athlete signs due to the ever increasing concern that it might be construed as an employment agreement. "With grants-in-aid increasingly in vogue in the 1950's, college officials found that the term *employee* was being interpreted by state officials applying state laws in the interest of the people, not college faculty representatives and athletic directors interpreting college rules in the interest of the college" (Byers, 1995 p. 69).

It is clear that the lower courts tend to view student-athletes as employees of the university while the appellate courts have overturned this view time and time again. "At many universities, including the University of Michigan, graduate student teaching assistants, who are compensated for classroom teaching, not only are recognized legally as employees but allowed to form unions for collective bargaining" (Duderstadt, 2000 p.198). It is ironic that those students compensated for academic activities are considered employees, while those students compensated for performing in highly profitable athletic "business" are not" (Duderdstadt, 2000 p.198).

As James Duderstadt, the President of the University of Michigan, stated in the above sentence the last ten years has seen a rise in the on campus union activity of graduate assistant students. In Los Angeles there has been an effort to form a union which represents the student-athletes interest. In early 2000 former University of California Los Angeles linebacker Ramogi Huma started the Collegiate Athletes Coalition (C.A.C.). The C.A.C. was formed to help student-athletes gain much needed benefits from the N.C.A.A. According to the N.C.A.A., student-athletes should feel grateful to be receiving a "full ride".

The C.A.C. position is that a full ride doesn't begin to justify the long hours spent earning money that benefits the university. While their public position is that they are an organization not a full fledged union it should be noted they have joined forces with the United Steelworkers of America to provide an infrastructure for their agenda. By definition a union is any organization that seeks to gain collective bargaining. This definition certainly seems to fit with the C.A.C.'s charter. While it has never recognized the C.A.C. publicly the N.C.A.A. has taken steps to pass legislation designed to appease current student-athletes.

One of the main goals of the C.A.C. is to get the N.C.A.A. to pass legislation proposed by California Senator Kevin Murray called the Student Athletes' Bill of Rights. This bill would insure that student-athletes have year round health coverage as well as additional spending money that would cover the cost of college attendance. The bill which was authored by former University of Colorado football player Jeremy Bloom would also give student-athletes a percentage of the sales of their athletic jerseys. The jersey royalty issue is an issue that continues to be a sore spot with current and former student-athletes. While N.C.A.A. rules prohibit the names of current players on the backs of jerseys it doesn't prohibit their number from being displayed.

The main grievance of the C.A.C. is that the N.C.A.A. refuses to reform its rules to actually benefit the student-athlete. Although this organization has been around for only a few short years it has made some significant strides in the current reform movement. One of the C.A.C. main problems is getting student-athletes to sign up for its services. Unlike professional baseball players who have struggled for years in the minor leagues before they start to make money college athletes tend to be more reserved. College athletes, especially in the major revenue sports tend to be pampered all through school. This fact makes them extremely reluctant to speak out against the system.

The argument against compensating student-athletes for their talents is similar to the one argued for years against university technology transfer rules. With technology transfer, universities along with faculty are allowed to profit from the discoveries made by professors in university owned facilities by patenting an idea and then commercializing it when the product goes to market. Roger Noll, an economist at Stanford University writes in Rethinking College Athletics (1991):

> College sports are already professionalized at universities that house their athletes separately, that advertise themselves as preparatory schools for a career in professional sports, and that fails to graduate nearly all its players.

Professionalization does not lie in how much someone is paid; it lies in the nature of the bargain between the university and a player. If athletes play little or no role in campus life, if they are not in any meaningful sense students, and if they are associated with the university only to participate in its athletic program, they are professionals, regardless of the amount they are paid (p. 208)

College athletics has become expensive. The cost of operating a Division I athletic department has more than doubled in the years 1993 – 2003 (Fizel, Fort, 2004, p.37). The revenue generated from the B.C.S. and the N.C.A.A. basketball championship has helped create an atmosphere of placing the importance of winning over the student-athletes best interest. "And each institution, once entered, will face powerful incentives to increase its expenditures in search of a competitive edge. This logic is in harmony with the observation that the revenues generated directly by college athletic programs fall far short of covering the costs in the overwhelming majority of cases" (Frank, 2004).

The creation of the Bowl Championship Series (B.C.S.) and other revenue generating mechanisms has established a new monetary goal which has replaced the athletic quest for excellence. "A frantic money oriented modus operandi that defies responsibility dominates the structure of big time college football and basketball" (Knight Report, 2002). Recent data has disputed an arms race in college athletics as it relates to operating budgets it clearly indicating spiraling costs related to both coaches salaries and facilities. A study by the Brookings Institute and commissioned by the N.C.A.A., states: "Increased spending on men's football and basketball does not produce medium term increases in winning percentages, and winning percentages does not produce medium term increases in net operating revenue" (Orszag, 2003).

Although the value of a college scholarship has remained unchanged the actual college scholarship has undergone many different changes over the years. One must take a historical look at the evolution of the scholarship to fully understand the changes that have taken place. In 1948 the N.C.A.A.'s athletic scholarship took the form of a Sanity Code. The Sanity Code included tuition and fees if the student-athlete showed financial need and met the schools entrance requirements like an ordinary student. According to most universities this amounted to a merit award in exchange for their athletic requirements. The student-athlete would be eligible for an athletic scholarship if he ranked in the top 25 percent of his high school graduating class. This was a guaranteed scholarship regardless of whether or not the student decided not to play. This rule failed in 1950 when many of the southern schools believing that the well endowed schools from the north could circumvent this rule due to an influential alumni base. It deserves mentioning that the Ivy League and the Big Ten supported the Sanity Code. This fact shows the growing mistrust not just between schools but between conferences as the academically oriented schools fought to keep the Sanity Code and the southern schools fought to adopt a grant-in-aid system. It was at the N.C.A.A. convention of 1956 that a grant-in-aid system was adopted by almost all universities participating in collegiate athletics. This was seen by most of academia as the first step toward a "pay for play" model. It was at this convention in 1956 that the delineation between an athletic scholarship and need based financial aid began to assert itself into college athletics. Prior to this convention most student-athletes attended school on need based financial aid. Need based financial aid amounts to a contractual agreement between the student and the institution (Gerdy, 2005). Under the contract, the student will continue to receive his or her financial aid regardless of what transpires on the athletics field As a result, the student is less beholden to the athletic departments competitive and business motives and thus freer to explore the wide diversity of experiences college offers. (Gerdy, 2005) After the convention of 1956 what began to replace need based financial aid were athletic scholarships. These athletic scholarships represent a contractual agreement between the student-athlete and the coach. This contract has little to do with education and everything to do with athletic performance and control (Gerdy, 2005) In this arrangement a coach tends to view the student-athlete as an employee that he or she has control over. The fact is when you are paid to play, regardless of the form of "payment", everything takes a back seat to the athletes performance (Gerdy, 2005)

It was during this time that the term student-athlete was adopted primarily to deal with the problem of trying to circumvent state employment laws which increasingly saw student-athletes as employees of universities. "One typical state law of that era provided that an employee is any person who engages to furnish his services for remuneration, subject to the direction and control of an employer" (Byars, 1995, p. 70).

As the definition of an athletic scholarship has changed over the years so has the way college coaches award them. "Coaches took another step toward professionalism in1973, up until then grants were for four years and could not be revoked. But the coaches wanted more control over athletes, including the ability to terminate their scholarship for poor performance" (Duderstadt, 2000, p197).

In today's college sports world the scholarships offered by coaches are typical one year renewable scholarships. These scholarships can be revoked for any reason be it either academically or athletically as long as the coach notifies the player prior to July1 of the upcoming year.

Over the last decade the N.C.A.A. has abolished symbols of athletic employment such as athletic dorms and limited the hours a team can practice. They have continued to make sweeping changes designed to ease the growing pressures on the student-athlete. This pressure is caused by an ever increasing commercialization of college athletics. Although college coaches and administrators are the monetary benefactors of the student-athletes work, there seems to be a growing sentiment among coaches that some form of compensation is overdue.

One suggestion that has gained a certain amount of momentum lately is the paying of college athletes that participate in the major revenue generating sports. This plan would create a new classification of student-athlete. Under this plan the so called B.C.S. conferences, which include the Big Ten, Big Twelve, Southeastern, Atlantic Coast, Pac Ten and Big East conferences, would become actual professional leagues and college athletes would be paid a salary. They could either accept this salary or take a scholarship from the school. The proposal has some advantages as it would fairly compensate athletes for their talents. It would also do away with the hypocrisy that currently surrounds college athletics by eliminating the fairly tale of the "student-athlete". It would serve to fairly compensate those athletes that have no desire to attend classes. "Since they would pay for play rather than for an education, they would not be cheated if they never received a degree or developed academic skills (Simon, 1985, p. 58).

The time has come to compensate our student-athletes for their services. Because of the talents of the student-athletes the universities athletic directors, coaches and school officials are paid more than they would in an open market. The N.C.A.A. could make some modest concessions such as a monthly stipend, year round health coverage and travel expenses. These concessions would go along way in appeasing current and future student-athletes who are starting to realize their value to the university.

One could draw a sharp correlation between today's student-athletes and major league baseball players in the 1960's. In the early days of the major league baseball players association the union was asking the team owners for reasonable requests. It was only after not getting any concessions from the owners that baseball players began making major demands and threatening strikes. In retrospect it would be interesting to see what would have happened had the baseball owners listened to the players and tried to form a compromise.

However, this proposal has some detractions as well. For one thing it would exclude all but the main revenue sports, therefore drawing a sharp distinction between revenue and non revenue sports. Something the NCAA has to date been loath to admit. One potential problem that is seldom discussed is the question of whether or not stakeholders such as alumni, faculty and other university supporters would support such a professional league concept. This is an important question as much of the pageantry of college athletics revolves around this groups. There are also potential ramifications for this move that deserve mentioning. At most Division I institutions the major revenue sports like football and basketball fund the non revenue sports. If the money making sports form their own league where is the funding for the non revenue sports going to come from?

A long time NCAA executive once was quoted as saying that the NCAA does two things well. The first is put on championships. The second is enforcing rules and regulations. If the major schools do ever decide to break off and form their own league then the question must be asked: What purpose will the NCAA have? Another major question is what defines a revenue sport? When this plan is mentioned it almost always includes just football and basketball. Universities define what makes a revenue sport differently. The University of Tennessee certainly considers women's basketball to be a revenue sport. The same could be said for hockey at the University of Wisconsin, softball at the University of Arizona and lacrosse at Johns Hopkins University.

In its currently state a university athletic department does not operate as a legitimate business per se with a profit motive bottom line. Business school professors would use the term "sustain the enterprise" in describing the mission of an athletic department. This term simply means the athletic departments chief concern is to pay its employees, host games and spend its budget. If the proposed idea were implemented it would change the mission of the athletic department to a profit oriented business. "Once the university consciously enters professional sports where the major goal is profit, doesn't its character change as well? (Simon, 1985, p.59). While this idea is probably not feasible under the current N.C.A.A. leadership implementing some aspects of this plan make sense.

Reasonable people can agree or disagree upon which model best suits college athletics however most people agree that college athletes needs to be properly compensated for their work. How that compensation is administered remains to be seen. While the rise in TV revenues as well as gate receipts continues to increase so does the belief that the compensation should come in a monetary form.

Perhaps most important is the belief that the N.C.A.A. needs to take a leadership position on this issue before a decision is made for them. As many third world dictators have learned, power is accrued to the organizations that parcel out benefits not hoard them. Those organizations that hoard power are usually overthrown.

REFERENCES

Andre, J. and James, D. (1991) *Rethinking College Athletics* Philadelphia: Temple University Press.

Byers, W. (1995). *Unsportsmanlike Conduct* Ann Arbor: University of Michigan Press.

Cohen, A. (1998). *The Shaping of American Higher Education* San Francisco: John Wiley and Sons.

Duderstadt, J. (2000) *Intercollegiate Athletics and the American University*: Ann Arbor: University of Michigan Press.

Fizel, J. and Fort, R (2004) *Economics of College Sports*: Westport: Praeger Publishing.

Frank, R. (2004) Challenging the Myth, Knight Foundation Commission On Intercollegiate Athletics Retrieved from *knightfdn.org.*

Friday, William C. and Hesburgh, Theodore (March 1991 – March 1993) *Commission on Intercollegiate Athletics*, Knight Foundation Retrieved March 10, 2005 from *knightfdn.org.*

Gerdy, J. (2005, January 5). Collegiate model needs more separation N.C.A.A. News Online.

National Collegiate Athletic Association. (2004) *APR Questions and Answers* Retrieved April 2, 2005 from *ncaa.org/academics_and athletics.*

Porto, B. (1985) Athletic Scholarship as Contracts of Employment. *Journal Of Sport and Social Issues,* 9, 20.

Sack, A. (1985) Worker's Compensation for College Athletes. *Journal Of Sport and Social Issues,* 9, 2.

Sperber, M. (1990) *College Sports Inc.* New York: Henry Holt and Company
Thelin, J. (1994) *Games Colleges Play* Baltimore: The Johns Hopkins Press.

Advances in Sports and Athletics. Volume 1   ISBN: 978-1-61122-824-3
Editor: James P. Waldorf   © 2012 Nova Science Publishers, Inc.

MOTIVATIONAL PROFILES OF SPORT FANS ATTENDING DIFFERENT LEVELS OF BASEBALL GAMES

*Amber L. Rickard, Frederick G. Grieve**
and W. Pitt Derryberry
Western Kentucky University, Kentucky, US

ABSTRACT

While a number of studies (e.g., James and Ross, 2004; Mehus, 2005; Wann, Grieve, Zapalac, and Pease, in press) have examined motives sport fans have for attending different sports, few have examined motives for attending different levels of the same sport (Bernthal and Graham, 2003). The present study was designed to examine motives for attending five different levels of baseball games—T-Ball, Little League, High School, College, and Minor League. Participants were 224 adult fans who attended a game at one of the five levels. They completed measures of sport fandom, team identification, and motivation for attending the game. Different motivational patterns were evident among the different levels. Implications for the findings are discussed.

Sport fans report attending different types of sports for a number of different reasons (Bilyeu and Wann, 2002; James and Ross, 2004; McDonald, Milne, and Hong., 2002; Mehus, 2005; Wann, 1995; Wann, Grieve, Zapalac, and Pease, in press). However, what is less well known is whether

---

* Please address correspondence to: Frederick G. Grieve, Department of Psychology, Western Kentucky University, 1906 College Heights Blvd, #21030. Bowling Green, KY 42101-1030. e-mail: rick.grieve@wku.edu

motivational patterns differ across different levels of the same sport. The present study was designed to address this lack.

Perhaps not surprisingly, sport fans report that they attend different types of sporting events for different reasons. Many of the reasons revolve around the qualities of the sport. For example, fans attending soccer games report higher levels of social and excitement motives for attending than fans who attend ski jump competitions (Mehus, 2005), which could reflect the qualities of the two sports.

James and Ross (2004) surveyed fans of collegiate sports and found significant differences among motives for attending different sporting events. Nine motives were examined: Entertainment, Skill, Drama, Team Effort, Achievement, Social Interaction, Family, Team Affiliation, and Empathy. Results indicated that there were significant differences across three sports. Spectators at the wrestling matches rated all of the motives higher than spectators at the baseball and softball games. Spectators at softball games rated all motives except social interaction higher than spectators at baseball games. Spectators at men's baseball, women's softball, and men's wrestling rated the sport-related motives (entertainment, skill, drama, and team effort) higher than the self-definition motives (achievement, empathy, and team affiliation). Consumers of men's baseball, women's softball, and men's wrestling also rated the sport related motives higher than personal benefit motives (social interaction and family).

McDonald, Milne, and Hong (2002) examined the motivational factors of consumers who watch and play sports. Using Maslow's five human needs as a framework, they developed a scale that evaluated 12 types of motivations for sport participation and spectatorship (achievement, competition, social facilitation, skill mastery, physical risk, affiliation, aesthetics, aggression, value development, self esteem, self actualization, and stress release) and surveyed 1,611 people about the reasons why they watch nine different sports (automobile racing, college baseball, professional baseball, college basketball, professional basketball, college football, professional football, golf, and ice hockey).

There were significant differences for nine of the motivations across sport. Participants who were fans of golf rated the achievement motive lower than fans of all other sports. Fans of auto racing and golf rated skill mastery as higher than fans of the other sports. Fans of auto racing and ice hockey rated physical risk as more important than fans of other sports. Affiliation was important for fans of auto racing moreso than fans of the other sports. Fans of basketball, hockey, and golf rated the aesthetic motive more highly than fans of other sports. Aggression was rated more highly by fans of auto racing and ice hockey than fans of other sports. The other motives did not display much variance, perhaps because they are more suited for participation in sports rather than spectating.

In a comprehensive examination of sport fan motives, Wann et al. (in press) examined the motives fans report for watching a given sport. They assessed eight different motives (escape, economic, eustress, self-esteem, group affiliation, entertainment, aesthetic, and family reasons) for watching 13 sports (professional baseball, college football, professional football, figure skating, gymnastics, professional hockey, boxing, auto racing, tennis, professional basketball, college basketball, professional wrestling, and golf). Participants included 1372 college students who completed the survey. Participants only responded to sports that they enjoyed and followed frequently.

The results indicated that aesthetic motivation was more important for fans of individual sports (e.g., figure skating, golf) while eustress, self-esteem, group affiliation, entertainment, and family reasons were more important motives for fans of team sports (e.g., football, baseball). For fans of nonaggressive sports (e.g., figure skating, baseball), aesthetics, again, was rated highly. For fans of aggressive sports (e.g., wrestling, football), economic, eustress, group affiliation, and entertainment were highly rated motives. Aesthetic motivation was also a high motive for fans of stylistic sports (e.g., figure skating, gymnastics). Fans of nonstylistic sports (e.g., hockey, tennis) rated economic, eustress, self-esteem, group affiliation, entertainment, and family reasons highly. Finally, the profiles of motives across sports were noted.

To date, only one study has examined fan motivation for attendance at different levels of a given sport. Bernthal and Graham (2003) explored the difference in fan motivation factors among fans attending Minor League baseball games and collegiate baseball games. A total of 522 fans, 188 from a Minor League game and 334 from a collegiate baseball game, completed an 11-item survey of the reasons they attended the game. From the survey, four motivational factors were established: Baseball (rivalries, quality of play, viewing outstanding players), Value (ticket price, overall cost of attendance including parking, concessions), Added Entertainment (promotions/giveaways, in-game entertainment such as mascots, sound effects.), and Community (family involvement, allegiance to home team). Results indicated that Minor League fans consider Value and Added Entertainment to be more important than collegiate fans. Collegiate fans considered Baseball and Community to be more important than did Minor League fans (Bernthal and Graham, 2003).

Two other factors that could influence attendance at a sporting event include team identification and level of sport fandom. Team identification is the extent to which a fan feels a psychological connection to a team and the team's performances are viewed as self-relevant (Branscombe and Wann, 1991). A number of positive outcomes have been associated with high levels of team identification, including feelings of self worth and life satisfaction (Branscombe and Wann, 1991), high self-esteem and social well-being (Lanter and Blackburn, 2004), and low levels of loneliness, depression, and other negative emotions (Wann, Dimmock, and Grove, 2003). In fact, Wann (2006) proposed the Team Identification Social Psychological Health Model as an explanation for the positive relationship between identification with a local sport team and social psychological health. In addition to, or perhaps because of, the psychological benefits they receive from identification, people who are highly identified with a specific team are more likely to attend sporting contests that involve that specific team than people with low levels of identification (Wann, Bayens, and Driver, 2004), regardless whether the game location was home or away (Wann, Roberts, and Tindall, 1999).

A second factor that could influence game attendance is sport fandom. People who describe themselves as fans of a given sport will be more likely to attend events in that sport than people who are not fans.

While the extant research on motivation to attend sporting events examines reasons people attend different types of sport, it does not address reasons people attend different levels of the same sport. For example, it is quite conceivable the fans attend children's sporting events (e.g., Little League baseball games) for different reasons than they attend professional games (e.g., Major League Baseball games). This study was designed to begin an examination of fan motivations for attending games at different levels of the same sport.

The research was designed to answer the question, "What motivates fans to attend sporting events of different levels?" There were two hypotheses for the current research. Hypothesis 1: It was expected that there would be different motivation profiles for fans attending different levels of sporting events. Hypothesis 2: It was expected that fans attending lower level sporting events would report lower identification with the teams than fans attending higher level sporting events.

METHOD

Participants

The sample consisted of 224 fans in the mid-south who attended five different baseball games at different levels. Of the 224 participants 122 were male and 102 were female. The sample was divided between five different levels of baseball. The sample consisted of 46 fans from a T-Ball game, 40 fans from a Little League baseball game, 46 fans from a High School baseball game, 48 fans from a College baseball game, and 44 fans from a Minor League baseball game. The sample contained 199 Caucasian participants, 14 African American participants, 4 Hispanic participants, 2 Native American participants, 2 Biracial/multiracial participants, and 2 participants that classified themselves as other for ethnicity. The demographic characteristics of participants attending the different level of baseball games are presented in Table 1.

Table 1. Demographics by Level

Motive	T-Ball	Little League	High School	College	Minor League
Age	43.50	39.18	45.98	49.27	41.05
Financial Status	3.83	3.23	4.10	3.91	3.54
Gender (%Male)	69.6%	70.0%	54.3%	27.1%	54.5%
Education (BA or less) 67.4%		89.7%	89.1%	64.6%	93.0%
Ethnicity (Caucasian) 78.3%		80%	95.7%	100.0%	88.6%

Notes: For Age the mean age is reported. For Financial Status the mean status is reported. Financial Status ranged from 1 (Very Poor, Not Enough to Get By) to 6 (Extremely Well To Do). For Gender the percent male and percent female is reported. For Education the percent with a Bachelors Degree or less is reported. For Ethnicity the percent that were Caucasian is reported.

Measures

Demographics. The demographics section consisted of 6 items to identify the age, gender, ethnicity, education level, and financial status of participants.

Motivation. The Sport Fan Motivation Scale-Revised (SFMS-R; Bilyeu and Wann, 2002) consists of 33 items that assess 11 different fan motives for attending sporting events: escape, economic, eustress, self-esteem, group affiliation, entertainment, family, aesthetic, similarity, representation, and support/perceived greater equality. Each subscale contains three items, with the exception of the family, similarity and representation subscales, which contain two items and the support subscale which contains six items. An example of an item from the SFMS-R is, "I like the stimulation I get from watching sports" The response options range from 1 (*low motivation*) to 8 (*high motivation*). The items on each subscale were summed and the total was divided by the number of items in the subscale. High scores on a subscale indicate high motivational level for that particular subscale (Wann, 1995). The SFMS-R is a reliable instrument, with Cronbach reliability coefficients for the 11 factors/subscales ranging from .61 to .94 for all the subscales.

Team Identification. The Sport Spectator Identification Scale (SSIS; Wann and Branscombe, 1993) contains seven items that assess the level of identification with a particular team; an additional item assesses which team the fan is supporting at the game. The responses range from 1 (*not important or low level of identification*) to 8 (*very important or high level of identification*). An example of an item is "How important to you is it that this team wins?" The items were summed to create a total score, and higher total scores indicate a high level of identification with a particular team. The SSIS is a valid and reliable instrument with an internal consistency of .91 and it related to other relevant variables as expected (Wann and Branscombe, 1993).

Fandom. The Sports Fandom Questionnaire (SFQ; Wann, 2002) contains five items that assess fans identification with his or her role as a sport fan. The responses range from 1 (*strongly disagree or low level of role identification*) to 8 (*strongly agree or high level of role identification*). An example of an item is "My life would be less enjoyable if I were not allowed to follow sports." The five item scores were summed to create a total score. Higher total scores indicate higher levels of fandom. The SFQ is a valid and reliable instrument with internal consistency of .96 and .94 test-retest reliability (Wann, 2002).

Procedure

Permission from the baseball team or league was obtained through a phone contact or e-mail before recruiting participants. The participants were recruited by asking fans over the age of 18 attending selected sporting events to participate in the research study. After providing verbal consent, participants were asked to complete a questionnaire packet. Within the packet were the demographics section, the SFMS, SSIS, and the SFQ. The participants completed the packet in one session that took 10 to 15 minutes.

RESULTS

Preliminary Analysis

Prior to examining the impact of different levels of a sport on motivational patterns preliminary analyses were completed. First, the five items of the SFQ were summed to create a single index of level of fandom for the participants. Next, the seven items of the SSIS were summed to create a single index of level of identification with the participants chosen team. Items for each of the SFMS-R motivation subscales were summed to create indices of motivation. Cronbach's Alpha was conducted on the three measures and all were found to have acceptable internal consistency. Cronbach's Alpha for the SFQ was .93. Cronbach's Alpha for the SSIS was .87. Cronbach's Alpha for the SFMS-R Aesthetic subscale was .78. Cronbach's Alpha for the SFMS-R Group Affiliation subscale was .67. Cronbach's Alpha for the SFMS-R Economic subscale was .86. Cronbach's Alpha for the SFMS-R Representation subscale was .87. Cronbach's Alpha for the SFMS-R Escape subscale was .93. Cronbach's Alpha for the SFMS-R Similarity subscale was .81. Cronbach's Alpha for the SFMS-R Self-esteem subscale was .67. Cronbach's Alpha for the SFMS-R Support/Equality subscale was .87. Cronbach's Alpha for the SFMS-R Family subscale was .57. Cronbach's Alpha for the SFMS-R Eustress subscale was .82.

Motivational Patterns

Comparisons across different levels. The first set of examinations involved a Multivariate Analysis of Variance (MANOVA) in which the levels served as the grouping variables and motivation subscale scores were employed as the multiple dependent measures. Means and standard deviations for SFMS-R subscales by levels appear in Table 2. The MANOVA yielded a significant multivariate effect, Wilks' Lambda $F (10, 224) = 2.78, p < .001, \eta^2 = .17$.

Since the MANOVA was significant, a series of univariate one-way Analyses of Variance (ANOVAs) was completed using each motivation subscale as the dependent variable. These tests were followed up by Scheffe post hoc tests to determine which levels differed from each other. The univariate one-way ANOVA on the aesthetic subscale resulted in a significant between-subjects effect, $F(4, 213) = 4.51$, $p = .002$, $\eta^2 = .09$. The post hoc analysis indicated that aesthetic motivation subscale scores were significantly higher for the high school ($p = .007$) and college ($p = .012$) level than the T-Ball level.

Table 2. Means (and Standard Deviations) for the Motivation Subscales by Level

Motive	T-Ball	Little League	High School	College	Minor League
AES	3.55a (1.67)	3.90ac (1.83)	4.91bc (2.02)	4.82bc (1.89)	4.12ac (1.72)
G A	4.02a (1.63)	4.66ac (1.88)	5.08bc (1.74)	5.04bc (1.86)	4.68ac (1.43)
ECO	1.21abc 0.69)	1.81ab (1.77)	1.29abc 0.86)	1.19ac (0.55)	1.40abc (0.96)
REP	2.66a (2.08)	3.68ab (2.54)	4.33ab (2.66)	3.24b (2.24)	2.95ab (2.26)
ESC	2.14a (1.53)	3.28ab (2.29)	2.96ab (1.99)	3.94b (2.20)	3.23ab (2.05)
SIM	2.27a (1.58)	3.53bc (2.19)	3.84bc (2.27)	3.95b (2.07)	2.65ac (1.93)
S-E	2.51a (1.34)	4.04bcd (1.87)	3.60bcd 1.72)	4.40bc (1.60)	3.10ad (1.64)
ENT	5.47a (2.04)	5.90ab (2.04)	6.32ab (1.38)	6.90b (1.16)	6.23ab (1.73)
S/E	2.68a (1.59)	3.82a (2.14)	3.64a (1.98)	3.75a (1.95)	2.87a (1.69)
FAM	4.38a (2.19)	5.59ab (1.93)	5.77b (1.80)	4.64ab (2.21)	5.31ab (2.10)
EUS	3.00a (1.56)	4.63bc (2.17)	4.46bc (2.10)	5.17bc (1.92)	4.16ac (2.26)

Notes: Standard deviations appear in parentheses below each mean. SFMS-R subscale scores range from 1 (*low motivation*) to 8 (*high motivation*). AES = aesthetic, G A = group affiliation, ECO = economic, REP = representation, ESC = escape, SIM = similarity, S-E = self-esteem, ENT = entertainment, S/E = support/equality, FAM = family, and EUS = eustress. Means with different superscripts are significantly different at the $p < .05$ level.

The univariate one-way ANOVA on the group affiliation motivation subscale resulted in a significant between-subjects effect, $F(4, 218) = 2.80$, $p = .027$, $\eta^2 = .05$. Post hoc analysis indicated that group affiliation subscale scores were significantly higher for the High School ($p = .04$) and College ($p = .05$) level than for the T-Ball level.

The univariate one-way ANOVA on the economic subscale resulted in a significant between-subjects effect, $F(4, 219) = 2.57$, $p = .039$, $\eta^2 = .05$. Post hoc analysis indicated that economic subscale scores were significantly lower for College level ($p = .05$) than for the Little League level.

The univariate one-way ANOVA on the representation subscale resulted in a significant between-subjects effect, $F(4, 221) = 3.46$, $p = .009$, $\eta^2 = .06$.

Post hoc analysis indicated that representation subscale scores were significantly higher for the College level (p = .009) than the T-Ball level.

The univariate one-way ANOVA on the escape subscale resulted in a significant between-subjects effect, F (4, 214) = 3.46, p = .009, η^2 = .09. Post hoc analysis indicated that escape subscale scores were significantly higher for the College level (p < .001) than the T-Ball level.

The univariate one-way ANOVA on the similarity subscale resulted in a significant between-subjects effect, F (4, 220) = 3.46, p = .009, η^2 = .11. Post hoc analysis indicated that Similarity subscale scores were significantly higher for the Little League (p = .05), High School (p = .003), and College (p = .001) level than the T-Ball level. Post hoc analysis also indicated that Similarity subscale scores were significantly higher for the Minor League level (p = .025) than the College level.

The univariate one-way ANOVA on the self esteem subscale resulted in a significant between-subjects effect, F (4, 216) = 3.46, p = .009, η^2 = .18. Post hoc analysis indicated that self esteem subscale scores were significantly higher for the Little League (p < .001), High School (p = .02), and College (p < .001) level than the T-Ball level. Post hoc analysis also indicated that self esteem subscale scores were significantly higher for the Minor League level than the College level.

The univariate one-way ANOVA on the entertainment subscale resulted in a significant between-subjects effect, F (4, 217) = 3.46, p = .009, η^2 = .08. Post hoc analysis indicated that entertainment subscale scores were significantly higher for the College level (p = .001) than the T-Ball level.

One-way ANOVA analysis on the support/equality subscale resulted in a significant between-subjects effect, F (4, 216) = 3.46, p = .009, η^2 = .07. Post hoc analysis indicated that support/equality subscale scores were lower for the T-Ball level than all the other levels, although none were statistically significant.

The univariate one-way ANOVA on the family subscale resulted in a significant between-subjects effect, F (4, 214) = 3.46, p = .009, η^2 = .07. Post hoc analysis indicated that family subscale scores were significantly higher for the High School level (p = .018) than the T-Ball level.

The univariate one-way ANOVA on the eustress subscale resulted in a significant between-subjects effect, F (4, 217) = 3.46, p = .009, η^2 = .13. Post hoc analysis indicated that eustress subscale scores were significantly lower for the T-Ball level than all the other levels (all ps < .05).

A one-way within-subject ANOVA was conducted on each motive by level. The univariate one-way ANOVA for the T-Ball level resulted in a significant within-subjects effect, $F (10, 220) = 32.54$, $p < .001$. The analysis for T-Ball level indicated that all motives were different from one another. The highest motive for fans at the T-Ball level games was the Entertainment motive as shown in Figure 1. The lowest motive for fans at the T-Ball level game was the Economic motive.

The repeated measure within-subjects ANOVA for the Little League level resulted in a significant within-subjects effect, $F (10, 360) = 24.81$, $p < .001$. The analysis for Little League level indicated that all motives were different from one another. The highest motive for fans at the Little League level games was the Entertainment motive as shown in Figure 1. The lowest motive for fans at the Little League level game was the Economic motive.

The repeated measure within-subjects ANOVA for the High School level resulted in a significant within-subjects effect, $F (10, 410) = 38.73$, $p < .001$. The analysis for High School level indicated that all motives were different from one another. The highest motive for fans at the High School level games was the Entertainment motive as shown in Figure 1. The lowest motive for fans at the High School level game was the Economic motive.

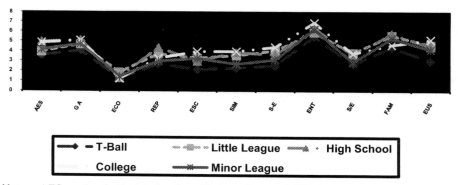

Notes: AES = Aesthetic Motivation, G A = Group Affiliation Motivation, ECO = Economic Motivation, REP = Representation Motivation, ESC = Escape Motivation, SIM = Similarity Motivation, S-E = Self-Esteem Motivation, ENT = Entertainment Motivation, S/E = Support/Equality Motivation, FAM = Family Motivation, and EUS = Eustress Motivation.

Figure 1. Means for the Motivation Subscales by Level.

The repeated measure within-subjects ANOVA for the College level resulted in a significant within-subjects effect, $F (10, 430) = 34.09$, $p < .001$. The analysis for College level indicated that all motives were different from one another. The highest motive for fans at the College level games was the

Entertainment motive as shown in Figure 1. The lowest motive for fans at the College level game was the Economic motive.

The repeated measure within-subjects ANOVA for the Minor League level resulted in a significant within-subjects effect, F (10, 400) = 39.51, p < .001. The analysis for Minor League level indicated that all motives were different from one another. The highest motive for fans at the Minor League level games was the Entertainment motive as shown in Figure 1. The lowest motive for fans at the Minor League level game was the Economic motive.

A MANOVA was conducted to determine if there were any differences between levels and resulted in F (4, 202) = 5.94, p < .001, η^2 = .10. This test was followed up by Scheffe's post hoc test to determine which levels differed from one another. Post hoc analysis also indicated that the T-Ball level is significantly different from the Little League, High School, and College levels but not the Minor League level (all ps < .05). The Little League, High School, College, and Minor League levels were not statistically different from one another.

Identification and Fandom

Two univariate one-way ANOVAs were conducted for the SSIS and the SFQ. These tests were followed up by Scheffe post hoc tests to determine which levels differed from each other. The results of these analyses are found in Table 3. The univariate one-way ANOVA on the SSIS resulted in a significant between-subjects effect, F (4, 215) = 16.02, p < .001, η^2 = .06. The univariate one-way ANOVA on the post hoc analysis indicated that the SSIS scores were significantly higher for the High School, and College levels than the T-Ball level (all ps < .001). Post hoc analysis also indicated that the SSIS score for the College level was significantly higher than the Little League level andthe Minor League level (p < .001).

DISCUSSION

The current study was designed to examine fan motivation for attending different levels of the same sport. There were two specific hypotheses under study. First, it was expected that there would be different motivation profiles for fans attending different levels of sporting events. Second, it was expected that fans attending lower level sporting events would report lower identification with the teams than fans attending higher level sporting events. The following results partially supported each hypothesis.

The first hypothesis was partially supported in that participants from the T-Ball and Minor League levels did not score highly on any of the motivation subscales. Overall, participants from the T-Ball level scored lower on all motives than the other levels. This could be due to fans at T-Ball games not being very invested in being a fan of the team. The SFQ mean, shown in Table 3, was lower for the fans at the T-Ball level than the other levels, which indicates that participants at the T-Ball games do not perceive themselves as baseball fans. The SSIS mean, shown in Table 3, was lower for T-Ball than all levels except the Minor League level, which indicates that people attending T-Ball and Minor League games are not highly identified with any particular T-Ball team.

Table 3. Means and Standard Deviations for the SSIS and SFQ by level

Level	SSIS Total	SFQ Total
T-Ball	27.98 (10.43)	16.65 (9.29)
Little League	36.92 (8.03)	21.84 (9.47)
High School	39.98 (9.35)	27.16 (10.02)
College	37.84 (12.95)	30.37 (8.73)
Minor League	26.36 (12.32)	22.48 (10.64)

Notes: Standard deviations appear in parentheses below each mean. SSIS = Sport Spectator Identification Scale responses range from 1 (*not important* or *low level of identification*) to 8 (*very important* or *high level of identification*). The total SSIS score ranges from 7 to 56. SFQ = Sports Fandom Questionnaire responses range from 1 (*strongly disagree or low level of role identification*) to 8 (*strongly agree or high level of role identification*). The total SFQ score ranges from 5 to 40.

An analysis of the different levels revealed that the participants at the High School, Little League, and College levels scored higher than the other levels on the motivation subscales. It is possible that fans at High School, Little League, and College level games are more invested in being a fan of the team. The SFQ mean, shown in Table 3, was higher for the High School and College levels than the other levels, which indicates that participants at the High School and College are invested in perceiving themselves as baseball fans. The SSIS mean, shown in Table 3, was higher for Little League, High School, and College levels than the Minor League and T-Ball levels, which indicates that people attending Little League, High School, and College games are highly identified with one of the teams playing in the game.

The second hypothesis was partially supported. An analysis of the different levels level of identification, see Table 2, revealed that fans attending High School games had higher identification with the team than other levels. College and Little League level fans also had a high level of identification with their teams. Fans attending Minor League and T-Ball games had the lowest level of identification with the team than other levels.

The results show that Little League, High School, and College baseball fans are similar in their motivational patterns and identification with being a baseball fan and a fan of a particular team. Also shown by the results is that T-Ball and Minor League Fans are very similar in their motivational patterns and identification with being a baseball fan and a fan of a particular team. It does not appear that the type of baseball played at each of these levels is similar— Minor League baseball differs in both quality and quantity from T-Ball baseball. However, it appears as though the importance that fans place on identification with the team and importance of attending games is similar between the two. Future research should examine why these similarities in identification and motivation exist.

The results show that, for all levels, statistically significant differences existed for the motives on the SFMS-R. However, the overall pattern of results was very similar. For all the levels of baseball, entertainment was the strongest motive and economic was the weakest motive for attendance. This indicates that the sport itself draws people to view it for specific reasons.

When the current research is compared to the Wann et al. (in press) findings for professional baseball, a similar pattern emerges. However, the pattern is not identical. The results of the current study indicate a much higher mean for the Family motivation than Wann et al. Such a difference could be because Wann et al. examined fans of Major League Baseball while the current study only examined up through the Minor League level. Thus, people could be motivated to watch Major League Baseball baseball for different reasons than Minor League baseball, just as they attend Minor League and College level baseball games for different reasons (Bernthal and Graham, 2003). Additionally, the difference could also be due to where the data was collected. The present study collected the data from fans who were actually in attendance at a baseball game, while Wann et al. collected data from fans away from the baseball park, and asked them why they usually attend games. Collecting data at the game could yield more valid results, because it is easier for the fans to note why they are attending a game rather than recall why they usually go to games once they are away from them.

The present results also parallel the findings of other researchers. Similar to the present findings, James and Ross (2004) found that consumers of men's baseball rated the Entertainment motive higher than other motives for following their respective teams. McDonald et al. (2002) found that the Self-Esteem motive was the lowest reported motive across all the sports. The current results also indicate that the Self-Esteem motive is the lowest motive.

In terms of identification, the results of the current study indicate that team identification is stronger for fans attending lower level baseball games than for those attending higher level baseball games. This stronger connection to the team for lower levels may be due to proximity to the team; that is most fans attending lower level games were more likely to have a close friend or family member who is on the team. With the higher levels, fans may not feel as connected to the teams because they do not personally know the players. These results are limited because the sample did not include people attending a Major League Baseball game, where identification with the team could be higher.

Still, these findings hold implications in regards to Wann's (2006) Team Identification-Social Psychological Health Model, which shows that high identification with a team increases a person's social psychological health. According to the model, social psychological health increases as a result of the social connections that people make because of their identification with a local team. However, to date, this model has only been tested by examining identification with college or professional teams. Based on these results, it is expected that the Team Identification—Social Psychological Health Model should also work with lower level teams. While it is not likely that people will encounter enough others identified with a Little League team, it is likely that this model will work with identification with high school teams.

While the data presented furthers our understanding of the motivational patterns found among fans at different levels of a sport, there is still much to be discovered about sport fan motivation. For instance, the current research only addressed fan motivation at different levels of baseball; fans of other types of sports could have different patterns of motivation. In addition, the participants for the study were drawn from those over the age of 18 in the mid-south United States; fans with different demographic characteristics may have different motives for attending sporting events.

Table 4. Means (and Standard Deviations) by Gender for Motives, Team Identification, and Fandom

Motives	Men	Women	F	P	Eta2
AES	3.82 (1.82)	4.96 (1.75)	19.53	<.001	.092
GA	4.56 (1.65)	4.88 (1.75)	1.69	.195	.009
ECO	1.34 (1.07)	1.43 (1.10)	.319	.573	.002
REP	3.17 (2.40)	3.50 (2.39)	.920	.339	.005
ESC	2.72 (1.92)	3.68 (2.21)	10.40	.001	.051
SIM	2.72 (2.02)	3.81 (2.11)	13.59	<.001	.066
S-E	3.31 (1.81)	3.85 (1.64)	4.74	.031	.024
ENT	5.88 (1.84)	6.64 (1.26)	10.84	.001	.053
S/E	3.12 (1.84)	3.54 (1.88)	2.40	.123	.012
FAM	5.48 (1.98)	4.86 (2.13)	4.45	.036	.023
EUS	3.88 (2.10)	4.32 (1.99)	10.61	.001	.052
FANtot	20.98 (10.23)	27.45 (9.72)	20.24	<.001	.095
Idtot	33.21 (11.66)	33.47 (12.30)	.024	.878	.000

Notes: Standard deviations appear in parentheses next to each mean AES = aesthetic, G A = group affiliation, ECO = economic, REP = representation, ESC = escape, SIM = similarity, S-E = self-esteem, ENT = entertainment, S/E = support/equality, FAM = family, and EUS = eustress, FANtot = fandom total, Idtot = team identification total.

The results of the current study only partially support the hypotheses. All the levels had differences within individual motives. However, the motivational patterns were similar in that the fans at all of the levels ranked Entertainment as their highest motive and Economic as their lowest motive. These similarities in levels show that baseball fans do not need to go to higher level games to obtain the entertainment that the results show fans desire. Fans can go to local or youth games and have the same entertainment without the cost or distance. In fact, the similarities found in this study could at least partially explain the popularity of youth sports, such as little league baseball, and high school sports with people who do not have children participating.

In conclusion, sport fans of all levels are highly motivated to attend baseball games for the entertainment value as well as to spend time with their friends and family. The sport itself seems to draw people to attend games with other individual factors also contributing to attendance. Fans attend baseball games for enjoyment of the game regardless of the teams they support. Fans may be in support of a particular team but, regardless of the game outcome the entertainment value of the game is not lost.

REFERENCES

Bernthal, M. J., and Graham, P. J. (2003). The effects of sport setting on fan attendance motivation: The case of Minor League vs. collegiate baseball. *Journal of Sport Behavior, 26*, 223-240.

Bilyeu, J. K., and Wann, D. L. (2002). An investigation of racial differences in sport fan motivation. *International Sports Journal, 6*, 93-106.

Branscombe, N. R., and Wann, D. L. (1991). The positive social and self concept consequences of sports team identification. *Journal of Sport and Social Issues, 15,* 115-127.

James, J. D., and Ross, S. D. (2004). Comparing sport consumer motivations across multiple sports. *Sport Marketing Quarterly, 13,* 17-25.

Lanter, J. R., and Blackburn, J. Z. (2004, September). *The championship effect on college students' identification and university affiliation.* Paper presented at the annual meeting of the Association for the Advancement of Applied Sport Psychology, Minneapolis, MN.

McDonald, M. A., Milne, G. R., and Hong, J. (2002). Motivational factors for evaluating sport spectator and participant markets. *Sport Marketing Quarterly, 11,* 100-113.

Mehus, I. (2005). Sociability and excitement motives of spectators attending entertainment sports events: Spectators of soccer and ski-jumping. *Journal of Sport Behavior, 28,* 333-350.

Wann, D. L. (1995). Preliminary validation of the sport fan motivation scale. *Journal of Sport and Social Issues, 19,* 377-395.

Wann, D. L. (2002). Preliminary validation of a measure for assessing identification as a sport fan: The sport fandom questionnaire. *International Journal of Sport Management, 3,* 103-115.

Wann, D. L. (2006). Understanding the positive social psychological benefits of sport team identification: The Team Identification-Social Psychological Health Model. *Group Dynamics: Theory, Research, and Practice, 10,* 272-296.

Wann, D., Bayens, C., and Driver, A. (2004). Likelihood of attending a sporting event as a function of ticket scarcity and team identification. *Sport Marketing Quarterly,* 13, 209-215.

Wann, D. L., and Branscombe, N. R. (1993). Sports fans: Measuring degree of identification with the team. *International Journal of Sport Psychology, 24,* 1-17.

Wann, D. L., Dimmock, J. A., and Grove, J. R. (2003). Generalizing the Team Identification – Psychological Health Model to a Different Sport and Culture: The Case of Australian Rules Football. *Group Dynamics: Theory, Research, and Practice, 7,* 289-296.

Wann, D. L., Grieve, F. G., Zapalac, R. K., and Pease, D. G. (in press). The impact of target sport on the motivational profiles of sport fans. *Contemporary Athletics.*

Wann, D., Roberts, A., and Tindall, J. (1999). Role of team performance, team identification, and self-esteem in sport spectators' game preferences. *Perceptual and Motor Skills,* 89, 945-450.

Advances in Sports and Athletics. Volume 1   ISBN: 978-1-61122-824-3
Editor: James P. Waldorf   © 2012 Nova Science Publishers, Inc.

CHARACTERISTICS OF SUCCESS IN MEN'S FOOTBALL AND MEN'S BASKETBALL AT THE DIVISION I LEVEL

Shane L. Hudson[*]
Texas A and M University, Texas, US

ABSTRACT

The push for student-athletes to graduate college has never been greater. Student-athletes are under more pressure to not only complete their degree but, to do it in a timely manner under NCAA guidelines. The intent of this study was to determine if men's football and men's basketball coaches at the university or college level utilize an assessment instrument when recruiting and evaluating potential student-athletes. Specifically studied through interviews were the characteristics that these coaches look for in successful and unsuccessful student-athletes, how they currently collect information during the recruitment period and whether collecting data on student-athletes is of importance or not. The population for this study consisted of current Division IA men's football and men's basketball coaches in the Big 12 Conference. The study helps to define through research and development an assessment instrument to more effectively define the needs of student-athletes prior to entering universities.

Through its first ten years, the Big 12 Conference has claimed 28 team and 310 individual NCAA titles and currently has over 4,600 student-athletes in 21 sports. Due to their athletic accomplishments and size the Big 12 Conference was used to determine whether coaches in men's basketball and

[*] Phone: (979) 845-8832; FAX: (979) 862-6489; Email: shudson@hlkn.tamu.edu

football utilize an assessment instrument in recruiting that helps define the character and potential success of the student-athlete. The ability to predict success is important because of statistics such as those put forward by the Knight Foundation Commission on Intercollegiate Athletics. According to their combined reports (1999),

> Nearly a third of present and former professional football players responding to a survey near the end of the decade said they accepted illicit payments while in college, and more than half said they saw nothing wrong with the practice. Another survey showed that among 100 big-time schools, 35 had graduation rates under 20 percent for their basketball players and 14 had the same low rate for their football players. (p. 4)

Today student-athletes are under more pressure to stay in school and complete their degrees and coaches are under more pressure to recruit student-athletes who will stay in school and out of trouble.

In the classroom

According to *The NCAA News* (2005), the philosophy of the NCAA is that colleges and universities should educate and graduate the student-athletes they recruit to their campuses. The NCAA has raised the stakes through aggressive legislation for recruiting student-athletes who are better prepared for collegiate life. Unfortunately there has been more talk than research on predicting the success of student-athletes (Sedlacek and Adams-Gaston, 1992). Crouse and Trusheim (1988) argued that high-school grades are better than the SAT at predicting college performance and that, while the SAT improves prediction significantly over high-school grades alone, the improvement is too small to be worth the effort (Baron and Norman, 1992). Without the ability to predict or assess student-athletes through standardized test scores, high school or junior college grades, universities must find alternative methods that best predict success from a holistic perspective.

Off the Field and Outside the Classroom

One cannot argue that athletes at colleges and universities are often in the news for scandalous, criminal, disruptive and controversial issues. Greg

Auman (2005) begins an article, "With scandals alleging criminal behavior at Colorado, Baylor and elsewhere focusing attention on the athletes schools recruit, universities are re-evaluating how they screen for character" (St. Petersburg Times online, 1). In 2006 there was the side-line clearing brawl between Miami and Florida International where Tim Reynolds from the Associated Press stated that this "was the third on-field incident in Miami's past seven games" (15). Officials from Miami, FIU, the Sun Belt and Atlantic conferences then issued 31 one-game suspensions. This trend is not new. In the 1980's a commission on intercollegiate athletics was formed so as to reform the current state of college athletics. According to the President of this commission, now called the Knight Commission on Intercollegiate Athletics, from 1988-1998, Creed C. Black stated that "In 1989, as a decade of highly visible scandals in college sports drew to a close, the trustees of the John S. and James L. Knight Foundation (then known as Knight Foundation) were concerned that athletics abuses threatened the very integrity of higher education" (1999, p. 2). Since then this foundation has done a positive job of correctly reporting the current state of college athletics, both the good and the bad.

PURPOSE OF THE STUDY

The intent of this study was to determine if men's football and men's basketball coaches at the university or college level utilize an assessment instrument when recruiting and evaluating potential student-athletes. Specifically studied through interviews were the characteristics that these coaches look for in successful and unsuccessful student-athletes, how they currently collect information during the recruitment period and the importance of collecting data on student-athletes. The study helps to define through research and development an assessment instrument to more effectively define the needs of student-athletes prior to entering universities and coaches will have additional data for meeting the needs of student-athletes.

Coaches and staff members that recruit at the university level should look at a multilevel performance model such as Swanson's Performance Diagnosis Matrix. Multilevel performance models were developed to reduce the "complexity of organizational systems to a more manageable form by creating taxonomic models of key performance variables" (Swanson and Holton, 2001, p. 188). This model in particular focuses on the organization, the process, and the individual as performance levels. "In order to achieve organization and individual performance, it is critical that all three performance levels are aligned" (Rummler, 1996, p. 29). The performance variables for each level are goals, system design, capacity, motivation and expertise. "These performance variables, matrixed with the levels of performance - organization, process, and/or individual - provide a powerful perspective in diagnosing performance" (Swanson and Holton, 2001, p. 194). The diagnosis of successful performance at each level can be determined by the answers to particular questions, which therefore can be used by institutions who seek to develop and encourage a performance based program. In as much, "the questions presented in the performance variable matrix help the diagnostician sort out the performance overlaps and disconnects" (Swanson and Holton, 2001, p. 194). For example, based on how a student-athlete answers these questions an organization can determine whether that particular student-athlete is the right fit for that particular institution, whether they can thrive and succeed, whether they have the drive to obtain a degree, and whether they have the motivation to succeed on the field. Therefore, identifying whether a recruit has those characteristics of success or performance variables prior to a university's investment in him or her could prove to be of great value.

METHOD

The goal in the data collection was to conduct unstructured interviews with the head coaches of each of the Big 12 teams to find out what they feel are predictors of success in student-athletes. Because the information is not directly observable, interviews were used to collect data. As Patton (2002) points out, "open-ended questions and probes yield in-depth responses about people's experiences, perceptions, opinions, feelings, and knowledge. Data consists of verbatim quotations with sufficient context to be interpretable" (p. 4).

A pilot study was conducted in July 2006 to help work out any possible problems with questions as well as method. The focus at this time was on contacting three coaches, not head coaches. Each coach conveyed the importance of the research and stated they were anxious to hear the results. As a condition of entry a letter of introduction was sent prior to asking for an interview. In as much, one of the pilot study coaches also suggested that the letter express an interest in an interview for research purposes. This coach was then used as a reference. The letter was simple, understandable and most importantly let the coaches know that there was something "in it for them."

Just as Erlandson et al. (1993) stated, "the accomplishment of successful entry also partially revolves around the field researcher's ability to explain his interests in terms that make sense to the members of the setting" (p. 72). The letter also had a former Division IA head football coach from the pilot study who endorsed the study and left his contact information if anyone felt the need to contact him. The letters were mailed to each head coaches' office on July 25th 2006.

Out of the 24 letters that were mailed, two responses were logged the following week. During the next month there were about two responses per week with the total sample response ending up at 9. A code system was used in order of responses, R 1-9. The R is coded for "respondent" and each one received a number in the order in which they were interviewed. Therefore, the first coach interviewed is coded R1 while the last coach interviewed is coded R9.

The phone interviews ranged from July 14th to September 18th and lasted anywhere from twelve minutes to thirty five minutes in length. Most head coaches referred the interviews to their assistant coaches whom the head coach trusted to provide accurate information therefore only on head coach was interviewed. The genders of the coaches interviewed were all male. Each interview took an extraordinary amount of time to coordinate due to the busy occupations of Division I A coaches. The data collection was started in early fall when Division I A football have two-a-day camps in preparation for the upcoming football season. Basketball was out of season and at first glance should have made contact less time consuming on their part. Rarely did the head coaches call personally; that happened only twice during the data collection process. The first head coach had his secretary call and setup an appointment 2 weeks in advance. The interview questions were:

1. What are the characteristics of a successful student-athlete (On and off the playing field)?
2. What are the characteristics of an unsuccessful student-athlete (On and off the playing field)?
3. How do you collect information regarding student-athletes prior to the student-athletes enrollment? Describe your current process?
4. Discuss the current issues involved in assessing student-athletes prior to college enrollment?

Understanding that data analysis is a messy and ambiguous process, emergent category designation was used to organize data into categories of ideas. These ideas were then formed into themes or constructs which illustrated what the coaches feel are predictors of student-athlete success. Consequently, a database was developed where topics, categories and statements moved around throughout the entire process.

The ability to use thematic analysis appears to involve a number of underlying abilities, or competencies. One competency can be called *pattern recognition*. It is the ability to see patterns in seemingly random information (Swanson and Holton, 2001). Patton cites content analysis as an example of analyzing text (interview transcripts, diaries, or documents) rather than observation-based field notes. Patton goes on to say that "content analysis is used to refer to any qualitative data reduction and sense making effort that takes a volume of qualitative material and attempts to identify core consistencies and meanings" (Patton, 2002, p. 453). In as much, content analysis was used to establish patterns in the interview transcripts.

FINDINGS

From analyzing the data the research found that the *coaches utilize different methods of assessing successful student-athletes,* most of which are not formalized, and that this is *the toughest part and most important* aspects of their jobs. The coaches tend to just go with a feeling or with their experience . as to what would indicate success. Every respondent made a statement or comment about one of these overall findings. One respondent stated that "there was no specific process" (R7) while another stated "no process is used" (R2). Others said that they "try to collect data but it is very difficult to do" (R4) and another said that all they have is a "regular line of questions" (R5) that they ask. According to (R1), he stated that trying to find successful students "is the toughest job that they have". Another respondent said "it is difficult to assess a high school student who is only 17 or 18 years old" (R9) while another coach stated that this process "is extremely important, everything ties into it" (R8). A coach said that they "will not offer until they get to know the kid, coach and family" (R3) while another coach said they "use a questionnaire to assess" student-athletes (R6). Therefore from the data analysis the research indicated a need for an assessment instrument with which coaches could utilize in assessing successful student-athletes.

Interview Question #1

The first interview question asked, "What are the characteristics of a successful student-athlete (On and off the playing field)?" From this question the data revealed that successful student-athletes, according to the nine respondents, are competitive, hard working, have some sort of family support, are leaders, take academics seriously, have character and are honest. "Driven to succeed in all areas. The best ones have a presence and are self motivated" (R8). Coaches, like student-athletes, are competitive and the research found that this specific characteristic, competitiveness, emerged from the data as most sought after by the coaches. Therefore, the first characteristic was identified as competitiveness. The constructs that support this theme were recognized as presence, self-motivation and determination. When this particular coach talked about success in all areas, he was referring to a student-athletes athletic ability, academic work, social life, and his character. When he talks about presence this refers to the student-athletes leadership abilities and how he handles himself on and off the field of play. Self-motivated athletes take care of business in the classroom, on the field and in the weight room. "Competitiveness drives them to do academic work better than they would if they weren't in athletics" (R7). In the competitive world of Division I college athletics, coaches are just as concerned about academics as they are about athletics. This particular coach felt that the student-athletes competitive nature gives him the extra determination and resolve he needs to achieve his academic and athletic goals. Other coaches clearly made a statement regarding the athletic realm by stating "We are looking for a guy who wants to win championships and comes from a good program" (R3). This coach doesn't appear to be as worried about how competitive this student is in the classroom and this aspect, academics, was not brought up during this part of the interview. Another respondent stated that he was looking for a young man who "hated to loose and loved to win" (R7). Again this was a direct reference to sports and being competitive. The competitive nature that student-athletes bring to their universities is for the most part a trait that is admired by their peers. Competitiveness is a quality that people look for in student-athletes and in people that are hired for jobs in almost every aspect of the highly competitive world in which we live. It is something that can be observed and has emerged as the most important aspect of success in student-athletes by the coaches contacted in the interview.

The next characteristic that emerged was that of hard worker. This doesn't seem too far removed from competitive but it emerged as a major theme under this research question. Furthermore, this characteristic is supported by the constructs of commitment, motivation and good work habits. This aspect seemed to be brought up regarding the student-athletes commitment to sport and everyday life. According to one respondent "players need to be motivated to work hard, and to play in the NBA is motivation" (R7). In order for athletic programs to be successful you need a "motivated athlete" (R2) and athletes with "good work habits" (R9). Without these essential elements coaches will likely struggle in the win and loss column and run the risk of being fired from their jobs before the student-athlete matriculates from a freshman to a senior. Research on the student-athlete begins in high school and the coaches are looking at every aspect of the meaning of work ethic. "We call the high school counselors and ask them if the student-athlete is in school everyday" (R6). From the coaches' perspective if a student-athlete can not get out of bed and go to school everyday, this directly relates to their motivation to succeed both academically and on the field or court.

The theme of family was important to the coaches interviewed and emerged from the research. It encompassed several constructs such as caring, having parents who are active in their lives, a good support system, stability, ability to adjust to adversity and having both a mother and father at home. This theme appeared to be a characteristic of successful student-athletes that some of the respondents were very passionate about. According to one respondent they are looking for "good guys that care about family and people. One or two parents with a solid household and are the parents active in the learning process" (R3)? When the parents have been active in the learning process the coaches feel that they will adjust easier to the pressures of making the grade academically at a major Division I A university. During the interviews the coaches made note of not only a strong presence of family but having both a mother and father at home. "We are looking for guys that have a support system in place with two parents" (R9). "Family is big. With mother and father, there is more emphasis on grades" (R6). Stability at home leads to students who adjust to adverse situations like the combination of academic rigor and intercollegiate athletics. It is up to the coaches to observe that environment when they visit the potential student-athletes home and when the student-athlete comes to campus for an official visit. Unfortunately, there is not enough time to observe the family in depth. The NCAA allows for limited contact with student-athletes during the recruiting process.

The theme of leadership is an important element and the coaches interviewed recognized that this intangible is very important to the success of their student-athlete. During the interview process the coaches did not go into detail of what leadership meant to them. However, I did identify the constructs of politeness, good citizenship and social ability as supportive of this theme. One respondent simply stated that "leadership was important" (R1). Another respondent stated that he wanted his student-athletes to be "polite and good citizens" (R3). "Poor social aspects and poor leadership" (R3) are under the microscope during the recruiting process and serve as an indicator for non-selection.

The academic aspect of a student-athlete was the next theme that emerged. Students who want to graduate and are responsible and who are a good fit with the university are the constructs that support this theme of academics. According to one respondent the student-athlete must be a "good fit with the university" (R1). This can encompass many variables and each coach will evaluate this differently at their institution. The academic fit would need to be a high priority. Another respondent stated that he is looking for student-athletes who "want to graduate and that it's not just about football" (R3). This construct is in correlation with the previous construct of being a hard worker. There is a correlation to being a hard worker on the field and in academics. He went on to say that "this is something that coaches talk about all the time" (R3). Most coaches want the best of both worlds. Great athletes and great students in the sports of men's football and men's basketball exist but with, for example, 119 Division I university's recruiting them; the competition to get these student-athletes on their campus is rigorous.

Character rounded out the information that emerged from this question and was recognized as a theme with the constructs of commitment, character, trustworthiness, no substance abuse and stays out of trouble. I had anticipated that the construct of "character" would be the number one topic that emerged due to the word character in the question that was asked to the coaches. One school in particular covered a lot on character and it was apparent during our conversation that the coach and their program were deeply committed to this one aspect. When he spoke his voice raised and he went into detail so quick and furiously that it was difficult to cover it all. According to this respondent, "character comes first (R6). They want to know every detail about a student-athlete before they bring him to their school. When looking at document analysis I found that they (R6) have a questionnaire and ask questions such as:

- Has he been suspended from school?
- Has he ever used drugs?
- Has he given a reason not to trust him?
- Would you worry if you allowed him to babysit your children?

If the answer is yes to 3 out of 4 questions then that is sufficient and they would not recruit or take him.

Other respondents simply wanted to know if the student-athlete was "an honest person" (R2). According to this respondent the coaching staff had a mental checklist that they used during the recruitment of a student-athlete. A formal process or checklist of what the coaches are looking for in regard to this question only existed with two out of the nine coaching staff interviewed. The rest simply went off their instincts or a mental checklist they developed after spending years in the field evaluating talent.

The constructs that support these characteristics or themes of a successful student-athlete are descriptive. The findings in the table show that there are several predictors that the coaches are looking for in prospective student-athletes.

Interview Question #2

When the coaches were asked the second question of "What are the characteristics of an unsuccessful student-athlete (On and off the playing field)?" they responded in much the same manner as in the previous question. According to (R3) "coaches are not looking for underachievers in the classroom, and personal life." This can only mean one thing if you look at the NCAA graduation rates for men's football and men's basketball. Coaches are not looking for underachievers in the classroom but student-athletes who underachieve are attending college and are struggling. Therefore the five themes that developed with this question were; undisciplined, lack of character, no competitive nature, and unstable family. In the undisciplined theme, coaches found that student-athletes who were undisciplined in behavior at home or within their family were also that way when they came to college. During the recruiting process coaches will visit the home on a "home visit" of the student-athlete. "If there is lack of discipline in the family" (R1) that is observable to coaches during this visit and the student-athlete can hurt his chances of attending that school. The manner in which a student-athlete treats his mother or father is a measure of how he will respond to authority figures on campus. Consequently, the constructs which support the theme of undisciplined is lack of family, respect for authority and following rules and guidelines, along with poor attendance at school or class, and laziness. In as much, (R2) stated that he looked for student-athletes that were not "lazy." This may seem easy to detect but he felt that one must spend a substantial time recruiting a student-athlete to clarify if this characteristic is factual. Coaches stated that they periodically talk to counselors and administrators regarding behavior in school. One respondent was concerned with "how they interact with their family and coach" (R6). Overall behavior and in some cases "not responding to authority" (R5) are factors during recruiting. Student-athletes often fail to realize how important their behavior is in the class room. A respondent defined undisciplined as "he doesn't go to school" (R5) and went on to say that without high school you can't go on to college. Life has parameters and boundaries and before a student-athlete enters a Division I institution coaches try to measure how well they have succeeded "following rules and guidelines" (R5). "Undisciplined student-athletes" (R2) often make it on to college campuses but many will not graduate due to the rigor and discipline required to complete a four year degree.

Emerging as the next theme was a lack of character. The constructs that support this theme of lacking in character are running with the wrong crowd, lack of trust, and inconsistencies or gaps in academics or character. For most of the coaches who I interviewed felt that in the recruiting of student-athletes, poor character was important in the decision to bring this student to campus. (R1) stated that character was important and "running with the wrong crowd was a sign of poor character" (R1). Trust was another major issue in any form and one respondent stated that recruiters want to know "can he be trusted" (R3)? "Has the kid been in trouble" (R3) is another routine question coaches ask when recruiting student-athletes. "Is there a gap (academic or character) wise" (R3)? This same respondent went on to say that "gaps get exposed in college" and recruiters can not afford to make many mistakes of this nature.

No competitive nature emerged from the interviews as the next theme, with constructs such as apathy, and intimidation. Overall the coaches made it apparent that student-athletes in the sport of men's football and basketball need to be competitive due to the competitive nature of the sports. Under no circumstance can student-athletes be "intimidated by competition on and off the field or lacking in competitive nature" (R4). Therefore, "apathy" (R2) is not a trait desired in the highly competitive nature of these sports.

An unstable family theme emerged as being a characteristic of an unsuccessful student-athlete. Coaches believe in a "good support system at home" (R4), thus providing an extra support system for coaches and administrators when the student-athlete arrives to campus. Therefore, the constructs in this theme were lack of role models and no foundation at home. Many factors play a role in the success of a student-athlete including a "foundation, with church as a factor and coaches as role models" (R6). This respondent stressed another particular aspect that was stressed is the "lack of role models in their lives" (R6). In as much, (R9) stated that they paid "close attention to how the student interacts with their family and coaches."

What was found in looking at the data through several methods is that there are particular characteristics that the coaches are looking for. In this question the research found several themes and constructs that are the opposite of what was stated in the previous question. When looking at the themes that were created between the two questions one can see that they are the opposites of each other (see Table 1). Out of the data given as characteristics of a successful student-athlete the themes that developed were ones of that student-athlete being competitive, having a supportive family structure and good character. While the themes that developed out of the data on characteristics of unsuccessful student-athletes were that of the student-athlete being undisciplined, lacking in character and having an unstable family. The other themes of a successful student-athlete; a hard worker, a leader, being honest, and supportive of academics, are also the opposite of the other theme of unsuccessful student-athletes, undisciplined.

Table 1. Comparison of themes for characteristics of successful and unsuccessful student-athletes

Successful Characteristics	Unsuccessful Characteristics
Competitive	Undisciplined
Hard Worker	Lack of Character
Family Support	No Competitive Nature
Leadership	Unstable Family
Support Academics	
Good Character	
Honesty	

Therefore the data from the first two questions show that coaches are looking for student-athletes who are competitive, have a strong family support, have good character and are disciplined or hard workers.

Interview Question #3

In the third question, "how do you collect information regarding student-athletes prior to the student-athletes enrollment and what is your current process?" it was found that most of the coaches did not have a formal process. Therefore, the theme with this question focused on how the coaches currently collect data on recruits. What the research found is that data is collected through discussions and talking, observing and using a questionnaire or form. Talking about or discussing the student-athlete with "as many people as you can" (R2) came up quite often. The most valuable people to discuss an athletes' potential for a program were coaches and high school counselors. Some respondents also liked to talk to anyone associated with the athlete to get a "random snapshot." Therefore the constructs that support this aspect of data collection were talking to coaches, counselors at their high school and others such as family and friends. It was also found that talking to student-athletes was very hard and difficult to do. A respondent stated that he always "talked to the high school coach first" but that it can be tough seeing that there are "1200 high school football players in the state alone" (R1). Another one also stated that he focused on "talking to the high school coach" (R7). Others went on to state that it "goes beyond the high school coach, recruiters need to talk to people walking in the hall of the school" (R8). A coach stated that he has to "talk to as many people as he can" to learn about the student (R2). In essence, (R2) felt that really hearing from multiple sources about a student was a good thing. The next construct was the counselor. Several coaches mentioned the fact that "they have a regular line of questions for them" and they usually prove to be valuable sources (R5, R9). One coach said "they gather athletic information after the students' sophomore year and try to get the students on campus as a junior" (R8). Due to NCAA rules, (R4) stated that they were limited in the amount of phone calls they can make to each student. According to one respondent, he felt that there was just not enough time and contact with the student-athletes and that he feels "we never really get to know them" (R5). He also went on to state that this process is so difficult because sometimes this student could be a "fifty, sixty, or seventy thoUSnd dollar investment" (R5). This aspect correlates with the final construct of this process being difficult to do as student-athletes are being recruited earlier and earlier in their high school careers.

The next construct for assessing student-athletes was student-athletes can be observed at camps, while at practice and on the playing field. I also noted that several of the coaches stated that one criterion they were observing was character. According to (R8), the camps "created a great avenue for athletic evaluation". It was also a place that he stated the coach could look at participation and "gain new leads" to learn about that particular student-athlete. Another respondent stated that observation is "the way coaches stay informed, by watching a player for up to three years" at practices and even "AAU games" (R7). He went on to state that "he wanted to see how that student reacts to certain situations" (R7). The character of the student-athlete was mentioned throughout the answers of the coaches as it had been brought up as well in the prior questions. When asked how they collect information, two coaches referred to fact that they sometimes focus on character. "Character is so important. We look at drug issues and so forth" (R5). Another respondent stated that "character is extremely important as part of the process" (R8). The coaches identified three main methods of collecting information; talking with people, observing the student-athlete, and sending a questionnaire. As stated earlier, most of the respondents acknowledged that this was the hardest part of their jobs and that there was not a specific process used. Most of the coaches indicated they used their instincts to determine whether a student-athlete would be successful at their institution. In as much, most of the coaches indicated their method of gaining information on prospective student-athletes was through talking to people.

Interview Question #4

In the fourth question, "discuss the current issues involved in assessing student-athletes prior to college enrollment?" the coaches identified once again that this was a tough part of their job. "This is the toughest job that we have" stated (R1). With this question four issues emerged from the interviews with many categories to support them. The issues of effects of the Academic Progress Rate (APR), it being a tough job, early commitment factors and character emerged. With the issue of APR the categories that developed from the data were increased pressure, having to be more selective and academics, or in other words, can this student make it academically? "The APR is a real-time assessment of a team's academic performance, which awards two points each term to scholarship student-athletes who meet academic-eligibility standards and who remain with the institution. A team's APR is the total points earned by the team at a given time divided by the total points possible" (Brown, 2005, 5). One coach stated that "APR is putting more pressure on everyone" (R5). During the recruiting process coaches are asking "can we keep him in school?" This of course makes recruiting student-athletes much more difficult in that they do not want to make a mistake during recruiting. He also went on to say that he would never compromise the program because of APR (R5). An example would be a student who makes the program suffer but the team keeps him so as not to loose points in the new APR system" (R5). One coach stated that "APR has no effect at this point" (R7).

The issue of assessing student-athletes as being a tough job emerged as the next category with constructs such as everything tying into it, it is difficult to do, one bad player affects everyone on the team, reflection of you, and product. Coaches spoke very passionately regarding this question and several felt it was the toughest job they have because of the consequences that at the very least could cost them their job. One coach described the process by stating that "it is difficult to assess a high school student who is 17 or 18 years old. The NFL, National Football League, misses on this all the time" (R9). His advice regarding the current process was to "take advantage of every phone call" (R9). Another coach felt that it was the "toughest job they have" and went on to say that "you just don't know the product you are getting" (R1). Continuing the same discussion (R1) stated that he felt that "there is no science to it. Three hundred and fifty kids in the state of Texas sign as Division I student-athletes." "The most important part is the total evaluation of the player" (R1). During the conversations about this the coaches' voices would raise and then abruptly lower back to normal. One respondent pointed out that it was "extremely important and everything ties into it" (R8). When he spoke further he also commented that "it is the life line" in coaching (R8).

Early commitment emerged as the next issue within this question. The constructs that support this theme were that of increased pressure, a need to start earlier, and maturity. "The problem with early commitments is that maturity is an issue. Physical development is big" (R7). Coaches have adapted to early commitments but many feel that "they are forced to make snap decisions" (R1). Student-athletes are growing mentally and physically during the recruiting process. In many cases it can be hard to predict the future and coaches are only permitted to have contact with student-athletes for short periods of time therefore making an assessment very difficult. According to one respondent, he felt that "more contact was good" (R4). This early commitment pressure on student–athletes does not help much and the fact is that student-athletes "feel the pressure to commit early" (R3). He went on to say that they will not offer until they get to know the kid, coach, and family. "Even though they commit early, coaches still evaluate" (R6). Coaches have adapted to this process by "getting to know student-athletes in the 9th and 10th grade" (R4). Another coach said that "they started tracking student-athletes in the 11th grade" (R6).

The final issue that developed with this question was the coaches' responses on the student-athletes character. They mentioned areas such as work ethic, academics, personality test and commitment. Character is an issue that has emerged throughout and this category remains consistent. One respondent felt that "academics, athletics, and character were important" (R1). Another felt that "character and work ethic were important and went on to say that he felt a personality test might have some merit. The question to the coaches would be, are they (the student-athletes) real" (R2)? Commitment is important and (R5) made the comment "don't bring people in that don't have the commitment." When it comes to assessing character issues two schools mentioned they had a formalized process. A respondent commented,

> We have four keys to success. Kids are rated and are given stars for how well they rate. They put all of this on a recruiting board, green is good, yellow is hold on, and red is stop. Character and ability are big as well as interest in the school (R3).

CONCLUSIONS AND RECOMMENDATIONS

What were identified through this research were the characteristics that coaches are looking for when recruiting student-athletes to their campuses. It was found that most coaches do not utilize a formal method or assessment tool when evaluating prospective student-athletes. However, with increased pressure on the institutional level for the sports of men's basketball and men's football to succeed and with increased pressure from the NCAA to have student athletes succeed academically, it is important for coaches to look at who they are recruiting. Recruiting successful student-athletes will not only benefit the organization or university but also have positive results for the team and the student-athlete themselves. Swanson informs us of the relationship between an individual and organization as well as the process that is chosen that predicts or produces positive performance. As Rummler and Brache (1988) state, an individual "is part of a human performance system. At issue is whether the job outputs have been correctly identified as the ones needed to support the process and whether the performance system will support the employee's efforts to achieve those outputs" (p. 49). Just as in this study, student-athletes are part of a system, the university. In addition, does the student-athlete have the characteristics, what will be outputs once they get on campus, to succeed? In as much, does the university have what it needs, the process, to help that student succeed once they get on campus?

As in Human Capital Theory, this study focuses on the capital of the student-athlete to a university or college. Therefore the more investments a university might put into a student-athlete the greater the return for the organization. In as much the same applies to the student-athlete, the more investments he makes on his education, athleticism, and character, the more positive the outcome will be. "Human capital theory suggests that individuals and society derive economic benefits from investments in people" (Sweetland, 1996, p. 341). In collegiate athletics this is very apparent. "Football success can greatly affect the overall welfare of a university" (Mandel, 2003, p. 5). Mandel goes on to quote the Kansas State president, Jon Wefald, who inherited the Division I A's losingest program and turned it into a top-ten contender;

When I got here, there was a sense of futility...If the old administration had stayed on here for three more years, I think football would have been dropped. We would have no marching band, and we'd be at about 12,000 students today. (p. 5)

"Instead, since 1986 Kansas State's enrollment has increased from about 13,000 to 23,000, its fundraising has gone from $7 million a year... to $83 million ... and the city of Manhattan's economy has grown exponentially" (Mandel, 2003, p. 5). Consequently, one can see the value of human capital society and the university can gain from the investment in these student-athletes. In as much one can see the detriment or consequences of a team who recruits individuals who do not measure up or even cause "bad publicity" for a university. Therefore, the ability to predict success in student-athletes is integral.

RECOMMENDATIONS FOR FURTHER RESEARCH AND LIMITATIONS

As for my recommendations for further research I suggest that my assessment instrument be field tested at select universities where coaches gather data during recruiting. This study should be replicated in a different conference using the same criteria to determine if results are similar. Further research should be conducted on all NCAA sponsored sports as well as the information gathered from coaches in the areas of (character, family, discipline, and leadership).

REFERENCES

Auman, Greg. (2005). Background checks vary; schools fear surprises. *St. Petersburg Times Online.* Retrieved March 8, 2005, from http://www.sptimes.com/2005.

Baron, J., and Norman, F. (1992). SATs, achievement tests, and high-school class rank as predictors of college performance. *Educational and Psychological Measurement, 52,* 1047-1055.

Brown, G. T. (2005, February 14). APR 101. *The NCAA News.* Retrieved October 5, 2005, from www.ncaa.org/wps/portal.

Crouse, J. and Trusheim, D. (1988). *The Case Against the SAT.* Chicago, IL: The University of Chicago Press.

Erlandson, D., Harris, E., Skipper, B., Allen, S. (1993). *Doing Naturalistic Inquiry.* Newbury Park, CA: Sage Publications.

Knight Foundation Commission on Intercollegiate Athletics. (1999). A call to action: Reconnecting college sports and higher education. Retrieved August 25, 2006, from www.knightfdn.org.

Mandel, S. (2003). College football's stakes, climate provoke serious battle. 2003 College Football Preview. Available from http://sportsillustrated.cnn.com.

NCAA News Online (2005). APR 101. Retrieved March 10, 2005, from the World Wide Web: http://www2.ncaa.org/media_and_events/association_news/ncaa_news_online/2005/02_14_05/front_page_news/4204n01.html

Patton, M. (2002). *Qualitative Research and Evaluation Methods.* ThoUSnd Oaks, CA: Sage Publications.

Rummler, G. A. (1996). In search of the holy performance grail. *Training and Development, 50*(4), 26-32.

Rummler, G. A. and Braache, A. P. (1988). The systems view of human performance. *Training, 25*(9), 45-53.

Sedlacek, W. E., and Adams-Gaston, J. (1992). Predicting the academic success of student-athletes using SAT and noncognitive variables. *Journal of Counseling and Development, 70,* 724-727.

Swanson, R. A. and Holton, E. F. III. (2001). *Foundations of Human Resource Development.* San Francisco, CA.: Berrett-Koehler.

Sweetland, S.R. (1996). Human capital theory: Foundations of a field of inquiry. *Review of Educational Research, 66*(3), 341-359.

Advances in Sports and Athletics. Volume 1   ISBN: 978-1-61122-824-3
Editor: James P. Waldorf   © 2012 Nova Science Publishers, Inc.

ALTERNATIVE DISPUTE RESOLUTION IN SPORT: A CONCEPTUAL APPROACH

*Mark E. Silver J.O. Spengler and Daniel Connaughton**

Dept of Tourism, Recreation and Sport Management,
University of Florida, Florida, US

ABSTRACT

Alternative dispute resolution (ADR) is an integral part of the sport industry. It allows leagues, teams, and players to resolve disputes that arise without using litigation. It is essential for people who work within sports to understand the value of ADR. The purpose of this article is to provide an extensive overview of ADR as it relates to sport. This article takes a conceptual approach in addressing the many aspects of ADR. The two major applications of ADR, arbitration and mediation, are discussed, with a focus towards arbitration. In order to properly utilize ADR one must understand the relevant statutes and cases. Therefore, federal and international laws, along with cases that define ADR are discussed. Additionally, this article will examine the benefits of ADR, what distinguishes mediation from arbitration, the arbitration process, how ADR is applied to amateur sports, how the Olympics and international sport community employ ADR, how US professional sports utilize ADR, and how new emerging hybrid forms of ADR are applied to sport-related disputes. In order to illustrate these concepts, recent sport examples are presented.

*M.E. Silver, BS, J.O. Spengler, JD, PhD, & D. Connaughton, EdD, University of Florida, Dept of Tourism, Recreation and Sport Management, P.O. Box 118208, Gainesville, FL 32611, (352) 392-4042. E-mail: danc@hhp.ufl.edu

The problem has arisen in sport countless times; a team decides to suspend their player for conduct unfit for the organization, or a player believes s/he should be paid more money based on their recent performance, or the construction of a new multi-million dollar stadium is being halted because of a disagreement between financier and contractor. If these matters were taken to court and resolved through traditional litigation, the case would likely not be decided within a short timeframe. All of the above issues, and the majority of disputes in sports, are often time sensitive (Greenberg, 2005). Even though the formal legal process will produce a resolution for the dispute, there is no saying how long, or how much money, it will take to get there. That is why businesses, especially those involved with sports, are increasingly utilizing alternative dispute resolution (ADR). ADR is an umbrella term that includes all of the "procedures for settling disputes by means other than litigation" (Epstein, 2002 p. 154). ADR incorporates two major subgroups: mediation and arbitration; with arbitration being the most often used (Epstein, 2002). The goal of ADR is to resolve a dispute between parties, by meeting those parties' needs within a timely fashion (Epstein, 2002). This paper will examine the benefits of ADR, what distinguishes mediation from arbitration, the arbitration process, the federal statutes that give power to arbitration, the case law that helped define arbitration statutes in America, how ADR is applied to amateur sports, how the Olympics and international sport community employ ADR, how US professional sports utilize ADR, and how new emerging hybrid forms of ADR are applied to sport facility disputes.

BENEFITS OF ADR

Why would anyone use ADR instead of taking the issue to court? In other words, what are the benefits of ADR to the sport professional? As stated before, the issues that arise in sports are usually time-sensitive and demand immediate resolution (Greenberg, 2005). Disputes with sports are considered time sensitive for two reasons. First, any delay in a sport dispute will cause both sides to lose large sums of money; both sides will save money every day they do not spend litigating. Secondly, there are disputes in sports that determine whether or not an athlete can continue competing. If it is not determined in a timely fashion whether an athlete can compete, the competitor may miss the game or tournament. Because of this, sports are turning to ADR more frequently to solve a variety of problems. There are five major benefits of using ADR over more traditional avenues of dispute resolution, such as litigation. These include speed, informality, privacy, finality, and cost effectiveness (Greenberg, 2005).

ADR is much faster then traditional litigation. It can take months for a case just to be assigned a trial date. Motions can extend this time period even more. Unlike the litigation process, ADR processes have strict timelines the parties must follow regarding filing of grievances, and a strict timetable that is followed concerning procedure. This includes the selection of a mediator or arbitrator, discovery period, and time allotted to reach a decision. According to the American Arbitration Association (AAA) a decision must be rendered within thirty days of the evidence period closing (Commercial Arbitration Rules, 2007). The amount of time that a decision must be rendered is decided prior to arbitration ever beginning. The second benefit of ADR is the informality involved. Contrary to the formal hearings of a courtroom, ADR usually takes place in a conference room occupied by both parties, and the mediator or arbitrator. This type of informal atmosphere may be less intimidating to an organization or athlete than the typical judge ruled courtroom. Although evidence in ADR hearings is presented in a similar fashion to traditional litigation, the evidence presentation process is far less formal. Thirdly, ADR provides an important concern of sport organizations and athletes, privacy. Since the only people usually present in an ADR hearing are the two disputing parties and the person/people presiding over the case, very little information typically reaches the public. This is extremely important for sport organizations and players because their disputes are closely observed by the media and public. Settlements are only made public if the contract between the two parties calls for it. This is usually the case in salary arbitration. The fourth benefit of ADR, in the case of arbitration, is the finality of the decisions rendered. An arbitrator's decision is usually final and binding, and only available for appeal for a few reasons, all of which will be addressed later. Lastly, ADR is cost effective. The hearing is shorter, with less legal presence, if any, and the possibility of appeals is remote. The combination of all of the aforementioned benefits makes ADR a cheaper option over litigation for dispute resolution (Greenberg, 2005).

MEDIATION AND ARBITRATION DISTINGUISHED

Mediation is, "… the submission of a dispute to an impartial facilitator who assists the parties in negotiating a voluntary, consensual settlement of their dispute" (Epstein, 2002 p. 158). In mediation, the two quarreling parties are essentially in control of the discussions. They are able to cease talks whenever they please. The purpose of mediation is to generate an environment that will contribute to the settlement of the argument at hand (Epstein, 2002). Ultimately, the relationship of the two parties involved must be preserved in order to continue closing in on a possible solution (Mowery, 2007). A mediator can accomplish this by trying to establish an open, respectful line of communication between the parties (Epstein, 2002). The mediation process involves meetings between the two parties, overseen by a mediator. The mediator is responsible for strictly facilitating the talks; he or she can not impose a solution on the parties (Mowery, 2007). Mediation talks can be divided into two different methods, caucus and conference (Fried and Hiller, 1997). In caucus talks the two parties are separated from one another, and talk to the mediator individually, while conference meetings consist of all parties discussing the issues together in one room (Fried and Hiller, 1997). During these meetings the parties are expected to discuss the problems they are experiencing, and what they believe should be done to resolve the conflicting issues. Hopefully, the two parties can agree on a viable solution on their own, although many times a mediator is requested to give his or her opinions and suggestions on possible solutions. Although typically not binding, mediation solutions can be written in the form of a contract, the violation of which could result in litigation (Epstein, 2002). Mediation can lead to dispute resolution, but this is not guaranteed. When a decision must be unequivocally resolved, businesses often turn to arbitration.

Arbitration, the most popular aspect of ADR in sports, is used to resolve a plethora of disputes by a wide array of organizations. Unlike mediation, arbitration will always result in a final solution to the problem. Arbitration is not concerned with preserving the relationship between the two parties as much as the mediation process is. It does not matter if the parties involved continue to talk after the arbitration hearing because the problem is resolved; however it would be beneficial for business if the relationship remains intact. During mediation you are not sure when and if the problem will be resolved so it is more essential to the process to keep the two parties in ongoing conversations. This can only happen if a relationship between the parties exists. Arbitration is "the submission of a dispute to a neutral decision maker (an arbitrator) for a final resolution of a disagreement" (Epstein, 2002 p.157). This decision can be binding or non-binding. This is determined within the contract or agreement the two parties have previously entered into. The contract or agreement between the parties can also determine whether the arbitration is voluntary or mandatory (Epstein, 2002). Epstein (2002) offers a sample arbitration clause that could appear in a contract:

> "Any controversy or claim arising out of or relating to this contract, or the breach thereof, shall be settled by arbitration administered by the American Arbitration Association in accordance with its Commercial [or other] Arbitration Rules [including the Emergency Interim Relief Procedures], and judgment on the award rendered by the arbitrator(s) may be entered in any court having jurisdiction thereof" (p. 170).

THE ARBITRATION PROCESS

The first step of the arbitration process is the notice of arbitration. This is done in the form of a written document. Most notices of arbitration have statutes of limitations that are outlined in the parties' contracts or agreements (Greenberg, 2005). The next step in the arbitration process is the response. The written response outlines whether the party responding to the initial notice agrees to the fact that the issue at hand is in fact subject to arbitration (Mowery, 2007). Once the notice and response is established, an arbitrator must be selected to oversee the proceedings and make the final ruling. The process of determining or selecting an arbitrator or panel of arbitrators can differ greatly from case to case. First, the manner in which an arbitrator is selected will almost always be defined in the contract or agreement the two parties have between them (Greenberg, 2005). Both parties are equally involved in the selection of a neutral arbitrator in order to ensure fairness (Epstein, 2002).

The AAA is a nongovernmental organization that provides neutral arbitrators to the public (Commercial Arbitration Rules, 2007). This is the most popular place that parties can secure an arbitrator, but is not the only organization of its kind. Typically, the two parties will either agree on one arbitrator to oversee the hearing, or each party may select their own arbitrator from an approved list. The two selected arbitrators will secure a third arbitrator to create an arbitration panel (Greenberg, 2005). This selection process can be done numerous ways, but the result is always a mutually agreed upon arbitrator or panel of arbitrators. A benefit of selecting an arbitrator is that the parties can select an individual(s) with expertise in the field, instead of a judge or jury that might not be familiar with sport practices. After the arbitrator(s) are appointed, the hearing commences. The AAA has created the Commercial

Arbitration Rules in order to regulate how arbitration hearings should be conducted (Epstein, 2002). Following these rules is extremely important because they are designed to maintain efficiency and fairness, while reducing the possibility of appeal. During the hearing, both parties will present documents, briefs, and witnesses like a normal trial, but it differs from a normal trial by being more relaxed and not providing transcripts in the fashion a trial would. In traditional litigation, the court compiles an ongoing transcript of what happens during the hearing. The transcript documents everything that is said and done over the course of a trial. The transcript is primarily designed to supply the appellate court with a description of whether the procedural rules were followed. Since an arbitration decision is rarely allowed to be appealed, there is no need for a transcript (Report of the Study Committee, 2003). Once both parties have presented their arguments, the arbitrator(s) will make a decision. The decision made is usually final and binding; however certain contracts allow for appeals, while others stipulate the decision as not appealable.

FEDERAL LAW

The US statute that initially outlines and defines arbitration, including why an arbitrator's decision can be appealed, is the US Federal Arbitration Act (FAA) of 1925 (US Federal Arbitration Act, 1925). The FAA applies to any contract or agreement between two parties, excluding those involving transportation workers. The purpose of the FAA was, and still is, to encourage businesses to utilize ADR as an alternative to traditional litigation (Epstein, 2002). Title 9, US Code, Sections 1-16 deals with domestic applications of the FAA. The foreign applications of arbitration within the United States are outlined in Sections 205-208 and 301-307 of the same US Code. Sections 205-208 deal with the enforcement and adoption of the Convention on the Recognition and Enforcement of Foreign Arbitral Awards of 1958; while Sections 301-307 are concerned with enforcing the Inter-American Convention on International Commercial Arbitration of 1975 (US Federal Arbitration Act, 1925). These statutes allow arbitration to be used in all areas of business, including sports. In regards to when an arbitrator's decision can be appealed and possibly dismissed, 9 USC. § 10 states that a decision can be vacated if:

"(1)... the award was procured by corruption, fraud, or undue means;" (2) "where there was evident partiality or corruption on the part of the arbitrators ... ;" (3) "where the arbitrators were guilty of misconduct in refusing to postpone the hearing upon sufficient cause shown[;]"(4) "where the arbitrators were guilty ... in refusing to hear evidence pertinent and material to the controversy;" (5) "where the arbitrators were guilty ... of any other misbehavior by which the rights of any participant have been prejudiced;" or (6) "where the arbitrators exceeded their powers, or so imperfectly executed them that a mutual, final and definite award upon the subject matter submitted was not made."

In summation, all of 9 USC. § 10's requirements for dismissal concern misconduct on behalf of the arbitrator(s). This is why arbitration decisions are difficult to appeal. Unless the arbitrator commits one of the six aforementioned actions, the decision rendered is final and binding. Without one of these infractions, the arbitrator's decision will not be dismissed.

Although the FAA of 1925 was the first US arbitration statute, it was not the last. In 1955, the American Bar Association ratified the Uniform Arbitration Act (UAA) (Uniform Arbitration Act, 1955). The purpose of this Act was to institute legal procedure and policy pertaining to arbitration (Mowery, 2007). The UAA has been implemented by 35 states (Uniform Arbitration Act, 1955). What the UAA does is create law that can legally support the enforcement of an arbitrator's decision (Uniform Arbitration Act, 1955). More recently the United States has enacted the Administrative Dispute Resolution Act of 1990 (ADRA), 5 USC.A. § 571-583 (Administrative Dispute Resolution Act, 1990). The ADRA was endorsed in order to require federal agencies to establish policies in regards to using ADR as a possible option for dispute resolution. The ADRA states that all government agencies have a "dispute resolution specialist" who determines in what situations it is appropriate to use ADR as a viable dispute resolution (Administrative Dispute Resolution Act, 1990). The objective of employing a specialist is to ensure actions are being taken that are in the best interest of both the public and the agency. This Act forces governmental agencies to have policies in place for ADR's possible use concerning "formal and informal adjudication, rulemakings, enforcement actions, the issuance and revocation of licenses or permits, contract administration, litigation brought by or against the agency, and other agency actions" (Epstein, 2002). The ADRA has expanded ADR from the businesses of America to the government itself.

CASE LAW INTERPRETATIONS OF ADR STATUTES

Since the FAA, UAA, and ADRA have been passed, there have been several landmark cases that helped define their rules and purpose. The most well known and significant litigation consisted of three US Supreme Court cases referred to as the Steelworker's Trilogy. On June 20, 1960, the Supreme Court gave their rulings on *United Steelworkers of America v. Warrior and Gulf Navigation Co., United Steelworkers of America v. Enterprise Wheel and Car Corp.,* and *United Steelworkers of America v. American Manufacturing Co.* In all three of these cases, the Supreme Court enforced the arbitration clause in the collective bargaining agreements between the parties. The Steelworker's Trilogy initiated principles "regarding the judicial review of arbitration awards" (Greenberg, 2005). These three cases are credited for allowing courts to enforce arbitration clauses found in collective bargaining agreements. The trilogy of cases had an additional impact on the way arbitration is conducted and judicially reviewed today. Within its ruling, the Supreme Court found that parties are only subject to arbitration on matters that were contractually agreed upon by both parties (Baker and Connaughton, 2005). Both Greenberg (2005) and Lipinski (2003) contend that there are two general rules that can be taken from the Steelworker's Trilogy. First, the cases establish that "grievances are presumed to be arbitrable" (Malin, 1990 p. 551). Secondly, the Steelworker's Trilogy further acknowledges that the decision of an arbitrator is extremely limited within a judicial review (Greenberg, 2005; Lipinski, 2003).

Another Supreme Court case that helped define the judicial review or appeal of an arbitrator's decision was *United Paper Workers International Union v. Misco, Inc.* In this case, a hazardous machine operator was found in the parking lot of his place of employment, in the back seat of a car containing marijuana smoke and a marijuana cigarette in the front ashtray. According to the collective bargaining agreement he had entered into, the use of narcotics or drugs at the workplace, or being under the influence at the workplace, would result in an immediate dismissal. The man's employer did in fact fire him once they were notified by the police about the arrest made on their property. As per the collective bargaining agreement, this grievance was set to be settled through arbitration. Once hearing both sides, the arbitrator found that the employee should be reinstated with pay for time missed, and returned to his previous seniority. The Arbitrator believed that the employer had not proved that the employee had ever possessed or used the marijuana, and therefore was not in violation of the drug rule within the collective bargaining agreement.

After hearing the arbitrator's decision, the employer appealed their case to United States District Court for the Western District of Louisiana. The district court reversed the arbitrator's decision stating that the award went against public interest, a reason some lower courts believe is cause for an arbitration award to be vacated, because having a hazardous machine operator on drugs was unsafe. The Court of Appeals which heard the case agreed with the District Court's decision. Eventually, the case reached the Supreme Court. The Supreme Court's decision reinforced the stance they had on judicial review of arbitration during the Steelworker's Trilogy cases. The Supreme Court ruled that the District Court and Court of Appeal erred in deciding what was against public policy. Even if they had the authority to do so, which the Supreme Court did not state, they both did not show enough evidence to even prove this was the case. Citing the fact that the arbitrator acted without fraud, and did not violate any of the outlined causes for vacating an arbitrator's award, the Supreme Court reversed the Court of Appeals decision, and allowed the arbitrator's original decision to stand.

ADR APPLICATION TO AMATEUR SPORTS

With ADR benefits, procedures, and statutes discussed, we now turn to the application of ADR as it pertains to sports. First is the use of ADR within amateur sport, specifically college athletics and the National Collegiate Athletic Association (NCAA). Since the United States does not recognize student-athletes as employees, student-athletes cannot enter into collective bargaining agreements. Therefore, ADR is often overlooked as a dispute resolution option (Greenberg, 2005). However, many scholars claim that ADR can be a viable option for student-athletes and universities because they enter into various contractual agreements, some of which might be interpreted as availing themselves to the arbitration clause. Fried and Hiller (1997) contend that three documents, the National Letter of Intent, scholarship agreements, and the student code of conduct, can all be used by student-athletes to explore ADR prior to litigation. Although there is a recent push for the use of ADR in intercollegiate athletics, the use of ADR in college athletics is very rare. However, one well known case involving the NCAA did address ADR. In *Law v. NCAA* (1995), coaches challenged the NCAA's Restricted Earnings Coach Rule that stated restricted earnings coaches were only allowed to earn $12,000 in an academic year, and $4,000 throughout the summer (Law v. NCAA, 1995). Law, and the other coaches, believed this rule violated the Sherman

Antitrust Act. The District Court granted summary judgment in favor of the coaches, stating that the Restricted Earnings Coach Rule violated the Sherman Act. The NCAA then motioned to appeal the judgment. Between the time of the District Court's decision and the start of the appellate trial, the NCAA and Law entered into ADR via mediation. Through the mediation process the two parties were able to reconcile their disputes in the form of a $54.5 million settlement paid to the coaches (Epstein, 2002). Although the history of ADR and NCAA is limited, there is a potential for greater use of ADR if the NCAA starts including arbitration and mediation clauses in thepreviously mentioned three documents. The NCAA itself has realized the benefits and possibilities that ADR represents for their Association. Since 2004, the NCAA has been discussing the possibility of introducing both arbitration and mediation for a variety of issues. They have submitted and voted on proposals that would require all members of the NCAA to agree to binding arbitration instead of legislation under the protection of the FAA. Although many subcommittees have been commissioned to help determine the best manner to initiate ADR practices, none have been officially enacted to date (Condition of Membership, 2004; Report of the NCAA, 2005).

ADR APPLICATION TO OLYMPIC AND INTERNATIONAL SPORTS

ADR in amateur sports is not limited to the collegiate level; in fact one of the most prestigious levels of sport competition in the world is considered an amateur sport, the Olympics. Unique predicaments arise concerning international competition. First, different nations have different legislative systems and laws, so international sport competitions and competitors face the problem of whose laws should be adhered to, the host nation or the athlete's country of origin (Mowery, 2007). The other major issue is that the problems that arise in international sport competition such as "positive drug tests of athletes, the challenges to technical decisions of officials made during competition, and the eligibility of athletes to compete in the Olympic Games," need to be decided under severe time constraints in order for an athlete to participate as scheduled (Gilson, 2006 p. 504). Just as in the US, international legislative processes are not quick, and the expedited process and binding finality of arbitration suits itself well for these situations.

Both the United States and international communities have addressed the issue of ADR in international amateur sport competitions. First, the United States compiled the Amateur Sports Act of 1978 (ASA), 36 USC.S. § 220501-220512 and §220521-220529, originally the Ted Stevens Olympic and Amateur Sports Act. The ASA not only established the United States Olympic Committee (USOC), it also outlined and defined its powers and obligations (Epstein, 2002). The ASA defines what constitutes an amateur athlete, international sport competitions, the purpose of national organizations pertaining to sports, and powers held by those organizations (36 USC.S. § 220501-220512). Additionally, the ASA requires the USOC to find "swift resolution of conflicts and disputes involving amateur athletes, national governing bodies, and amateur sports organizations..." (Epstein, 2002 p. 160). This part of the ASA shows why arbitration is a desired method of dispute resolution within US international competition.

In 1983, five years after the US enacted the ASA, the International Olympic Committee (IOC) established the Court of Arbitration for Sport (CAS) (Epstein, 2002). The purpose of the CAS is to remedy the problem international competitions face with jurisdiction, by offering the same arbitration process to all nations and athletes. In order to maintain a neutral status and be independent from the IOC, the International Council of Arbitration for Sport (ICAS) began overseeing the CAS in 1993 (Nafziger, 2002). The CAS is recognized as the leader in international dispute resolution (Gilson, 2006). An important fact that supports CAS being a leader is that their decisions are "recognized as developing a *lex sportive*," which means their rulings establish precedence concerning international sport law (Gilson, 2006). The CAS hears cases brought forth by "international athletes, national governing bodies, national Olympic committees, and sport federations" (Mowery, 2007 p. 413).

Much like the typical arbitration process, CAS arbitration must be agreed upon by both parties prior to the hearing. In order to secure arbitration as the only dispute resolution method used by Olympic participants, the Olympic Games began requiring athletes to sign a document that binds them to arbitration through the CAS if a grievance should arise (Gilson, 2006). Similarly, International Federations that govern sports also demand athletes to sign a contract ensuring all grievances will be appeased through the CAS (Nafziger, 2002). Arbitrators are selected in a similar fashion to what was discussed during the arbitration process; parties can choose an arbitrator(s) from a list provided by the CAS. The CAS has three separate divisions that hear disputes: Ordinary Arbitration, Appellate Arbitration, and Ad Hoc

(Gilson, 2006). A typical case would first go to the Ordinary Division of the CAS, then, if one party disagrees with the decision they can take their case to the CAS's Appellate Division. These divisions of the CAS are located in LaUSnne, Switzerland; New York City, New York; and Sydney, Australia (Mowery, 2007). The Ad Hoc Division of the CAS was established in 1996. Its purpose is to solve any disputes that arise during the Olympic Games, Commonwealth Games, and other international competitions (Nafziger, 2002). The CAS's Ad Hoc division establishes a presence at the Games themselves, so that arbitration hearings can be conducted onsite and in an expedited fashion (Nafziger, 2002). Since 2001, the CAS has decided over 250 arbitration hearings and that number only continues to rise (Nafziger, 2002).

Although originally designed to resolve Olympic issues, the CAS also hears cases from other organizations such as the World Anti-Doping Agency (WADA) and European Football Championships. One such case, decided January 24, 2007, involved WADA and a Portuguese soccer player Mr. Nuno Assis Lopes de Almeida. Mr. Almeida was initially suspended by the Portuguese Football Federation (FPF) for six months, but that punishment was eventually dismissed by the federation's judicial board. One month later WADA sought a 2-year suspension in the CAS. The FPF, on behalf of Almeida, argued against the suspension by claiming that WADA lacked authority to appeal the dismissal, the testing procedure was unreliable, the sample was not transported quickly enough, and any suspension should not exceed the original six month suspension. The CAS ruled in favor of WADA and suspended Almeida for 12 months. They also ruled that the FPF must cover the legal and other costs of WADA in the amount of 5,000 Swiss Franc (*WADA v. Almeida,* 2007).

ADR APPLICATION TO US PROFESSIONAL SPORTS

Although all four of the US major sport leagues, the National Basketball Association (NBA), the National Hockey League (NHL), Major League Baseball (MLB), and the National Football League (NFL) are self-governed, they still require ADR in order to function efficiently and effectively. This section will address the NHL's and MLB's use of salary/labor arbitration and the NBA's and NFL's use of arbitration for disciplinary decisions.

In any business, labor disputes will eventually develop between management and its labor force. Professional sports are no exception. Recently, the NHL became the first professional sports team to cancel their entire season due to a labor dispute. This labor dispute was over the discrepancy between the amount of money and benefits the players wanted, compared to what owners and management were willing to give. The resolution of the dispute led to a new collective bargaining agreement (CBA) with new arbitration provisions (Yoost, 2006). The CBA was, and still is, an agreement between the NHL and the National Hockey League Players Association (NHLPA), the players' union. The other three major US leagues also utilize a CBA to govern the business relationship between owners and the players. However, only the NHL and MLB utilize arbitration in salary disputes, but they both have their own unique versions. The NHL was the first league to use arbitration to resolve a salary dispute back in 1970, three years prior to the MLB adding arbitration to their CBA (Yoost, 2006).

In both leagues, arbitration starts with the two parties disagreeing on the salary of a player. Both parties inherently agree to decide all salary disputes via arbitration because this is defined in their CBA. In the NHL, only players were allowed to file for arbitration under the old CBA; under the new CBA both owners and players can file for an arbitration hearing. The only other difference under the NHL's new CBA pertaining to salary arbitration is that players are eligible to request arbitration after four years in the league, instead of three. In both the NHL and the MLB, once the parties agree that arbitration is necessary to resolve the salary dispute, an arbitrator(s) must be selected. The leagues differ in the manner in which they do this. The NHL has a system in place wherein the NHL and NHLPA annually select eight arbitrators from the National Academy of Arbitrators to hear all disputes that arise in that year, with only one arbitrator presiding over a case. While the MLB and its players' association also select a group of arbitrators annually, each case has a panel of three arbitrators that hears the dispute. In the NHL and MLB, both parties in a dispute have an equal role in the arbitrator selection process. Another difference between the two leagues is the amount of salary that can be awarded (Yoost, 2006). The MLB has a "final-offer" system. The final-offer system states that each party in the dispute suggests the salary they believe appropriate; once hearing their cases, and looking at the salaries of other players in the league with comparable statistics and performance, an arbitrator can choose one of the two amounts. Yoost (2006) provides the following example, "… [if] the ballplayer asks for $750,000 and the owner offers $500,000, the arbitrator must choose either $750,000 or $500,000, one or the other" (p. 501). The amount the arbitrator chooses is final and binding, and not available for appeal. A real life parallel to this example is the San Diego Padres second baseman Todd Walker and his February 21, 2007 salary arbitration. At the beginning of the arbitration proceedings Todd Walker submitted his request of $3.95 million to the arbitration panel, while the club was arguing his salary be $2.75 million (Staff, 2007). After analyzing Walker's career numbers, the arbitration panel decided that the $3.95 million he requested was closer to the value that Walker deserved. As a result of the hearing, Walker earned $3.95 million that year to play second base for the Padres (Staff, 2007).

Although an arbitrator in the NHL goes through a similar process of analyzing the salaries, performance, and statistics of comparable players in the league, the arbitrator is given the power to grant any amount they please. Also, the amount awarded is not binding. The owner's of the NHL have the opportunity to utilize the "walk-away" clause, which allows them to disregard the arbitrator's decision within 72 hours of its announcement. However, if the team has multiple ongoing arbitration hearings, they are permitted to wait until all of the hearings have been concluded before deciding whether or not to walk-away. The teams can only do this three times in a two season span. If the contract being arbitrated was for one-year, then the player would become an unrestricted free agent. If it was for two years and the team chose to walk-away, then the player would remain on the team for one year under the salary awarded by arbitration, and then become an unrestricted free agent (Yoost, 2006). An example of the "walk-away" clause being used by a team is the August 5, 2006 salary arbitration decision of David Tanabe. At the time of the $1.275 million decision, Tanabe was a defenseman for the Boston Bruins. In an effort to keep their payroll below $36 million, the Bruins decided it would be in their best interest to walk-away from the arbitrator's decision. As a result, Tanabe became an unrestricted free agent and less than a month later signed with the Carolina Hurricanes (Bruins Walk Away, 2006). The NHL CBA states that the salary of a player who signed a contract as an unrestricted free agent, testimonials, videos and media reports, the financial state of the team, and the team's payroll as it relates to the salary cap are not admissible as evidence at a salary arbitration hearing (Fitzpatrick, 2006). Although salary arbitration is typically the type of ADR most reportedin the media, it is not the only reason why a team, player, or league may utilize arbitration.

By nature, sport is an aggressive activity. Realizing this, professional sport leagues establish clauses within their CBA that outlines what on-the-field and off-the-field actions warrant disciplinary action. The groups responsible for handing down a disciplinary action can either be the athlete's team or the league office they belong to. Two highly publicized disciplinary cases, one from the NBA and the other from the NFL, will be examined in order to show

how players use arbitration to appeal punishments they receive. The first case concerns the suspensions handed down by the NBA's Commissioner, David Stern, regarding a fight that took place in a game between the Indiana Pacers and the Detroit Pistons. On November 19, 2004, in Detroit, a brawl erupted between members of the Indiana Pacers and both the Pistons players and fans. In total, 9 suspensions were handed down by Commissioner Stern, with Ron Artest, Stephen Jackson, and Jermaine O'Neal receiving the harshest punishments. As a result, the National Basketball Players Associations (NBPA) filed an appeal to the NBA's Grievance Arbitrator (Baker and Connaughton, 2005). According to Article XXXI, section 8, of the NBA's CBA, only the commissioner is allowed to hear an appeal for "on the court" disciplinary violations, making the request to the Grievance Arbitrator unusual (NBA CBA, 2006). In this special situation the Grievance Arbitrator contended he had arbitrability over the dispute (Baker and Connaughton, 2005). However, Commissioner Stern believed that Article XXXI, section 8, of the NBA's CBA applied to this case and refused to attend the hearings. In the end the Grievance Arbitrator decided:

> "....the dispute is arbitrable before the Grievance Arbitrator, and is not within the exclusive jurisdiction of the Commissioner, because the conduct in question did not take place "on the playing court" within the meaning of Article XXXI, Section 8 of the Collective Bargaining Agreement; and (iii) the Commissioner had just cause for his suspensions of defendants Artest, Jackson and Johnson, but did not have just cause to suspend defendant O'Neal for twenty-five games. The Grievance Arbitrator reduced defendant O'Neal's suspension to fifteen games" (NBA v. NBPA, 2005).

Commissioner Stern appealed the Grievance Arbitrator's decision to New York's District Court. As seen in previous appeals of arbitrator's awards in court, the District Court upheld all of the arbitrator's decisions. Although on the court disciplinary rulings are rarely subject to arbitration in the NBA pursuant to their CBA, this example highlights both arbitrability, and how in the right situation arbitration can be called upon to resolve disciplinary disputes.

The second case involves the NFL, the Philadelphia Eagles, Terrell Owens, and the National Football League Player's Association (NFLPA). In this case, the Philadelphia Eagles suspended Owens, a wide receiver, for four games, and then informed Owens that he would not play for the remainder for the season. The Eagles felt this was necessary because Owens was affecting the team negatively by "...skipping mini-camp and team meetings, ignoring coaches and fellow players and publicly criticizing the team, the Eagles organization and his colleagues" (Matter, 2005 p. 3). The NFLPA, on the behalf of Terrell Owens, immediately filed for appeal to the Notice Arbitrator. According to Article IX, Section 6 of the NFL CBA, the arbitration hearing will be heard by a panel of 4 arbitrators that were all decided upon by both the NFLPA and the NFL Management Council (NFL CBA, 2006). Article XXVII, Section 7, states that if the two sides cannot agree on a panel of arbitrators, then they will be selected from the list of currently serving Non-Injury Grievance Arbitrators (NFL CBA, 2006). In this dispute the arbitrator was asked to answer two questions: "[1] Was the four-week disciplinary suspension for just cause; if not, what should the remedy be, and [2] Was it a violation of the CBA for the Club to exclude the Player from games and practices, following the four-week suspension" (Matter, 2005 p. 1). The arbitrator ruled that the suspension was for just cause. The arbitrator also determined that because of Owens' disruptive behavior, compounded with the fact that he would be paid while being benched for the remainder of the season, the punishment would not violate the NFL's CBA (Matter, 2005).

HYBRID FORMS OF ADR AND SPORT FACILITY LEASES

Although traditional sport and business arbitration typically occurs between management and its labor force, a recent trend in sports is the utilization of arbitration to resolve contractual disputes involving facility leases. Some sport facility leases, such as the one utilized by the Minnesota Wild, require the two parties enter mediation for a specific amount of time before an issue can proceed to litigation (Greenberg, 2005). Facility lease disputes tend to use new hybrid forms of ADR such as Mediation-Arbitration (Med-Arb) and Arbitration-Mediation (Arb-Med). Med-Arb is usually used when several issues are being disputed. What happens is the two parties enter mediation talks and resolve any issues they can. Any issues that remain after the mediation period are subject to arbitration. The same is true for Arb-Med, except that the arbitration process is held prior to mediation (Epstein, 2002). An example of Med-Arb in a sport facility lease is the Carolina Hurricanes' lease clause that states,

"If the parties have not resolved the Dispute through the Mediation within 60 days after the Request... [then] the Dispute shall be submitted to arbitration (the "Arbitration") for resolution by an arbitrator or a panel of arbitrators ..." (p. 106).

Facility leases often have clauses within them that state specific situations, usually constructional disagreements, which are eligible for expedited arbitration (Greenberg, 2005). Expedited arbitration is similar to normal arbitration, except the timeframe in which it is conducted is even faster. The reason construction is usually subject to expedited arbitration, as supposed to normal arbitration, is that the delay of construction has the potential of costing both parties millions of dollars. The amount of time between the initial notice and the hearing is reduced greatly, and the arbitrator may be predetermined. The Philadelphia Phillies have an arbitrator that presides over any expedited arbitration hearing until "he resigns or is replaced by written agreement of the parties" (Greenberg, 2005 p. 110). With its expansion to new facets of sport, it is easy to see that ADR will continue to impact the sport industry in new ways.

CONCLUSION

As long as there is sport, ADR will be utilized as an efficient, cheap alternative to litigation. From the statutes that established it, to the cases that define it, ADR continues to gain more legal backing. It is used in amateur sports such as the Olympics, and is a vital aspect of all the four major US sports' CBAs. Sport organizations have come to appreciate the value of ADR so much that they now use it in other areas of their business such as facility lease agreements. With its prolonged use, ADR will continue to evolve, hence the new practices of Med-Arb and Arb-Med. Without arbitration, sport franchises would have to pass the additional costs of litigation to ticket holders and fans. Fans may read about arbitration cases and are often unaware that ADR is actually saving them money. Additionally, sports will never stop searching for disputes that can be effectively settled via ADR. Sports will always have disputes between its participating members and ADR will always have a place in sports.

REFERENCES

Administrative Dispute Resolution Act of 1990, 5 USC.A. 581.

Baker, T. A., and Connaughton, D. P. (2005). The Role of Arbitrability in Disciplinary Decisions in Professional Sports. *Marquette Sports Law Review*, 16(1), 123-155.

Bruins Walk Away From Tanabe. (2007). Retrieved August 25, 2007, from http://puckstopshere.blogspot.com/2006/08/bruins-walkaway-from-tanabe.html.

Commercial Arbitration Rules. (2007). Section R-41: Time of Award. Retrieved October 21, 2007, from http://www.adr.org/sp.asp?id=22440#R41.

Condition of Membership–Mandatory Binding Arbitration. (2004). Retrieved August 12, 2007, from http://www.ncaa.org/membership/governance/divsion_III.management_council/2004-4/s36_arbitration.htm.

Epstein, A. (2002). Alternative Dispute Resolution in Sport Management and the Sport Management Curriculum. *Journal of Legal Aspects of Sport*, 12, 153-173.

Federal Arbitration Act of 1925, 9 USC. Retrieved March 24, 2007, from http://www.adr.org/sp.asp?id=29568.

Fitzpatrick, J. (2006). NHL Salary Arbitration Explained. Retrieved August 25, 2007, from http://proicehockey.about.com/od/nhlfreeagents/a/arbitration.htm

Fried, G., and Hiller, M. (1997). ADR in Youth and Intercollegiate Athletics. *Brigham Young University Law Review*, 631-652.

Gilson, E. T. (2006). Exploring the Court of Arbitration for Sport. *Law Library Journal*, 98, 503-514.

Greenberg, M. J. (2005). Alternative Dispute Resolution in Sports: Alternative Dispute Resolution in Sport Facility Leases. *Marquette Sports Law Review,* 16, 99-122.

Law v. NCAA, 134 F.3d 1010 (10th Cir. 1998).

Lipinski, T. (2003). Major League Baseball Players Ass'n v. Garvey Narrows the Judicial Strike Zone of Arbitration Awards. *Akron Law Review*, 36, 325-362.

Malin, M. H. (1990). Labor Arbitration Thirty Years After the Steelworkers Trilogy. *Chicago-Kent Law Review,* 66, 551-570.

Matter of the Arbitration Between Terrell Owens and the National Football League Players Association v. the Philadelphia Eagles and the NFL Management Council, (2005). Retrieved March 24, 2007, from http://tom.mcallister.ws/2005/11/24/full-text-of-the-terrell-owens-arbitration-settlement/.

Mowery, R. J. (2007). Alternative Dispute Resolution: Arbitration, Negotiation, and Mediation. In. D.J. Cotten & J.T. Wolohan (Eds.). Law for Recreation and Sport Managers (4th ed., pp. 409-418). Dubuque: IA: Kendall/Hunt.

Nafziger, J. A. R. (2002). Dispute Resolution in the Arena of International Sports Competition. *The American Journal of Comparative Law*, 50, 161-179.

Nat'l Basketball Ass'n v. Nat'l Basketball Players Ass'n, No. 04 Civ. 9528, 2005 WL 22869 (S.D.N.Y., 2005).

National Basketball Association Collective Bargaining Agreement. (2006). Retrieved March 24, 2007, from http://www.nbpa.com/cba_articles.php.

National Football League Collective Bargaining Agreement. (2006). Retrieved March 24, 2007, from http://www.nflpa.org/CBA/CBA_Complete.aspx.

Report of the NCAA Executive Committee Subcommittee on Mandatory Binding Arbitration. (2005). Retrieved August 12, 2007, from http://www.ncaa.org/Membership/governance/assoc-wide/executive_committee/docs/2005/2005-08/s10_mand-bind.htm.

Report of the Study Committee on Trial Transcripts. (2003). Retrieved October 21, 2007, from http://www.mass.gov/courts/trialtransrep.pdf.

Staff. (2007). *Final 2007 Arbitration results*. Retrieved August 25, 2007, from http://www.bizofbaseball.com/index.php?option=com_contentandtask=viewandid=719andItemid=78.

Ted Stevens Olympic/Amateur Sports Act of 1978, 36 USC.A. 383.

Uniform Arbitration Act of 1955.

United Paperworkers International Union, Afl-Cio, Et Al. v. Misco, Inc., 484 US 29 (1987).

United Steelworkers of America v. Am. Mfg. Co., 363 US 564 (1960).

United Steelworkers of America v. Enter. Wheel and Car Corp., 363 US 593 (1960).

United Steelworkers of America v. Warrior and Gulf Navigation Co., 363 US 574 (1960).

World Anti-Doping Agency (WADA) v. Portuguese Football Federation (FPF), CAS 2006/A/1153 (January 24, 2007). Retrieved August 12, 2007, from http://www.sports-arbitration.com/tp-070129105711/post-070130152038.shtml.

Yoost, S. M. (2006). The National Hockey League and Salary Arbitration: Time for a Line Change. *Ohio State Journal on Dispute Resolution;* 21, 485-537.

Advances in Sports and Athletics. Volume 1   ISBN: 978-1-61122-824-3
Editor: James P. Waldorf   ©2012 Nova Science Publishers, Inc.

JUST NOT ON MY TURF: STUDENT-ATHLETES' PERCEPTIONS OF HOMOSEXUALITY

*Amy Sandler**

University of Nevada, Las Vegas, US

ABSTRACT

NCAA certification guidelines now stipulate that member institutions must have policies, support opportunities, and educational programs in place to ensure a safe environment for student-athletes with diverse sexual orientations. This research measures student-athletes' general level of homophobia. The results indicate that student-athletes are comfortable with other people being gay or lesbian, but they would not be comfortable if they found themselves attracted to someone of the same-sex, or if someone of the same sex was attracted to them. If coaches and athletic administrators are aware of how student-athletes perceive sexual orientation, they can be more intentional in choosing educational programming to meet specific needs of each team.

Gay, lesbian, and bisexual (GLB) student-athletes often face marginalization from their closest associates on campus: their coaches, teammates, and fellow student-athletes. Rotella and Murray (1991) found that both athletes and coaches are tremendously homophobic and heterosexist, with the mere mention of the subject often resulting in strong emotions and apprehension. But the male and female student-athlete experience around

---

* Contact Information: 2229 Ramsgate Drive, Henderson, NV 89074, amy.sandler@unlv.edu, 702-917-8991 (cell) 702-895-5700 (fax)

sexual orientation tends to be vastly different due to particular gender assumptions and expectations. For female student-athletes, the lesbian label stems from their athletic success as women in a male-dominated environment. When it comes to sexual orientation, they often enter their specific athletic environment under a cloud of suspicion until they prove their heterosexuality. Male student-athletes, however, face the opposite predicament. Because they have reached what many consider to be the pinnacle of masculinity as elite athletes, societal expectations dictate that they must therefore also be heterosexual. Although the expectations around sexual orientation differ for male and female student-athletes, there are consequences for all who face these circumstances.

Scholarly research reveals a hostile climate for GLB student-athletes, coaches, and administrators (e.g., Kauer and Krane, 2006; Rotella and Murray, 1991; Wolf-Wendel, Toma, and Morphew, 2001). These studies offer accounts of student-athletes, coaches, and administrators' experiences around issues of sexual orientation in the athletic environment. Rotella and Murray (1991) claim that any person who is concerned about athletic performance and human ability must be sensitive to the impact of homophobia because of its negative impact on team cohesion.

But when student-athletes feel accepted as they are, Schlossberg's (1989) theory of mattering and marginality dictates that a positive and effective transition results. Schlossberg's work should be of particular interest to athletic administrators and coaches who aspire for their student-athletes to succeed both inside and outside of the athletic arena. Essentially, Schlossberg (1989) asserts that students are more prone to succeed when they feel that others care about them as individuals. Conversely, they may fail or fall short of their potential when they feel marginalized. Rotella and Murray (1991) align with Schlossberg's (1989) claim, noting the positive effect that all forms of diversity can have on personal achievement and team success.

For this research, the following definitions apply. Homophobia is "the affective, irrational dislike of lesbians and gay men" (Hill, 2006, p.4). Homonegativism concerns "learned beliefs and behaviors towards nonheterosexuals and is demonstrated through negative stereotypes, prejudice, and discrimination" (Krane, 1997, p. 145). Heterosexism is "the assumption that the world is and must be heterosexual at the same time that it rationalizes the existing distribution of power and privilege that flows from this assumption," (Rothenberg, 2007, p.120).

If coaches and administrators are aware of how student-athletes perceive sexual orientation, they can be more intentional in choosing co-curricular educational programming specific to the needs of their team. Whereas prior studies address individual experiences with or perceptions about issues related to sexual orientation in athletics, the purpose of this study is to assess specific team climates around sexual orientation.

BACKGROUND

Jacobson (2002) considers athletic departments to be the most homophobic environment on the college campus. Wolf-Wendel, Toma, and Morphew (2001) said, "The extent to which those in athletics openly express hostility to gay men and lesbians seems above and beyond that found on other parts of campus" (p.466). In their research, an example of such enmity is highlighted in Gill et al.'s (2006) study of attitudes and sexual prejudice in sport and physical activity. In surveying 150 exercise and sport science students, the Kinsey Scale was utilized to determine the sexual orientation of the sample population. The Kinsey Scale uses a rating continuum from zero to six for respondents to indicate their sexual identity, with zero indicating an exclusively heterosexual identity and six indicating an exclusively homosexual identity. In the results, Gill at al. (2006) shared that on the Kinsey Scale question, a number of respondents circled the "zero" multiple times in addition to noting that they were "definitely, exclusively" heterosexual (p.559). The respondents took no such action for any other demographic question. The results reflected an attitude toward gay men and lesbians significantly lower than the other seven inquired upon populations in that study. More specifically, males expressed the most negative attitudes toward gay men. Such findings are consistent with previous research and spark the need for further inquiry regarding climate around issues concerning sexual orientation in athletic environments (Wolf-Wendel, Toma, and Morphew, 2001).

Specific examples of homophobia in athletics facilitate a framework that addresses where, how, and finally why such perceptions are fostered. Wolf-Wendel, Toma, and Morphew (2001) found that men and women responded differently when asked about homosexuality in athletics. More specifically, they found that men were more likely to share whether or not they would feel comfortable with a gay team member. Female coaches and student-athletes, however, were well aware of the stereotypes attributed to them specifically as women in athletics and were more likely to address those stereotypes. Wolf-Wendel, Toma, and Morphew (2001) shared how homophobia directly affected one athletic director's decision to add a women's swimming team.

When faced with adding another sport to meet the terms of Title IX, "he chose swimming over softball because they did not want to bring a lot of those [lesbian] people" (p.469). Whether or not administrators and coaches are consciously aware of the situation, previous research reveals that athletic departments are fostering a hostile climate for GLB student-athletes (e.g., Gill et al. 2006; Jacobson, 2002; Rotella and Murray, 1991; Wolf-Wendel, Toma, and Morphew, 2001).

Different Assumptions for Male and Female Athletes

When asked about the issue of homosexuality, one male football player stated, "Myself, I can communicate with a gay person but I am not for communicating with them every day and letting them touch me. I don't want to talk about their sexual tendencies…that is their problem" (Wolf-Wendel, Toma, and Morphew, 2001, p.469). A female student-athlete said that when she was being recruited by her coach, "the coach made it clear that there were no lesbians on the team" (Wolf-Wendel, Toma, and Morphew, 2001, p.469). In their study on stereotypes with 15 female student-athletes, Kauer and Krane (2006) found that the most common stereotype women encountered was the lesbian label. One heterosexual basketball player in their sample noted the following: "One night, I was at a club and a [male basketball player] came up to me, and he was like, 'aren't you guys like all gay, why are you guys dancing, shouldn't you be home" (p.46). A softball player in their research suggested that if she turned down an interested male, then she was automatically assumed to be gay. Furthermore, two student-athletes in the study implied that having short hair only escalated lesbian assumptions. Another softball player in the study who identified herself as bisexual, said, "If someone is rude to us and we make a comment back, the first thing out of their mouths is, 'oh you stupid dyke'…" (Kauer and Krane, 2006, p.46). Essentially, these comments reflect that female athletes must go to lengths to prove their heterosexuality, often facing dire consequences until attaining such status. But regardless of their sexual orientation, the homonegativism imparted on female student-athletes causes unnecessary frustration and harm and can have significant effects inside and outside of the sporting environment.

Baird (2002) says that when a woman outwardly displays athletic characteristics, her femininity becomes suspect. Griffin (1992) emphasizes the fears associated with such perceptions, reporting female athletes' shame associated with the lesbian image of women's sports. But for males, Jacobson

(2002) notes the opposite assumption. Male athletes are presumed to be heterosexual because of their athleticism. In fact, Baird says that for men, "Athleticism and homosexuality have come to be seen as mutually exclusive" (p.33). As a result, there are negative consequences for male athletes as well in that the presumption of heterosexuality marginalizes gay male athletes and fosters a hypermasculine, heterosexist, and homonegative atmosphere.

Religion and Sport

In her book, *Strong Women, Deep Closets*, Griffin (1998) introduces the conflict that emerges when athletic organizations grant fundamentalist Christian organizations access to coaches and student-athletes. *Athletes in Action (*AIA) and *Fellowship of Christian Athletes* (FCA) are two of the more prominent organizations that recruit student-athletes to help spread fundamentalist Christian teachings. In discussing the FCA's affiliation with the Women's Basketball Coaches Association (WBCA), Griffin (1998) says, "By providing a forum for the FCA to distribute antigay literature and air their views on homosexuality, the WBCA and other sports governing bodies who sponsor FCA events provide tacit, if not explicit, approval of discrimination..." (p.118). One example was at the 1996 WBCA national conference when then University of Alabama assistant basketball coach, Cheryl Littlejohn, was on a panel in which she shared her beliefs on the contradictions between homosexuality and the Bible's teachings (Griffin, 1998). Despite this overt opposition to diverse sexual orientations, the WBCA continues to foster an amicable working relationship with both the FCA and AIA (e.g., WBCA, 2007). More recently, the University of Florida settled a lawsuit with a former lesbian student-athlete who was kicked off the softball team after she alleged that the head coach "created an atmosphere of alienation for anyone not sharing her Christian beliefs and outed other coaches and players as lesbians..." (Buzinski, 2005). These examples expose the impact that fundamentalist religious organizations and coaches can have on student-athletes' experiences and personal development.

On a more positive note, there are recent signs of progress between organizations working to end discrimination against gay, lesbian, bisexual, and transgender (GLBT) people in sport and Christian sport organizations. Aiming to demonstrate that members of Christian sport organizations and GLBT advocacy organizations can coexist in a climate of respect, if not agreement, the two groups collaborated on a panel at the 2008 WBCA convention titled,

Seeking Common Ground in Athletics, A Conversation Among Lesbians, Christians, and Christian Lesbians.

Conceptual Framework

This literature review presents the so-often invisible climate around sexual orientation in college athletics. Schlossberg's theory of mattering and marginality is significant because it offers an appropriate framework for understanding the importance of seeing each student-athlete as an individual. Student-athletes who are marginalized or 'considered other' begin to feel as if they do not matter (Krane, 2001; Schlossberg, 1989). One symptom of marginalizing practices that Schlossberg (1989) identifies is that "individuals become 'obsessed' with the problem of marginality and this becomes their dominant mode of thinking and behavior" (p.7). Thus, GLB student-athletes in a homonegative environment often feel compelled to negotiate their sexual orientation at a time when they simply might want to be validated for their athletic skills or for their multiple identities. It is critical, however, to note that this research presents only one side of this issue. The researcher was unable to find scholarly research demonstrating results from athletic environments that are inclusive of all student-athletes, regardless of sexual orientation.

METHOD

Participants and Sampling

Participants in this study included 34 male and female student-athletes (all representing the same sport) from an urban, NCAA division one institution in the southwestern portion of the United States. Descriptive statistics were compiled for each respondent's year in college, race/ethnicity, religion, and religious importance. For this study, the researcher utilized purposive sampling. Babbie (2007) suggests that this sampling method allows the researcher to determine the most appropriate and representative population for the study. Because the researcher was looking to understand student-athletes perceptions about sexual orientation, student-athletes were intentionally sought out as survey respondents for the study.

Instrumentation

The student-athletes were administered the Index of Attitudes Toward Homosexuals (IAH). According to Hudson and Ricketts (1980), the IAH is a 25-item survey with five-point likert scale responses that range from strongly agree to strongly disagree. Once the responses to the 25 statements are tallied, total scores will range between zero and 100. The lower the score, the less likely the respondent is to experience anxiety about being in close environment with someone who is homosexual. The inverse is true for those who score higher.

Validity and Reliability

To control for respondents' biases, the survey instrument offers both positive and negative statements about gay people and their social relations. According to Walmyr Publishing (n.d.), the IAH received scores of .90 or better for its reliability and has a "very good to excellent validity coefficient." Hinkle, Wiersma, and Jurs (2003) consider a reliability value of .90 or better to signify a "very high correlation" (p.109). In a pilot study of 300 college students, Hudson and Ricketts (1980) determined the IAH to have an alpha coefficient of .90. In the same study, the IAH had high content and factorial validity. According to Babbie (2007), "validity refers to the extent to which an empirical measure adequately reflects the real meaning of the concept under consideration" (p.146). A similarity between the Hudson and Ricketts study and this study is that both samples drew from adults in a university setting.

Procedures

Upon consultation with the participating institution's associate athletic director, the researcher contacted and subsequently met with the men and women's coaches, at which time any issues concerning the survey were openly addressed. The coaches agreed to allow the student-athletes to be surveyed; however, they asked that the teams be separately surveyed. In addition, one of the coaches specifically requested that the researcher not ask the student-athletes to indicate their sexual orientation in the demographic section. While the researcher honored these requests, future research should examine what environmental factors led to the coaches' wishes.

With permission from the coaches, the researcher met with the two teams separately, where intentions for conducting the study and an informed consent letter were read prior to distributing the surveys. Approval was granted from the Institutional Review Board at the institution's Office for the Protection of Human Subjects.

RESULTS

For all data analyses, the statistical package for the social sciences (SPSS) version 15.0 (2007) was utilized. This study population (N=34) included nearly equal numbers of male (18, 52%) and female (16, 48%) student-athletes, all of whom were in good academic standing. The respondents were mostly first-year (14, 41.2%), second-year (9, 26.5%) and third-year (10, 29.4%) students, with only one (2.9%) fourth-year student in the sample. Seventy-nine percent (27) of the respondents identified as Caucasian/non-Hispanic, with the Hispanic (3, 8.8%) and African American (3, 8.8%) representation totaling approximately 18 percent of the study population. One student (2.9%) self-identified as multi-racial/bi-racial. A majority of the students identified as Catholic (16, 47.1%), with Protestant/Christians (10, 29.4%) being the second largest religious identity amongst the student-athletes. Seven students (20.6%) indicated that they did not identify with any religion at all, and one student (2.9%) circled the "other" option, but did not indicate a specific religion. The majority of the respondents indicated that their religion was either somewhat important (15, 44.1%) or important (12, 35.3%). Nearly equal numbers indicated that religion was either very important (3, 8.8%) or not important at all (4, 11.8%). There were no statistical differences among the athletes according to race/ethnicity, religion, religious importance, or year in college.

Utilizing the t-test and a significance level of $p < .05$, the means of the men's team and women's team were significant regarding their level of homophobia. The mean for the men's team was 54.22 (SD = 15.73, p = .05) and the mean for the women's team was 41.31 (SD = 14.46, p = .05). According to Hudson and Ricketts (1980), these results suggest that as a group, the men's team is considered low-grade homophobic and the women's team is considered low-grade non-homophobic (see Figure 1).

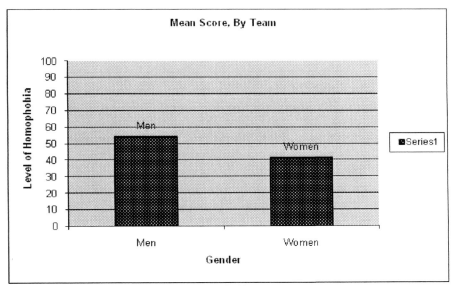

Note. 0 = Non-Homophobic, 100 = Homophobic.

Figure 1. Mean score comparisons on the Index of Attitudes Toward Homosexuals.

More than one-fourth (9) of the respondents indicated that they would feel comfortable being seen in a gay bar. However, additional t-test results indicated that as a team, male student-athletes would be significantly (p = .03) less comfortable (x = 3.83, SD = 1.20) being seen in a gay bar than female student-athletes (x = 2.88, SD = 1.20).

Both the men's team (x = 2.56, SD = .98) and the women's team (x = 2.56, SD = 1.26) agreed that they would be comfortable if they learned that their daughter had a lesbian teacher. However, as a team the men indicated that they would be significantly (p = .02) less comfortable (x = 3.72, SD = .96) than the women (x = 2.75, SD = 1.39) if they learned that their son's male teacher was gay.

Frequencies

The mean scores reveal that members of both teams indicated that they would be uncomfortable if they found themselves attracted to a person of the same sex (men, x = 4.67, SD = .49; women, x = 3.81, SD = 1.22). Only three student-athletes (8.8 %) said that they would be comfortable, and 30 student-athletes (88.2 %) indicated that they would be uncomfortable if they found themselves attracted to a person of the same sex. In response to the statement, *"I would feel comfortable knowing I was attractive to members of the same sex,"* as a team (although non-significant), the women leaned toward the "neither agree nor disagree" response (x = 3.13, SD = 1.20) and the men reflected a "disagree" response (x = 4.00, SD = .97).

For the statement, *"I would feel comfortable if I learned that my best friend of my sex was homosexual,"* 70.6 percent (24) of the student-athletes indicated that they either agreed, strongly agreed, or were indifferent and 29.4 percent (10) indicated that they disagreed or strongly disagreed.

DISCUSSION

When the researcher proposed the study to the head coach of the men's team, the coach suggested that he believed his sport to be one of the more liberal sports. Contrary to his perception, this study confirms previous research findings, which hold that men have negative attitudes towards gay men (e.g., Gill et al., 2006; Wolf-Wendel, Toma, and Morphew, 2001). The mean scores for both the men and women's teams in this study indicated that student-athletes are comfortable working with both male and female homosexuals in the context of their sport. But as a team, the men are significantly less comfortable working with male homosexuals than they are working with female homosexuals. The male student-athletes hold similar beliefs regarding their future children, particularly their male children. As a team, the female student-athletes indicated that they would be comfortable if they learned that their daughter's female teacher was a lesbian or if their son's male teacher was homosexual. These findings raise an important question: Why would male student-athletes be comfortable if they learned that their daughter's teacher was a lesbian, but uneasy if a male homosexual was teaching their son?

Homophobia: A Manifestation of Sexism

Pharr (1988) notes that there are two realms where it is acceptable for men to be affectionate with one another: These two exceptions occur in competitive athletics and during wartime crises. Though such expressions might be considered natural after a critical turning point in a game or battle, it is culturally unacceptable to carry such behaviors beyond these two settings. Pharr indicates that when gay men are affectionate towards one another outside of the cultural boundaries, they are considered to not be "real men," thus denigrating male dominance and superiority over women. Perhaps Pharr's (1998) point explains why the majority of the men in this study tend to be homophobic towards other men.

Riddle Homophobia Scale

The Riddle Homophobia Scale is an attempt to expand the notion of homophobia through the use of different points along a scale (Riddle, 1985). Although the Riddle Scale was not created to complement IAH results but rather to understand levels of homophobia in a social setting, conceptually it appears that the student-athletes in this sample fall across the spectrum of the Riddle Homophobia Scale. The majority of them, however, are between acceptance and support of gay men and lesbians (see Figure 2). Characteristics of the *acceptance* stage include that there is still something to be accepted. Individuals in this stage might say, "I don't care if you are gay or lesbian, just don't shove it in my face." Individuals in the *support* stage might not themselves be comfortable with the idea of homosexuality, but they recognize and might work to reverse the inequalities imposed upon on those who do not identify as strictly heterosexual.

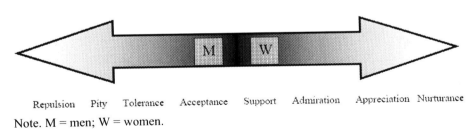

Repulsion   Pity   Tolerance   Acceptance   Support   Admiration   Appreciation   Nurturance

Note. M = men; W = women.

Figure 2. Conceptualizing the Riddle Homophobia Scale.

The results suggest that the student-athletes appear to be more at ease with homosexuality when it does not threaten or compromise their own sexual identity. The researcher asserts that movement along the scale will be dependant upon two factors: (1) positive interactions with gay male and lesbian peers and role models, and (2) intentional, departmentally supported educational programming around GLB concerns. Although the men's team is less accepting than the women's team, the athletes' openness in certain stated scenarios and the reasons stated above indicate that great potential exists for positive movement along the Riddle Homophobia Scale.

Discomfort with Personal Identity

Although the study population was limited not only in number but also to one team sport, the findings unveil new data regarding how these student-athletes would feel if they found themselves attracted to or attractive to someone of the same sex. These two issues sparked the most angst from the respondents. A significant majority of the student-athletes in this sample either disagreed or strongly disagreed with the statement: *I would be comfortable if I found myself attracted to members of my sex.* Only three students indicated that they would be comfortable. Secondly, when the table was turned and the survey said, *I would be comfortable knowing I was attractive to members of my sex,* the women were significantly more comfortable. However, both teams revealed discomfort with these two statements. There are explanations for why the students responded this way. First, most literature focusing on sexual orientation issues in college athletics maintains that the athletic environment is either the most homophobic place on the college campus or that athletes and coaches are tremendously homophobic and heterosexist (e.g., Jacobsen, 2002; Wolf-Wendel, Toma, and Morphew, 2001; Rotella and Murray, 1991).

Schlossberg's (1989) theory of mattering and marginality encompasses the notion that all students, including those who identify as GLB or who are questioning their sexual orientation, are more likely to succeed when their individual identity is valued. This inverse is true for those who feel marginalized. Regardless of one's sexual identity, the mindset of the student-athletes and behaviors consistent with such beliefs inherently sets up an atmosphere in which the student-athletes might accept homophobia, homonegativism, and heterosexism as the norm and therefore choose not to challenge it. Thus, while they demonstrate that they are comfortable with others' being GLB, it appears that their identity development, particularly if they might be questioning their sexual orientation, is not fostered in this environment and therefore hindered.

Limitations

Although some of the results are consistent with previous research (e.g., males are more homophobic than females and tend to be less comfortable with male homosexuals), the sample is limited in number and therefore generalizing beyond the scope of this inquiry should be done with caution. Also, the majority of the students surveyed were Caucasian and Christian. The population lacks racial diversity and reflects the cultural encapsulation that these particular student-athletes may experience. Finally, the survey instrument was limited to perceptions of homosexuality only.

IMPLICATIONS FOR FUTURE RESEARCH AND POLICY

The findings are consistent with previous research in that negative perceptions about gay men and lesbians exist in college athletics, with males holding more hostile views towards other gay men (Jacobsen, 2002; Wolf-Wendel, Toma, and Morphew, 2001; Rotella and Murray, 1991). It is important to comprehend why these perceptions continue as well as how they are fostered. In addition, how does environment, particularly with an emphasis on "team", impact student-athletes' identity development? Results from this study motivate the question: In team sports, are individual identities marginalized in an effort to encourage student-athletes to conform to perceived team norms? Furthermore, because gender identity and sexual orientation are perceived as naturally interconnected in the United States and especially in sport, future research should consider gender identity, including transgender issues. Other areas for inquiry include the difference in perceptions of sexual orientation between religious affiliations and/or between Caucasian students and students of color in college athletics. Inquiry into these populations can help researchers and practitioners understand the origins of perception. For example, Wall and Washington (1995) state that "much of the heterosexism and homophobia that is experienced or felt is justified first by religious teachings" (p.70). Their research focuses particularly on the relationship between the African American community and the Christian Church, noting that "for many years the church has been one of the central places of truth, goodness, and solidarity (p. 70). These statements unveil the complexities concerning homophobia and heterosexism in the African American and religious communities, and in many cases, the intersection of both. In addition, inquiries into athletic environments that are inclusive of GLB students could potentially inform best practices.

CONCLUSION

Homophobia, homonegativism, and heterosexism affect individuals no differently than racism, sexism or any other systemic oppression against a minority population. Those sensitive to or on the receiving end of these acts understand the unnecessary harm that it causes. In college athletics, the proactive option is to create a safe and inclusive environment for all student-athletes. In fact, the National Collegiate Athletic Association (NCAA) not only includes sexual orientation as a protected class in its non-discrimination policy, for certification it now requires that member institutions report policies, support opportunities, and educational programs that are in place to ensure a safe environment for student-athletes with diverse sexual orientations (NCAA, 2006).

Education as a Tool for Learning and Inclusion

Townsend (1997) considers education to be one of the greatest impetuses in the struggle to end homophobia. Despite the new NCAA certification guidelines, Gill et al. (2006) says that diversity training and multicultural instruction is minimal for future sport and physical education professionals. The NCAA, the National Center for Lesbian Rights (NCLR), and the Women's Sports Foundation's – It Takes a Team! Project, each offer tailored educational programming around these issues. Additionally, the National Association for Girls and Women in Sport endorses Barber and Krane's (2007) recommendations for creating a positive climate for girls and women in sport.

Although the road to equality remains uncertain, it appears that the NCAA recognizes the importance of diversity. But for many in college athletics, the topic of sexual orientation remains divisive, if not off limits. Unfortunately, those personally affected are often silenced for fear of losing their job, their friends, or their position on the team. In aspiring to promote the development of all student-athletes, athletic administrators and coaches should intentionally integrate strategies for providing educational opportunities around sexual orientation awareness and understanding.

REFERENCES

Babbie, E. (2007). *The practice of social research.* (11th ed.). Belmont, CA: Thomson Wadsworth

Baird, J.A. (2002). Playing it straight: an analysis of current legal protections to Combat homophobia and sexual orientation discrimination in intercollegiate athletics. *Berkeley Women's Law Journal, 31-67.*

Barber, H., and Krane, V. (2007). Creating Inclusive and Positive Climates in girls and Women's sport: position statement on homophobia, homonegativism, and heterosexism, *16, 1,* 53.

Buzinski, J. (2005). Florida settles with lesbian athlete. Retrieved October 27, 2007, from http://www.outsports.com/campus/20040227zimbar disettlement.htm

Gill, D.L., Morrow, R.G., Collins, K.E., Lucey, A.B., and Schultz, A.M. (2006). Attitudes and sexual prejudice in sport and physical activity. *Journal of Sport Management, 20,* 554-564.

Griffin, P. (1992). Changing the game: homophobia, sexism, and lesbians in sport. *Quest, 44,* 251-265.

Griffin, P. (1998). *Strong women, deep closets: Lesbians and homophobia in sport.* Windsor, ON: Human Kinetics.

Hill, R.J. (2006). Challenging homophobia and heterosexism: Lesbian, gay, bisexual, Transgender, and queer issues in organizational settings. *New Directions for Adult and Continuing Education, 112.*

Hinkle, D.E., Wiersma, W., and Jurs, S.G. (2003). *Applied statistics for the behavioral Sciences.* (5th ed.). Boston: Houghton Mifflin

Hudson, W.W., and Ricketts, W.A. (1980). A strategy for the measurement of homophobia. *Journal of Homosexuality, 5, 4,* 357–372).

Jacobson, J. (2002, November 1). The loneliest athletes. *The Chronicle of Higher Education, 49, 10,* pA33.

Kauer, K.J., and Krane, V. (2006, Spring). "Scary dykes" and "feminine queens": Stereotypes and female college athletes. *Women in Sport and Physical Activity Journal, 15, 1,* 42-55.

Krane, V. (2001). One lesbian feminist epistemology: Integrating feminist standpoint, queer theory, and feminist cultural studies. *The Sport Psychologist, 15,* 401-411.

NCAA. (2006). Division one athletics certification self study instrument. Retrieved September 3, 2007, from NCAA Web site: http://www.ncaa.org/library/membership/d1_self-study_instr/2006-07/2006-07_self-study_instrument.pdf

Pharr, S. (1988). *Homophobia: A weapon of sexism.* Iverness, CA: Chardon Press.

Riddle, D. (1985). "Homophobia Scale." In Opening Doors to Understanding and Acceptance. In K. Obear and A. Reynolds. Boston: Unpublished essay.

Rotella, M., and Murray, M. (1991). Homophobia, the world of sport, and sport psychology consulting. *The Sport Psychologist, 5,* 355-364.

Rothenberg, P.S. (2007). *Race, class, and gender in the United States: An integrated study* (7th ed.). New York: Worth Publishers.

Schlossberg, N.K. (1989). Marginality and mattering: Key issues in building community. *New Directions for Student Services, 48,* 5-15.

Townsend, K.D. (October, 1997). Coaches wanted: lesbians need not apply. *Lesbian News, 23, 3,* p.24.

Wall, V.A., and Washington, J. (1995). Understanding gay and lesbian students of color. In Evans, N.J., and Wall, V.A. (1995). *Beyond tolerance: gays, lesbians and bisexuals on campus.* Pp. 67-78. Lanham, MD: American College Personnel Association.

Walmyr Publishing Company. (n.d.). Assessment Scales. Retrieved September 20, 2007, from http://www.walmyr.com/scales.html.

Wolf-Wendel, L.E., Toma, J.D., and Morphew, C.C. (2001). How much difference is too much difference? Perceptions of gay men and lesbians in intercollegiate athletics. *Journal of College Student Development, 42, 5,* 465-479.

Women's Basketball Coaches Association (2007). WBCA Convention Schedule 2007. Retrieved October 27, 2007, from http://www.wbca.org/upload/Convention%20Program%20Schedule%202007.pdf

Advances in Sports and Athletics. Volume 1   ISBN: 978-1-61122-824-3
Editor: James P. Waldorf   ©2012 Nova Science Publishers, Inc.

NEW TECHNOLOGY HOLDS PROMISE FOR THE FUTURE APPLICATION OF PSYCHOPHYSIOLOGICAL METHODS FOR THE ENHANCEMENT OF PERFORMANCE DURING SPORT AND EXERCISE

David L. Neumann[*]

School of Psychology, Griffith University and Centre of Excellence for
Applied Sport Science Research, Queensland Academy of Sport,
Nathan, Queensland, Australia

COMMENTARY

Psychophysiology is the study of psychological processes through the measurement and interpretation of physiological responses (Cacioppo, Tassinary, Berntson, 2007). The realisation of the relationship between the so-called "mind" and "body" has encouraged the application of psychophysiology in various areas of psychology, including sport psychology (see Hatfield and Hillman, 2000). Unfortunately, methodological problems have limited the application of psychophysiological techniques to the study of sport. The gross body movements in most sports cause considerable degradation in the quality of the physiological recordings. The obtrusiveness of the electrode attachments and the wiring of the electrodes to a data acquisition system can also severely impede the athlete's mobility and performance. It is perhaps not surprising that

[*] Address for correspondence: David Neumann, School of Psychology, Griffith University (Gold Coast Campus), Mail: GRIFFITH UNIVERSITY QLD, Queensland, 4222, Australia, E-mail D.Neumann@griffith.edu.au, Facsimile +61(0)7 5552 8291, Telephone +61(0)7 5552 8052

most psychophysiological research has been concerned with sports that involve minimal movements, such as pistol shooting (e.g., Mets, Konttinen, and Lyytinen, 2007). However, a range of new technological advances are giving encouragement for future applications of psychophysiological methodology in sport.

New data filtering and processing techniques have been developed to greatly improve signal quality. A case in point is the recording of heart rate, which has shown to be sensitive to both physical and psychological states in exercising individuals (e.g., Szabo, Peronnet, Gauvin, and Furedy, 1994). Commercially available equipment can record heart rate averaged across several seconds or more using non-invasive and robust devises that can be worn on the wrist like a watch or as a strap around the chest. Such techniques are useful, but can be limited when more precise measurement of heart rate is required. In many cases, heart rate needs to be time locked to certain behaviours (e.g., the onset of a baseball pitch) or indices derived from the biosignal that underlies heart rate (e.g., T-wave amplitude) are required. In such cases, the electrocardiogram (ECG) itself must be acquired.

Although the ECG is a relatively large biosignal, it can still be difficult to obtain clear recordings in active athletes due to the noise created by muscle activity and artefacts created by movement. Improvements in the quality of the recording electrodes to allow for a firmer attachment and improved conductive gels can reduce artefacts caused by moderate movements at the source. New data processing techniques are providing additional solutions. Noise may be removed in many cases using digital signal processing techniques such as wavelets (Celka and Gysels, 2006), nonlinear methods (Schreiber and Kaplan, 1996), adaptive filtering (Thakor and Zhu, 1991), and principal components analysis (Moody and Mark, 1989). Motion artefacts that persist in the signal may also be removed with some success using these modern digital signal processing techniques (e.g., Renevey, Vetter, Krauss, Celka, and Depeursinge, 2001). Significant challenges still remain for smaller biosignals, such as the electroencephalogram, although future technologies hold promise for improvements in the quality of even these biosignals.

The use of an electromyographic signal to cancel out muscle and motion artefacts from the ECG was recently demonstrated during a rowing task (Celka and Kilner, 2006). Rowing is a continuous and energetic task that greatly impacts on the recording of ECGs from the chest. For such recordings, the biosignals generated by the pectoral and surrounding muscles and movement artefacts are a problem. To recover the ECG during rowing, the electromyogram recording of the distal pectoral muscle was used to provide a reference signal for motion and muscle activity cancellation. This additional reference information, in combination with band-pass and adaptive filters, allowed the ECG to be recovered even during highly vigorous rowing by trained rowers. I have applied the same technique during a cricket batting task. Although cricket batting represents a different task to rowing (e.g., it is a discrete task of relatively clear ECG recordings punctuated by sudden and rapid movements), the ECG during the entire task could be recovered successfully using the relatively low-complexity technique of Celka and Kilner (2006). It should also be noted that such techniques could be used the other way around, that is, by using concurrent recordings of ECG and cancellation techniques to improve the quality of electromyographic recordings.

Another technological advancement that encourages further psychophysiological study in sport is the increased simplicity of the data acquisition equipment. In addition to becoming less expensive, the recording equipment has become easier to set up. Interfacing with a computer no longer necessitates the use of input/output cards and complicated calibration settings. There are now several commercially available systems that interface with a computer by using plug-and-play universal serial bus (USB) connections. Such technology also allows the standard laptop computer to be used for data acquisition. Finally, the recording equipment is becoming smaller in size, thus increasing the portability of the system when used during on-field studies of a sport.

Perhaps one of the most significant technological advances for sport application has been the development of new wireless portable or telemetry systems. Such systems allow the athlete to be physically separated from the data acquisition equipment. As such, the athlete is afforded greater freedom of movement and can be less conscious of avoiding the wires and damaging the equipment. This can be particularly important for psychological research because researchers want to avoid a situation in which the measurement technique changes the behaviours they were designed to observe. Also from a researchers perspective, wireless systems can allow psychophysiological measurements to be taken in many sports that have been unable to be studied in the past. Portable wireless systems can be used stand-alone in that the same unit can acquire the biosignal, do some signal processing, and store the information for later retrieval. Improved technology has increased the storage capacity of portable systems, thus allowing for recordings to be made for longer periods or at higher sampling rates. Telemetry systems can be used to acquire the biosignal and send this information via a wireless protocol to a receiving station for signal processing and storage. Such telemetry systems can allow for more sophisticated data processing techniques to be used and for on-line monitoring of the athletes psychophysiological responses.

The adoption of new technological advancements in the psychophysiological study of sport has the potential to increase our understanding of performance-related psychological factors. Psycho-physiological methods can provide unique information about psychological factors in sport that can be difficult to measure using self-report or behavioural observation. Moreover, psychophysiological techniques provide an excellent interface between the psychological and physical demands of many sports. Biofeedback, the process in which an individual's biological state is played back to an athlete to help them gain control over a mental state or motor actions (Blumenstein, Bar-Eli, and Tenenhaum, 2002), is particularly well positioned to produce improvements in sports performance through the application of new technology. By using information obtained from biofeedback during the actual sport performance, rather than during simulated or post-session periods, a greater correspondence between performance and psychological state can be achieved. Moreover, by using new technological advancements in psychophysiological recording techniques, biofeedback information can be more accurate and applied in a wider variety of sports.

REFERENCES

Blumenstein, B., Bar-Eli, M., and Tenenbaum, G. (Eds.) (2002). *Brain and body in sport and exercise: Biofeedback applications in performance enhancement.* New York: John Wiley and Sons.

Cacioppo, J. T., Tassinary, L. G., and Berntson, G. G. (2007). Handbook of psychophysiology (3rd ed). New York: Cambridge University Press.

Celka, P., and Gysels, E. (2006). Smoothly adjustable denoising using a priori knowledge. *Signal Processing, 86,* 2233-2242.

Celka, P., and Kilner, B. (2006). Carmeli's *S* index assesses motion and muscle artefact reduction in rowers' electrocardiograms. *Physiological Measurement, 27,* 737-755.

Hatfield, B. D., and Hillman, C. H. (2001). The psychophysiology of sport: A mechanistic understanding of the psychology of superior performance. In R. N. Singer, H. A. Hausenblas, and C. M. Janelle (Eds.), *Handbook of Sport Psychology* (pp. 363-386). New York, NY: John Wiley and Sons Inc.

Mets, T., Konttinen, N., and Lyytinen, H. (2007). Shot placement within cardiac cycle in junior elite rifle shooters. *Psychology of Sport and Exercise, 8,* 169-177.

Moody, G., and Mark, R. (1989). QRS morphology representation and noise estimation using the Karhunen-Loève transform. *Computers in Cardiology, 16,* 269-272.

Renevey, P., Vetter, R., Krauss, J., Celka, P., and Depeursinge, Y. (2001). Wrist-located pulse detection using IR signals, activity and nonlinear artefact cancellation. *Proceedings of the 23rd Annual International Conference of the IEEE, 3,* 3030-3033.

Schreiber, T., and Kaplan, D. (1996). Nonlinear noise reduction for electrocardiogram. *Chaos, 6,* 87-92.

Szabo, A., Peronnet, F., Gauvin, L., and Furedy, J. J. (1994). Mental challenge elicits "additional" increases in heart rate during low and moderate intensity cycling. *International Journal of Psychophysiology, 18,* 197-204.

Thakor, N., and Zhu, V. (1991). Application of adaptive filtering to ECG analysis: noise cancellation and arrhythmia detection. *IEEE Transactions on Biomedical Engineering, 38,* 785-794.

Advances in Sports and Athletics. Volume 1   ISBN: 978-1-61122-824-3
Editor: James P. Waldorf   ©2012 Nova Science Publishers, Inc.

IDENTIFICATION WITH MULTIPLE SPORTING TEAMS: HOW MANY TEAMS DO SPORT FANS FOLLOW?

Frederick G. Grieve[1]*, Ryan K. Zapalac[2], Amanda J. Visek[3], Daniel L. Wann[4], Paula M. Parker[5], Julie Partridge[6] and Jason R. Lanter[7]

[1]Western Kentucky University, Bowling Green, Kentucky, US
[2]Sam Houston State University, Huntsville, Texas, US
[3]The George Washington University, Washington D. C., US
[4]Murray State University, Murray, Kentucky, US
[5]East Stroudsburg University, East Stroudsburg, Pennsylvania, US
[6]Southern Illinois University, Illinois, US
[7]Kutztown University, Berks County, Pennsylvania, US

ABSTRACT

The current study examined the identification with multiple sport teams by sport fans, as a potential means to maintain these positive benefits of identification by switching identification to another sports team. Sport fans were predicted to report following fewer teams closely compared to moderately, and fewer teams moderately compared to casually. Additionally, sport fans were predicted to be higher identified with teams they followed closely compared to those teams moderately followed, and more identified with moderately followed teams compared to teams they followed casually. The first hypothesis was not supported,

---

* Please address correspondence to: Frederick G. Grieve, Department of Psychology, Western Kentucky University, 1906 College Heights Blvd, #21030. Bowling Green, KY 42101-1030. rick.grieve@wku.edu

as participants reported following more teams closely compared to moderately and casually. The second hypothesis was supported, as· participants reported being more identified with the teams they closely follow compared to the moderately and casually followed teams. Implications of these findings for sport researchers and sport marketers are discussed.

Identification with a local sport team has been shown to have important psychological consequences (Wann, 2006). Sport fans who highly identify with a team, or who feel a strong psychological connection with the team (Wann and Branscombe, 1993), report higher levels of psychological health, including lower levels of loneliness (Wann, Dimmock, and Grove, 2003; Wann, Martin, Grieve, and Gardner, in press), higher levels of social self-esteem and social well-being (Lanter and Blackburn, 2004), lower levels of depression, alienation, and experiences of negative emotion (Wann et al. 2003), higher levels of openness, conscientiousness, and extroversion (Wann, Dunham, Byrd, and Keenan, 2004), and lower levels of fatigue, anger, tension, and confusion (Wann, Inman, Ensor, Gates, and Caldwell, 1999). These benefits are derived through the social connections, or social support, highly identified fans experience vis a vis their identification (Wann, 2006).

However, in order to benefit from being strongly, or highly, identified with a local sports team, individuals must cope with team losses. Fans who are not highly identified with a team are not affected by a team loss as the loss is not meaningful to them (Branscombe, Ellemers, Spears, and Doosje, 1999). Highly identified fans, on the other hand, are often strongly affected by team losses, as noted by the intense negative emotional reactions many have to a team loss (Bernhardt, Dabbs, Fielden, and Lutter, 1998). Thus, they have a need to cope with a team loss in order to continue to receive the psychological and physiological benefits of team identification.

There are a number of coping mechanisms available for highly identified fans. One coping method is through derogating the outgroup (Wann, 2006). Fans of a team that loses are more likely to become angry with game officials, members of the opposing team, or even fans of the opposing team (Rubin and Hewstone, 1998). Another coping method is through Cutting Off Reflected Failure (CORFing; Snyder, Lassegard, and Ford, 1986), in which fans emotionally and psychologically distance themselves from teams after a team failure. The opposite of CORFing is Basking In Reflected Glory—BIRGing (Cialdini et al., 1976); thus, fans often refer to "us winning" and "them losing" when discussing team performances. Finally, fans can Cut Off Future Failure (COFF; Wann, Hamlet, Wilson, and Hodges, 1995), in which they do not become overly excited about a team's current performance due to the possibility of poor performance in the future.

One form of CORFing (i.e., distancing oneself from a team) is to change the cognitive focus from one team to another. For example, if a fan is identified with two National Football League teams, such as the Tennessee Titans and the Detroit Lions, and one of these teams were to lose on a given Sunday while the other team won, that fan could, conceivably, change focus from the losing team to the winning team. There is some data to suggest that this phenomenon occurs. Grieve, Wann, and Zapalac (in press) presented participants with a vignette describing the end of the season and asked participants to indicate to what extent they would perform seven different activities. Several of the activities involved changing focus from the losing team to another team, such as rooting for the team that defeated their favorite team or changing their focus from one sport to another. Participants were likely to indicate that they would participate in many of these activities.

However, in order for this switch in focus to take place, sport fans must follow more than one team. Such a phenomenon seems likely. With the expansion of the competitive seasons in virtually all sports (e.g., baseball's spring training begins in February while the World Series has been pushed back to late October) and the creation of new sport leagues (e.g., Arena Football League, Major League Soccer, Women's National Basketball Association), there are multiple sport seasons occurring concurrently. It seems logical, then, that sport fans would be following, and would be identified, with more than one team at any given time. However, to date, there is no empirical support for this hypothesis.

Therefore, the present study was designed to address the gap in this area of the literature. Two hypotheses were formulated. First, it was hypothesized that participants would report following fewer teams very closely than they would report following teams either moderately or casually; further, participants would report following fewer teams moderately than casually. Second, it was hypothesized that identification would be strongest for teams that participants follow closely than for teams they follow moderately or casually; further, participants would report higher identification for teams they follow moderately than casually.

METHOD

Participants

Participants for this study included 986 college-age participants from seven different universities in the eastern United States. Participants for the study included 445 women (45.1%) and 538 men (54.6%), while 3 participants (0.3%) did not indicate gender. In terms of racial/ethnic background, 810 participants (82.2%) identified themselves as Caucasian, 113 (11.5%) identified themselves as African American, 18 (1.8%) identified themselves as Asian American, 2 (0.2%) identified themselves as American Indian, 3 (0.3%) identified themselves as Pacific Islander, 20 (2.0%) identified themselves as Hispanic, and 2 (0.2%) people did not indicate race/ethnicity. The mean age of the sample was 20.74 years (SD = 2.89) and the mean education level fell at the sophomore year of college (M = 14.23 years; SD = 1.33).

Measures

Demographics. Participants completed a short demographic survey that included questions about age, race, gender, education level, and home town.

Team Survey. Participants also completed three questions that asked them to list the teams that they follow at different levels (i.e., closely, moderately, and casually). Specifically, the first question asked them to list the teams that they follow closely (e.g., know the teams' records, can name most of the players on the teams). The second question asked participants to list the teams that they follow moderately (e.g., generally know if the teams are playing well or not, but not the exact record; know some, but not all of the players on the teams). The final question asked participants to list all of the teams that they follow casually (e.g., are interested in having the teams do well, but do not actively follow them; may look up the teams' records every once in a while; know one or two players on the team). In the cases of all three levels of followship, the teams cited could have been from multiple levels of competition (i.e., collegiate, professional, etc.). Thus, participants were not directed to focus their responses on one specific level, but were asked to take a more holistic view on the teams they choose to follow closely, moderately, and casually.

Team Identification. The Sport Spectator Identification Scale (SSIS; Wann and Branscombe, 1993) was used to measure participants' degree of identification with their self-reported sport teams. The SSIS contains seven self-report items rated on an eight-point Likert-type scale (1-low, 8-high; scale anchors vary depending on the item). Higher scores indicate higher levels of team identification. The SSIS has been shown to have sound psychometric properties (Wann, Melnick, Russell, and Pease, 2001) in a wide range of cultural settings (e.g., Theodorakis et al., 2006; Uemukai et al., 1995). Internal consistency scores (e.g., Cronbach's alpha) for the SSIS are consistently at or greater than .90 and the scale has documented test-retest reliability as well as criterion validity (Wann and Branscombe, 1993).

Procedure

Following Institutional Review Board (IRB) approval participants were recruited to voluntarily participate in the study. After giving informed consent, participants completed the demographic questionnaire followed by the Team Survey. Participants were then instructed to select the first team they listed from the Team Survey for each of the three different levels (i.e., closely, moderately, casually) and asked to complete the SSIS for each team. The SSIS was thus completed once each for the first team listed in the closely, moderately, and casually lists. Participants were then debriefed and released. Data collection sessions lasted approximately 15 to 20 minutes.

RESULTS

Cronbach's alpha was calculated for the SSIS. Alpha reliability coefficients for the SSIS were consistently high across all different measurement points. The alpha for the SSIS for teams participants followed closely was $\alpha = .88$; for teams participants followed moderately, $\alpha = .90$; and for teams that participants followed casually, $\alpha = .92$.

Participants reported a large range of teams that they followed closely, from 0 teams to 20. They reported following from 0 to 22 teams moderately, and from 0 to 11 teams casually. Ranges for the SSIS at all levels (closely, moderately, and casually) ranged from 7 to 56.

To evaluate the first hypothesis, a series of paired t-tests was conducted using the number of reported teams at each level as the dependent measure. Because three different t-tests were performed, a Bonferroni correction (Pedhazur, 1982) was used to decrease the chance of a Type I error. Therefore, alpha was set at $p < .016$. Results of the paired t-tests indicated that participants reported following significantly more teams closely ($M = 2.83$, $SD = 2.01$) than they did moderately ($M = 2.20$, $SD = 1.58$), t (953) = 9.59, $p < .001$, $d = .40$. Results also indicated that participants reported following significantly more teams closely ($M = 2.80$, $SD = 2.02$) than they did casually ($M = 1.61$, $SD = 1.13$), t (917) = 17.57, $p < .001$, $d = 1.08$. Finally, results indicated that participants reported following significantly more teams moderately ($M = 2.23$, $SD = 1.60$) than they did casually ($M = 1.61$, $SD = 1.13$), t (917) = 12.20, $p < .001$, $d = .52$. Please note that the different Ns resulted because some participants did not list a team under one of the three categories, and, therefore, there were different numbers of participants for each of the analyses.

To evaluate the second hypothesis, a series of paired t-tests was conducted using reported identification with teams at each level as the dependent measure. Again, a Bonferroni correction was calculated to decrease the change of Type I error and alpha was set at $p < .016$. As shown in Figure 1, results indicated that participants were significantly more identified with teams they followed closely ($M = 46.71$, $SD = 7.98$) than with teams they followed moderately ($M = 31.17$, $SD = 10.36$), t (873) = 39.94, $p < .001$, $d = 1.50$. Results also indicated that participants reported that they were significantly more identified with teams they followed closely ($M = 46.71$, $SD = 7.99$) than with teams they followed casually ($M = 20.33$, $SD = 10.84$), t (809) = 58.06, $p < .001$, $d = 2.43$.

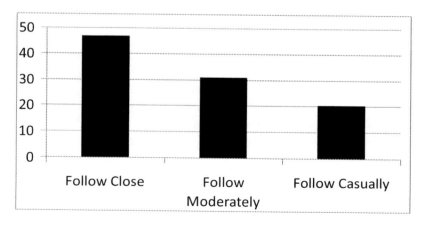

Figure 1. Reported level of team identification, as measured by the SSIS, for the first team that fans reported to follow closely, moderately, and casually.

Finally, results indicated that participants reported that they were significantly more identified with teams that they followed moderately (M = 30.93, SD = 10.15) than teams they followed casually (M = 20.39, SD = 10.81), t (840) = 26.54, p < .001, d = .97.

DISCUSSION

The present study was conducted to better understand the degree to which fans follow and identify with multiple sport teams. Specifically, it was hypothesized that: (1) participants would report following fewer teams closely than they would report following either moderately or casually; with participants reporting following fewer teams moderately than casually; and (2) team identification would be strongest for teams participants follow closely than for teams they follow moderately or casually, with participants reporting higher identification for teams they follow moderately than casually.

Interestingly, results did not support the first hypothesis. In fact, the results were the exact opposite of what was proposed: fans reported following more teams closely and fewer teams moderately and casually. Results would suggest that sport fans in this sample allocate most of their cognitive resources to following teams closely than to following teams moderately or casually. This could also be a matter of time and resources. Meaning, individuals do not have an infinite amount of time to devote to following all teams of interest. Therefore, they may decide to allocate their time to following the teams with which they are highly identified and those that are most meaningful to them. Any remaining time is then spent following teams that are not as meaningful to them.

The results indicated that people in this sample follow approximately three teams closely, two teams moderately, and one and a half teams casually. Thus, in terms of being able to switch focus (or identification; see Grieve et al., in press), results would suggest that individuals do have some latitude. For instance, if one of the teams they follow closely is performing poorly, they can CORF with that team by switching their focus to another team. However, this coping strategy only works if the teams they follow are in-season and competing at the same time (i.e., both teams are football teams or one team is a football team and one is a basketball team). If the teams are not active at the same time (i.e., one team is a football team and another is a baseball team, or what could be termed "dormant identification"), the switching strategy becomes more difficult to perform. Future research should examine whether sport fans are able to switch focus from one sport season to another.

These findings may also further explain findings by Hirt and colleagues (1992). In this study, the authors found that individuals that strongly identified with a sport team can often find it difficult to dissociate with a team when that team is unsuccessful, thus impacting their perceived self-competencies and self-esteem. This may connect with the findings of the current study through the number of teams that participants follow closely. For instance, by utilizing the switching strategy, or CORFing with the unsuccessful team, the participant can then alter focus to another one of the teams they follow closely, thus protecting their own self-esteem and positively impacting their own psychological health and well-being (Wann, 2006). Future research should examine this switching strategy in more depth to determine: (a) whether a relationship exists between the performance of the team, (b) the number of teams a fan is highly identified with, and (c) the point at which they switch their focus to another one of "their" teams.

Further, the finding that fans report high levels of identification with multiple teams has interesting implications for Wann's (2006) Team Identification – Social Psychological Health Model. According to Wann's framework, fans acquire important social connections via their identification with sport teams which, ultimately, can facilitate social well-being. Empirical support for the positive relationship between team identification and well-being in strong, as noted previously (e.g., Lanter and Blackburn, 2004; Wann, Martin et al., in press; Wann et al., 2003). However, Wann, Keenan, and Page (in press) recently found that college students with high levels of identification with two of their university's sport teams reported a more positive well-being profile than those identifying strongly with only one team (the most negative profiles were reported by persons with low levels of identification with both teams). Thus, fans may reap additional benefits by identifying strongly with multiple teams. The current research indicates that this benefit may be available for many fans because such a large proportion of the current sample reported strong attachments to multiple teams.

Results supported the second hypothesis. Participants reported being more highly identified with the teams that they follow closely than teams they follow moderately or casually. While it is tempting to state that identification precedes level of following, this relationship is correlational in nature. For instance, perhaps fans begin following a team closely and through doing so later develop an identification with the team. This would be consistent with what Kolbe and James (2000) describe as an internalization process whereby sport fans come into contact with the team before becoming identified with it.

Regardless of how the team identification occurs, the differences between levels of identification were highly meaningful. The effect size difference (Cohen's *d*) for team identification between teams fans follow closely and teams fans follow moderately and casually were on the order of one to two standard deviations difference. While these findings may seem to be common sense (e.g., of course people are going to be more highly identified with teams that they follow more closely), this is the first empirical evaluation of different levels of identification. Most sport fan research (i.e., Grieve et al., in press; Kolbe and James, 2000; Lanter and Blackburn, 2004; Wann et al., 2004; Wann and Grieve, 2005) has examined identification with a single team. So, while it was anticipated that people would identify at different levels with teams they follow at differential rates, this question had not been empirically evaluated to date.

Practical Implications

These findings also have some rather significant marketing implications. For example, the findings of the current study suggest that not only are fans highly identified with the teams they follow closest, but they are also identifying with *additional* teams, which is of significant interest. This propensity of a fan to be highly identified with many teams provides the sport marketer with an accessible population to help drive revenue generation as opposed to the fan that is only identified with one team. In such cases, Mahony, Madrigal, and Howard (2000) suggest that reinforcement strategies should be utilized in which the fan's high level of identification is maintained and cultivated in order to increase yield and promote brand loyalty. The authors suggest that economic incentives and intrinsic rewards can be effective marketing tactics to help maintain consumer loyalty to the team the person is identified with.

This could be an especially useful approach when a fan is identified with two teams that compete in a similar league or geographical area. For example, a highly identified fan of both the New York Jets of the National Football League (NFL) and the New York Mets of Major League Baseball (MLB) could be influenced by a marketing approach that provides certain economic incentives that the other team might not. As a result, the fan may choose to become a more dedicated consumer of the team that has made a more demonstrative effort to reinforce their identification, which can then result in other ancillary benefits such as decreased price sensitivity and decreased performance-outcome sensitivity (Sutton, McDonald, Milne, and Cimperman, 1997). Through such marketing tactics, attendance and consumption patterns often increase resulting in additional revenue for the sport organization (Mullin, Hardy, and Sutton, 2007).

It is also interesting to note that although respondents were not as highly identified with the other teams they followed less frequently (i.e., teams they followed 'moderately' and 'casually'), they still listed them as teams of interest. This could be a rather visible example of the *escalator concept* (Mullin, Hardy, and Sutton, 1993; 2007) in practice. Briefly, the escalator concept often classifies sport spectators and fans into three broad categories (with further classification provided within certain categories) based on their attendance and participation patterns. These three categories include: (a) nonconsumers (i.e., nonaware, minsinformed, and aware), (b) indirect (or media) consumers, and (c) consumers (i.e., light, medium, and heavy). The level of attendance and participation increases along a linear path with nonconsumers being classified as those that choose not to participate or attend while the heavy consumer is very active. It could be that participants in the sample are being "moved" up or down the escalator based on the organization's marketing efforts.

Unfortunately, where participants in the current study may be classified on the "escalator" cannot be discerned because factors such as attendance, participation, and purchasing variables were not measured. Further, all participants were college students, and they may differ in their identification with sport teams and consumption of sporting events than people who are not college students. However, the findings of the present study do provide an exciting foundation for future research to examine consumption patterns for spectators and fans that follow multiple teams closely, moderately, and casually. Future research such as this may assist sport marketers in devising marketing tactics that would help move the moderate or casual fan up the sport consumer escalator and potentially expand the customer base for a given franchise or team. In addition, future research could focus on seasonal factors related to sport followship and identification. Such research may focus on whether a sport consumer shifts their identification to another team that is currently "in season" or if they maintain the same level of interest even when their team is not engaged in competition (i.e., "offseason").

REFERENCES

Bernhardt, P. C., Dabbs, J. M., Fielden, J. A., and Lutter, C. D. (1998). Testosterone changes during vicarious experiences of winning and losing among fans at sporting events. *Physiology and Behavior, 65,* 59-62.

Branscombe, N. R., Ellemers, N., Spears, R., and Doosje, B. (1999). The context and content of social identity threat. In N. Ellemers, R. Spears, and B. Doosje (Eds.), *Social identity* (pp. 35-58). Oxford, UK: Blackwell.

Cialdini, R. B., Borden, R. J., Thorne, A., Walker, M. R., Freeman, S., and Sloan, L. R. (1976). Basking in reflected glory: Three (football) field studies. *Journal of Personality and Social Psychology, 34,* 366-375.

Grieve, F. G., Wann, D. L., and Zapalac, R. K. (in press). Sport fans' responses to the end of the season. *International Journal of Sports Marketing and Management.*

Hirt, E., Zillmann, G., Erickson, G.A., and Kennedy, C. (1992). Costs and benefits of allegiance: Changes in fans' self-ascribed competencies after team victory versus defeat. *Journal of Personality and Social Psychology, 63(5),* 724-738.

Kolbe, R. H., and James, J. D. (2000). An identification an examination of influences that shape the creation of a professional team fan. *International Journal of Sports Marketing and Sponsorship, 2,* 23-37.

Kolbe, R. H., and James, J. D. (2003). The internalization process among team followers: Implications for team loyalty. *International Journal of Sport Management, 4,* 25-43.

Lanter, J. R., and Blackburn, J. Z. (2004, September). *The championship effect on college students' identification and university affiliation.* Paper presented at the annual meeting of the Association for the Advancement of Applied Sport Psychology, Minneapolis, MN.

Mahony, D. F., Madrigal, R., and Howard, D. (2000). Using the Psychological Commitment to Team (PCT) Scale to segment sport consumers based on loyalty. *Sport Marketing Quarterly, 9(1),* 15-25.

Mullin, B.J., Hardy, S., and Sutton, W.A. (1993). *Sport marketing.* Champaign, IL: Human Kinetics.

Mullin, B.J., Hardy, S., and Sutton, W.A. (2007). *Sport marketing* (3rd ed.) Champaign, IL: Human Kinetics.

Pehazur, E. J. (1982). *Multiple regression in behavioral research: Explanation and prediction* (2nd Edition). Ft. Worth, TX: Holt, Rinehart, and Winston.

Rubin, M., and Hewstone, M. (1998). Social identity theory's self-esteem hypothesis: A review and some suggestions for clarification. *Personality and Social Psychology Review, 2*, 40-62.

Snyder, C. R., Lassegard, M., and Ford, C. E. (1986) Distancing after group success and failure: Basking in reflected glory and cutting off reflected failure. *Journal of Personality and Social Psychology, 51*, 382-388.

Sutton, W. A., McDonald, M. A., Milne, G. R., and Cimperman, J. (1997). Creating and fostering fan identification in professional sports. *Sport Marketing Quarterly, 6(1),* 15-22.

Theodorakis, N. D., Vlachopoulos, S. P., Wann, D. L., Afthinos, Y., and Nassis, P. (2006). Measuring team identification: Translation and cross-cultural validity of the Greek version of the Sport Spectator Identification Scale. *International Journal of Sport Management, 7(4)*, 506-522.

Uemukai, K., Takenouchi, T., Okuda, E., Matusmoto, M., and Yamanaka, K. (1995). Analysis of the factors affecting spectators' identification with professional football teams in Japan. *Journal of Sport Sciences, 13,* 522.

Wann, D. L. (2006). Understanding the positive social psychological benefits of sport team identification: The Team Identification – Social Psychological Health Model. *Group Dynamics: Theory, Research, and Practice, 10*, 272-296.

Wann, D. L., and Branscombe, N. R. (1993). Sports fans: Measuring degree of identification with the team. *International Journal of Sport Psychology, 24,* 1-17.

Wann, D. L., Dimmock, J. A., and Grove, J. R. (2003) Generalizing the Team Identification–Psychological Health Model to a different sport and culture: The case of Australian rules football. *Group Dynamics: Theory, Research, and Practice, 7*, 289-296.

Wann, D. L., Dunham, M. D., Byrd, M. L., and Keenan, B. L. (2004) The five-factor model of personality and the psychological health of highly identified sport fans. *International Sports Journal, 8*, 28-36.

Wann, D. L., and Grieve, F. G. (2005). Biased evaluations of in-group and out-group spectator behavior at sporting events: The importance of team identification and threats to social identity. *The Journal of Social Psychology, 145*, 531-545.

Wann, D. L., Hamlet, M. A., Wilson, T., and Hodges, J. A. (1995). Basking in reflected glory, cutting off reflected failure, and cutting off future failure: The importance of identification with a group. *Social Behavior and Personality: An International Journal, 23,* 377-388.

Wann, D. L., Inman, S., Ensor, C. L., Gates, R. D. and Caldwell, D. S. (1999). Assessing the psychological well-being of sport fans using the Profile of Mood States: The importance of team identification. *International Sports Journal, 3,* 81-90.

Wann, D. L., Keenan, B., and Page L. (in press). Testing the Team Identification – Social Psychological Health Model: Examining non-marquee sports, seasonal differences, and multiple teams. *Journal of Sport Behavior.*

Wann, D. L., Martin, J., Grieve, F. G., and Gardner, L. R. (in press). Social connections at sporting events: Attendance and its positive relationship with state social psychological well-being. *North American Journal of Psychology.*

Wann, D. L., Melnick, M. J., Russell, G. W., and Pease, D. G. (2001). *Sport fans: The psychology and social impact of spectators.* New York: Routledge Press.

Advances in Sports and Athletics. Volume 1   ISBN: 978-1-61122-824-3
Editor: James P. Waldorf   ©2012 Nova Science Publishers, Inc.

MOTIVATIONS OF INTERNATIONAL STUDENT-ATHLETES TO PARTICIPATE IN INTERCOLLEGIATE ATHLETICS

Stephanie G. Jones[1], Gi-Yong Koo[1], Seungmo Kim[1], Damon Andrew[2] and Robin Hardin[1]*
[1]University of Tennessee, Tennessee, US
[2]Troy University, Troy, Alabama, US

ABSTRACT

The purposes of this study were to (a) explore motives of international student-athletes who come to the United States to participate in intercollegiate athletics, and (b) examine differences in motives of international student-athletes based on selected socio-demographic attributes (e.g., gender, types of scholarship received, types of sports participation and region of the world). An exploratory factor analysis revealed four motivation factors: intercollegiate athletics attractiveness, school attractiveness, desire for independency, and environmental attractiveness. Data analysis indicated differences in motivation factors based on types of sports participation and region of the world. The study will help coaches and athletic administrators understand international student-athletes' motivational factors, which play a critical role in recruiting these international student-athletes. Knowing why an international student-athlete wants to participate in intercollegiate athletics in the United States will aid coaches in developing specific

---

* Correspondence to: Robin Hardin, Ph.D. University of Tennessee, 1914 Andy Holt Avenue, 335 HPER Bldg. Knoxville, TN 37996-2700. (865) 974-1281 Office. (865) 974-8981 Fax ; E-mail : robh@utk.edu

recruiting plans to attract these athletes. This information will also assist coaches in satisfying those needs once the student-athlete is competing in intercollegiate athletics.

The number of international athletes has increased substantially in Major League Baseball (MLB), the National Hockey League (NHL), and the National Basketball Association (NBA) over the past decade. The MLB commissioner announced that the opening day of the 2007 MLB season featured 246 international players on the 25-man rosters of the 30 MLB teams. The number indicated that 29% of the MLB players were not born in the United States, which resulted in a 2% increase compared to the 2006 season. More surprisingly, 3,098 international baseball players accounted for 46.2% of the players in the Minor League Baseball (MiLB) (National pastime takes on international flavor, 2007). There were 82 international players in the NBA on the 2005-06 season rosters, accounting for 19% of the total players. This was an 8.9% increase compared to the 2000-01 season (NBA Players from around the World, 2006). The NHL had approximately 30% of its 720 players born outside North America for the 2007-08 season (Burnside, 2007). Professional sports teams have pursued competitiveness through recruiting the most talented international athletes who are performing at high levels in their own countries' leagues.

The phenomenon of recruiting international athletes to improve team performance is not limited to professional sports. It has occurred and become common in intercollegiate athletics and even high school sports in the United States (Ridinger, 1996). According to the latest National Collegiate Athletic Association (NCAA) report on international student-athletes, which was published in 1996, the number of international student-athletes at all NCAA institutions increased from 6,883 to 8,851 and the average number also increased from 8.55 students per institution to 10.52 between 1991-1992 and 1995-1996. Even though updated data regarding the number of international student-athletes has not been reported since 1996 by the NCAA, it is easily noticed that the number of international student-athletes has drastically increased in various sports for the past 10 years. In some sports like tennis and soccer, the roles of international student-athletes have become extremely important for their team's performance due to their superior talent over domestic athletes. The Intercollegiate Tennis Association (ITA) reported in April 2004, that 65 of America's best 100 college tennis players were international student-athletes, and some universities, such as Baylor, Virginia Commonwealth, and Tulane, rarely have American tennis players in their programs (Greviskes, 2004). Given the situation highlighted above, international student-athletes are without a doubt an integral part of American intercollegiate sports. However, there have been only few studies (Bale, 1991; Berry, 1999; Ridinger, 1996; Ridinger and Pastore, 2000a; Ridinger and Pastore, 2000b; Ridinger and Pastore, 2001; Stidwill, 1984) in the sport management literature on the issue of international student-athletes. The present study empirically attempts to examine influencing factors of international student-athletes in deciding to attend colleges in the United States to compete in intercollegiate athletics.

INTERNATIONAL STUDENT-ATHLETES

The first appearance of international student-athletes in intercollegiate athletics in the United States occurred when a small number of Canadian student-athletes participated in track and field competitions in the early 1900s (Ridinger and Pastore, 2000a). However, the recruitment of international student-athletes was uncommon and only limited to Canadian athletes in a small number of sports until World War II (Stidwill, 1984). Some sport-oriented universities began to have a growing interest in recruiting international student-athletes in the 1960s and 1970s. African countries were targeted because of the success those athletes had in track and field, and universities won several national championships due to the dominant performance of African runners (Stidwill, 1984). As many universities rushed to recruit African runners to be competitive in track and field, especially long distance events, 35% of the men's NCAA track and field athletes were athletes from African countries by 1978 (Hollander, 1980). The successful stories of these international student-athletes naturally stimulated coaches and institutions who simply wanted to be competitive against other opponents to recruit international student-athletes in not only track and field, but also in sports such as golf and tennis (Berry, 1999). Usually, the primary reason or benefit that coaches prefer to recruit international student-athletes is that international student-athletes have experience at higher levels of competitions in their countries before they come to the United States. In some sports, their outstanding abilities and experiences in their early competitions are good enough to take the team to a championship level (Ridinger & Pastore, 2001). Some coaches also insist that international student-athletes are more mature and work harder for their goals than American athletes. Thus, the attitudes of international student-athletes could become an example for American student-athletes (Asher, 1994).

Meanwhile, there are also some controversial issues surrounding the recruiting of international student-athletes. First, some people argue that domestic students and international students are not on a level playing field. European athletes playing tennis or soccer have been trained by club sport systems which often provide much higher levels of competition. These student-athletes end up dominating games and matches with better skills and experiences over United States student-athletes, who primarily had scholastic-level experiences. Second, the eligibility issue of foreign student-athletes has received attention because many European athletes have played in professional leagues while they were participating in the club sport system. In the early 1960s, student-athletes in their late 20s or even 30s from other countries were competing in intercollegiate competitions against young domestic athletes who had just graduated from high school (Ridinger, 1996). This situation initiated arguments on age limits of student-athletes and about allowing individuals play in the NCAA if they had been playing professionally. Finally, international student-athletes take athletic scholarships away from United States students. For example, 30% of tennis scholarships go to international student-athletes (Greviskes, 2004). Even though the NCAA has yet to consider any restrictions on the amount of grant funding for international student-athletes, some athletic associations have tried to protect domestic student-athletes by instituting a rule to limit amount of grant funding toward international student-athletes. For example, the National Junior Collegiate Athletic Association (NJCAA) instituted a rule that no more than 25% of grant funding should be awarded to international student-athletes in 1991 (Ridinger & Pastore, 2001).

MOTIVES OF INTERNATIONAL STUDENT-ATHLETES

Little research on international student-athletes in American intercollegiate athletics has been conducted, although the number of international student-athletes have continuously increased and played vital roles throughout various collegiate sports. One topic of study has been to investigate the motivations of international student-athletes to participate in intercollegiate athletics in the United States (Bale, 1991; Berry, 1999; Stidwill, 1984). Most studies (Bale, 1991; Berry, 1999; Ridinger, 1996; Stidwill, 1984) found that one of the primary motivations of international student-athletes who come to American colleges is to gain an education via a scholarship opportunity. International student-athletes are attracted by the fact that they can become educated, while still participating in sport activities through athletic scholarships in the United States (Ridinger, 1996). Unlike other countries, the United States has developed a unique educational system offering opportunities to gain both academic and athletic achievement simultaneously.

Stidwill (1984) researched track and field athletes in his study and found that having the opportunity of experiencing high levels of competition and the well-organized training by expert coaches in American colleges were motives for coming to American colleges, as well as gaining an education. His findings could be supported by the fact that athletic programs in American colleges provide better facilities and coaching staffs that international athletes are not able to experience in their countries. The endless support from the institution is attractive to international student-athletes. In addition, Stidwell found no differences between domestic student-athletes and international student-athletes in terms of being motivated by receiving an education and gaining experience and training.

Bale (1991) studied 200 swimmers and track athletes from Britain, Sweden, and the Netherlands to examine the stressors that might lead an international athlete to come to the United States and participate in an NCAA athletics program. Bale found that international student-athletes wanted to come to the United States for their athletic career because of poor training facilities, lack of quality coaches, and limited training time in their own countries. He also found that the student-athletes were also attracted by the level of competition in the United States, and that American culture and lifestyle had an impact on the decision. Other significant factors identified by Bale were the influence of friends in the United States, the sport and academic reputation of the college, and the influence of coaches.

Berry (1999) examined these motivational factors using 61 international student-athletes from 11 different sports and three different regions of the world. While the previous two studies only focused on one or two sports to understand the motivations of international student-athletes, Berry collected data from various sports. He classified the motivational factors into four categories: athletic, academic, influence-related, and social/environmental. Berry compared the means of those factors and concluded that the athletic motive was most important over academic, influence-related, and social/environmental motives. Male and female student-athletes generally showed similar patterns. In addition, Berry found that student-athletes showed different patterns of motivations based on their region of the world. For example, South African students reported higher social/environmental factors and academic reasons, while English students were motivated to hone their athletic skills in the United States.

Ridinger and Pastore (2000b) proposed a framework to identify factors associated with international student-athletes' adjustment to American colleges. In the strict sense, the study was not about the motivations of why international student-athletes come to the United States, but the motivations of international student-athletes from previous motive studies were utilized to interpret the findings by the authors in this study. Five adjustment elements were proposed by the researchers: academic adjustment, athletic adjustment, social adjustment, personal-emotional adjustment, and institutional adjustment. Ridinger and Pastore (2000b) also compared the level of adjustment to college among three sub groups in their follow-up study: international student-athletes, international non student-athletes and domestic student-athletes. The authors found international student-athletes reported the highest mean score among sub groups in terms of academic and other adjustments to college. International student-athletes tend to work hard academically because they primarily have chosen to come to the United States in order to receive an education with financial support while participating in their chosen sport (Bale, 1991; Ridinger, 1996; Stidwill, 1984).

Even though previous research had identified possible motivations of international student-athletes to migrate into the United States, there were several limitations. First, most studies, except one (Berry, 1999), only examined one or two specific sports, and these motives may be sport-specific. Second, there was no research including all regions of the world due to the small number of international student-athletes in their study samples. Third, much of the research that has been conducted on the motivations of international student-athletes is quite dated and may not accurately reflect the motives of today's athletes. Finally, the methods that the studies utilized to analyze their data strongly relied on descriptive statistics, which are limited in their ability to examine statistical differences among group, so it is difficult to say that their findings really existed as they concluded. Therefore, the primary purposes of this study were to extend past research by measuring international student-athletes' motivations to come to the United States to participate in intercollegiate athletes, and to expand the knowledge of international student-athletes by examining differences in motives according to socio-demographic attributes. The current study attempted to recruit a large number of international student-athletes from three NCAA Division I – Football Bowl

Subdivision conferences and incorporate more sophisticated statistical techniques to examine motivations in terms of gender, type of sport, and regions of world origin. The following research questions were proposed in relation to the foregoing discussion.

1. Why do international student-athletes come to the United States to participate in intercollegiate athletics?
2. Are there differences in motives of international student-athletes to come to the United States to participate in intercollegiate athletics based on selected socio-demographic attributes?

METHODOLOGY

Instrument Development

The questionnaire for the current study consisted of two parts. The first part consisted of seven demographic questions including age, gender, region of world origin and scholarship status. The second part consisted of 29 items that may have contributed to the international student-athletes' decision in coming to the United States in order to participate in intercollegiate athletics. The researchers included selected items from a previous survey by Berry (1999) and added related items based on qualitative interviews with international student-athletes in order to attempt to get a wider range of motivation items on the questionnaire. All of Berry's original items were included in a pilot test to check for the validity of the questionnaire. Based on participant feedback from the pilot study, some of those items were deleted, thus leaving 29 items for motivational factors. The items for the motivations were developed with seven point Likert-type scales anchored by "Not important at all" (1) and "Extremely important" (7).

Participants and Survey Procedure

The sample for this study consisted of international student-athletes at institutions from three NCAA Division I – Football Subdivision conferences. International student-athletes were identified on the rosters of the athletic teams of the particular institutions chosen for study. Internet survey methodologies were incorporated in this study (Dillman, 2000). E-mail addresses for 397 international student-athletes from the three conferences were obtained through their institutes' Web sites. E-mails containing the link to the online survey and related instructions were sent to the selected sample. E-mail reminders were sent three times, five days apart, to the sample. The response was rate 53.4% (N = 212).

Data Analysis

The analysis of the data from the online survey was completed using the SPSS 13.0 computer program. Descriptive statistics were employed to assess the respondents' gender, types of scholarship received, types of sports participation, and region of world origin, while an exploratory factor analysis (EFA) was used to identify the underlying structure of a relatively large set of international student-athletes motivation variables. Since the classification of international student-athletes based upon socio-demographic attributes did not result in enough number of observations for each group in order to employ parametric statistics, the Mann-Whitney and Kruskal-Wallis tests were applied to examine how international student-athletes' motivation factors are different according to the socio-demographic attributes, respectively (Siegel and Castellan, 1988). Therefore, for this analysis, socio-demographic attributes (e.g., gender, types of scholarship received, types of sports participation, and region of the world) were considered as the independent variables and four identified motivation factors as the dependent variables.

RESULTS

Demographics of International Student-Athletes

Table 1 shows the socio-demographic profile of international student-athletes participating in this study. The mean age of the respondents was 20.47 (SD = 1.59) and all respondents' ages ranged from 18 to 25. Of the 212 respondents, more than half (63.3%) were females, and the majority (93.4%) of international student-athletes received a partial (24.8%) or full (68.6%) scholarship. The group of international student-athletes was comprised of 61.4% of individual-sports participants and 38.6% of team-sports participants. Respondents in this study competed in 17 different sports, but 73.3% of them participated in the top five sports: tennis (20.5%), swimming and diving

(15.7%), rowing (14.3%), track and field (12.4%), and golf (10.5%). Finally, while the respondents came from 49 different countries, 45.7% of them were from countries in Europe, followed by 38.6% of them from countries in North and South America.

Table 1. Demographics of International Student-athletes (N = 212)

Mean Age	M	SD
	20.47	1.59
Gender	N	%
Male	77	36.7
Female	133	63.3
Scholarship	N	%
Full-scholarship	144	68.6
Partial-scholarship	52	24.8
No-scholarship	14	6.7
Top five sports	N	%
Tennis	43	20.5
Swimming and diving	33	15.7
Rowing	30	14.3
Track and field	26	12.4
Golf	22	10.5
Home continents	N	%
Europe	96	45.7
America	81	38.6
Oceania	14	6.7
Africa	10	4.8
Asia	9	4.3

Substructures of International Student-Athletes Motives

Exploratory factor analysis (EFA) using a principal-component analysis extraction technique was conducted to assess factors that help explain how international student-athletes characterize their motivation in their participation in intercollegiate athletics in the United States. It was expected that student-athlete motives would be intercorrelated so an oblique (OBLIMIN) rotation with a default delta parameter of 0 was utilized.

In Table 2, the results of the EFA identified a four-factor model providing a reasonable compromise between model parsimony and adequacy of fit according to the "Kaiser rule." The assumed factor model accounted for 66.14% of the total variance of the variables and almost all of the individual variables explained reasonably well, possessing communalities ranging from 0.54 to 0.78. The four factors were labeled as intercollegiate athletics attractiveness, school attractiveness, desire for independency, and environmental attractiveness.

The percent variance explained by the model was higher compared to Mathes and Gurney's (1985) five-factor model, which only explained 51% of the total variance of student-athletes' choices of schools. In this study, intercollegiate athletics attractiveness explained 31.23% of the variance followed by school attractiveness which explained 15.06%. Desire for independency accounted for 11.60%, and environmental attractiveness explained 8.24% of the variance.

Three items associated with the attractive features of US intercollegiate sports loaded on the first factor, which was labeled intercollegiate athletics attractiveness. Statements for the intercollegiate athletics attractiveness factor included: "competition level of US athletics," "sport season schedule," and "NCAA college conference." Six items related to the various academic and athletic services provided from an institution loaded on the second factor, which was labeled school attractiveness. Statements for the school attractiveness factor included: "library resources," "campus dining and meal plan opportunities," "closeness of athletic facilities to campus," "athletic therapy resources/personal trainers," "academic advising opportunity," and "information technology operations (e.g. wireless campus)." Three items related to the possibility of being independent loaded on the third factor, which was labeled desire for independency. Statements for the desire for independency factor included: "chance to gain independence from home," "chance to leave hometown," and "possibility to leave parental influence at home." Finally, three items related to the living environment loaded on the fourth factor, which was labeled environmental attractiveness. Statements for the environmental attractiveness factor included: "location of university," "size of city," and "weather/climate of city."

Table 2. Exploratory Factor Analysis

Motivation Factors	Factor Loadings			
	1	2	3	4
Factor 1 – Intercollegiate Athletics Attractiveness				
competition level of United States athletics	.791			
NCAA college conference	.747			
sport season schedule	.691			
Factor 2 – School Attractiveness				
athletic therapy resources / personal trainers		.848		
closeness of athletic facilities to campus		.827		
academic advising opportunity		.799		
campus dining and meal plan opportunities		.737		
information technology operations		.737		
library resources		.697		
Factor 3 –Desire for Independency				
possibility to leave parental influence at home			.875	
chance to gain independence from home			.870	
chance to leave hometown			.863	
Factor 4 – Environmental Attractiveness				
location of US College				.860
size of city				.833
weather/climate of city				.738

Means, Standard Deviations, and Correlations of Motives

.

The means, standard deviations, and correlation matrix of spectator motives are shown in Table 3. Intercollegiate athletics attractiveness ($M =$ 5.02, $SD = 1.28$) was the most important motivation factor for international student-athletes followed by school attractiveness ($M = 4.85$, $SD = 1.32$), environmental attractiveness (M = 4.41, SD = 1.31), and desire for independency (M = 3.94, SD = 1.71).

Internal consistency was examined for each of the four motivation factors. Initial reliabilities of each category for the instrument ranged from .76 for environmental attractiveness to .86 for school attractiveness, exclusive of the measure of intercollegiate athletics attractiveness (α =.62), indicating an acceptable level of reliability (Nunnally & Bernstein, 1994). While all four motives were significantly correlated to each other, these correlations fell within the recommended threshold of r < .50, which satisfied the issue of linear dependency (George & Mallery, 2000). Thus, an examination of the correlation coefficients indicated good discriminant validity among the four motivation factors.

Table 3. Correlation Matrix, Means, and Standard Deviations of Spectator Motives

Motivation Factors	Factor 1	Factor 2	Factor 3	Factor 4	Mean	Std. Dev.
Intercollegiate athletics attractiveness	(.616)				5.02	1.28
School attractiveness	.415***	(.862)			4.85	1.32
Desire for independency	.296***	.191**	(.843)		3.94	1.71
Environmental attractiveness	.296***	.251***	.192**	(.756)	4.41	1.31

Notes. * p < .05, ** p < .01, *** p < .001; Cronbach Alphas in parentheses and italics along the diagonal.

Effects of Demographics on Motivational Factors

The study examined potential motivation difference on the basis of four socio-demographic attributes: gender, region of the world, types of scholarship received, and types of sport participation. Results of the Mann-Whitney test and Kruskal-Wallis test indicated that the equality of the average rank of type of sport participation and region of world origin were statistically different while gender and types of scholarship received were not significantly different.

Differences in motives based on the participation of team vs. individual sports. In order to examine the differences in motives based on the types of sports participation, student-athletes were classified as either team-sports participants or individual-sport participants. As seen in Table 4, the average ranks for intercollegiate athletics attractiveness, school attractiveness, desire for independency, and environmental attractiveness were listed separately for both groups. Since the rank of 1 is assigned to the smallest value, the average rank was smaller for team sports participants for all motivation factors, excluding desire for independency. Results of the Mann-Whitney Test showed that the main effect of types of sports on intercollegiate athletics attractiveness ($U = 4179.50$, $p = .014$) and environmental attractiveness ($U = 4209.50$, $p = .017$) were statistically significant at the .05 level while those on school attractiveness ($U = 4843.00$, $p = .373$) and desire for independency ($U = 4712.00$, $p = .231$) were not statistically significant. Thus, international student-athletes participating in individual-sports were more motivated by intercollegiate athletics attractiveness and environmental attractiveness than international student-athletes participating in team sports.

Table 4. Differences in Motives based on Sport Type

Motivation factors	Types of Sports	N	Mean Rank	Mann-Whitney-U	p
Intercollegiate athletics attractiveness	Team	81	92.60	4179.50*	.014
	Individual	129	113.60		
School attractiveness	Team	81	100.79	4843.00	.373
	Individual	129	108.46		
Desire for independency	Team	81	111.83	4712.00	.231
	Individual	129	101.53		
Environmental attractiveness	Team	81	92.97	4209.50*	.017
	Individual	129	113.37		

Notes. Grouping variable: Gender; *p < .05, **p < .01, ***p < .001.

Differences in motives based on the region of the world. The average ranks for intercollegiate athletics attractiveness, school attractiveness, desire for independency, and environmental attractiveness are separately shown in Table 4 in terms of the region of world origin of the international student-athletes. Descriptively, the average rank was higher for student-athletes from

Africa than those from other areas in relation to the four motivation factors, excluding school attractiveness.

Results of the Kruskal-Wallis test indicated a significant main effect of region of world origin on intercollegiate athletics attractiveness, $\chi^2(4, 210) = 13.09$, $p = .011$, and environmental attractiveness, $\chi^2(4, 210) = 13.40$, $p = .009$, with no significant effects on school attractiveness, $\chi^2(4, 210) = 7.15$, $p = .128$, and desire for independency, $\chi^2(4, 210) = 2.06$, $p = .724$. Further analysis from the Mann-Whitney test provides additional support for results of the Kruskal-Wallis test. For instance, support for the main effect of region of the world was found by the differences in intercollegiate athletics attractiveness and environmental attractiveness being statistically significant between: (a) Africa and America ($U = 758.50$, $p = .004$; $U = 225.00$, $p = .022$), (b) Africa and Europe ($U = 257.00$, $p = .015$; $U = 192.00$, $p = .002$), and (c) Africa and Oceania ($U = 27.50$, $p = .011$; $U = 14.50$, $p = .001$). As a result, student-athletes from Africa were more motivated by intercollegiate athletics attractiveness and environmental attractiveness than student-athletes from America, Europe, and Oceania.

Table 5. Differences in Motives based on World Origin by Continent

	Continents	N	Mean Rank	χ^2	p
Intercollegiate athletics attractiveness	Europe	96	109.91	13.09*	.011
	America	81	93.92		
	Oceania	14	89.71		
	Africa	10	156.55		
	Asia	9	130.56		
School attractiveness	Europe	96	106.76	7.15	.128
	America	81	99.94		
	Oceania	14	86.54		
	Africa	10	135.40		
	Asia	9	138.33		
Desire for independency	Europe	96	107.28	2.06	.724
	America	81	102.72		
	Oceania	14	90.79		
	Africa	10	121.10		

	Asia	9	117.06		
Environmental attractiveness	Europe	96	96.26	13.40**	.009
	America	81	112.36		
	Oceania	14	83.11		
	Africa	10	159.15		
	Asia	9	117.56		

Notes. Grouping variable: Continents; $*p<.05$, $**p<.01$, $***p<.001$.

DISCUSSION AND CONCLUSION

In this line of research, previous studies had examined the motivations of international student-athletes to participate in intercollegiate athletics in the United States (Bale, 1991; Berry, 1999; Stidwill, 1984). For coaches and athletic administrators to recruit and attract international student-athletes, it is very important to identify why international student-athletes participate in intercollegiate athletics. Results from this study identified a four-factor model explaining the international student-athletes' motives (e.g., intercollegiate athletics attractiveness, school attractiveness, desire for independency, and environmental attractiveness) and indicated differences in motives attributable to the types of sport participation and region of world origin of the international student-athletes. The present study uncovered a number of important findings.

First, the motivational factors extracted from this study were similar to some of the results in other studies. The previous studies revealed that one of the major motives of international student-athletes is to gain academic and athletic achievement (Bale, 1991; Berry, 1999; Ridinger, 1996; Stidwill, 1984). These findings supported the notion that the potential opportunities related to the academic and athletic success (e.g., athletic therapy resources/personal trainers, closeness of athletic facilities to campus, academic advising opportunity, campus dining and meal plan opportunities, information technology operations, library resources) motivate international student-athletes to come to the United States to participate in intercollegiate athletics. The United States has developed a unique educational system offering opportunities to gain both academic and athletic achievement at the same time, thus placing them in an ideal setting to recruit international student-athletes.

Stidwill (1984) indicated international student-athletes in track and field would like to experience the high levels of competition and well-organized training from the American intercollegiate athletics system. Bale (1991) also demonstrated international student swimmers and track athletes from Britain, Sweden, and the Netherlands have an inclination to come to the United States as a consequence of poor training facilities, lack of quality coaches, limited training time, and the level of competition in their own countries. This was consistent with the findings of the present study in that international student-athletes were motivated by intercollegiate athletics attractiveness, andintercollegiate athletic programs in the United States have been known to offer a better intercollegiate athletic system and schedule and higher level of competition.

Environmental attractiveness was also an important motive for international student-athletes, as it was the third highest motive among the four extracted. Environmental attractiveness was consistent with Berry's (1999) social/environmental factor. This motive describes the influence that environmental attributes have on international student-athletes' school consideration. In other words, international student-athletes might want to participate in American intercollegiate athletics because of the location of school, size of city, and climate of the city.

The last motive was desire for independency. This factor ranked as the lowest motive among the four extracted, and its mean score was lower than the scale average. The findings indicated that the possibility of leaving their parental influence, gaining independence, or leaving their hometown might be motives for international student-athletes to come to the United States to participate in intercollegiate athletics, but this motive is not strong compared to the others identified in this study.

Second, the differences that emerged in motivational factors in individual sports and team sports provide some interesting insight into the motivations of international student-athletes. Respondents participating in individual sports are more motivated by intercollegiate athletic attractiveness and environmental attractiveness that respondents participating in team sports. The notion of intercollegiate athletic attractiveness does fit with individual sports. The competition level at the intercollegiate level is high and athletes from other countries may not be able to get the same level of competition in their home countries as they can in the United States. These student-athletes want to improve their skills, and the way to do that is to compete against competitors with equal or higher skill levels. While this is not such an issue with team sports, individual development cannot be measured as easily in a team setting than in an individual setting.

In addition, environmental attractiveness is important because the climate varies throughout the United States, so golfers can choose a university that allows for year-round play. Tennis players can play year-round in many parts of America as well. Track and field is also dependent on weather conditions for student-athletes to train year-round. The majority of the respondents in the study participated in individual sports that are primarily contested outdoors, so location and weather were justifiably more important for individual sport participants.

Third, in this study, the international student-athletes from Africa were significantly motivated by intercollegiate athletics attractiveness and environmental attractiveness than student-athletes from other areas (e.g., America, Europe, and Oceania). These findings were partially supported by Berry's (1999) study. He employed four motivational factors (e.g., athletic, academic, influence-related, and social/environmental) and concluded that international student-athletes showed different patterns of motives based on the region they call home. In particular, he found that South African students were highly motivated by social/environmental factors. This phenomenon could be explained by the reasons that the majority of student-athletes from Africa participated in individual sports (e.g., golf, tennis, track and field, and swimming and diving). The notion of intercollegiate athletic attractiveness and environmental attractiveness are understandably more significant for individual sport participants, as discussed previously. Therefore, the significantly different motives derived from African student-athletes were closely related to the differences emerged in motivational factors in individual sports and team sports.

In view of the fact that an understanding of international student-athletes' motives has been recognized as a crucial strategy for coaches and institutions who want to be competitive in their sports, the significant motives derived from this study will play a vital role in the success of recruiting international student-athletes. However, the current study only focused on international student-athletes in NCAA Division I schools and does not represent entire international student-athlete population. Therefore, further research on this topic should be conducted at Division II and Division III institutions as well in order to better understand motives of international student-athletes in those competitive divisions. In addition, most research, including the current study, on international student-athletes has been limited to understand motivational factors of international student-athletes to participate in intercollegiate athletics in the United States. Researchers should examine other aspects of international student-athletes other than motives. For example, future studies should examine international student-athletes' satisfaction after experiencing intercollegiate athletics. Additionally, future studies might examine the perception of domestic student-athletes regarding the recruitment of foreign student-athletes because, as discussed earlier, there have been some controversial issues surrounding the recruiting of international student-athletes.

REFERENCES

Asher, K. (1994). Multi-cultural cultivation. *Coaching Volleyball*, 18-23.

Bale, J. (1991). *The Brawn Drain: Foreign Student-Athletes in American Universities*, Urbana, IL: University of Illinois Press.

Berry, J. R. (1999). *Foreign student-athletes and their motives for attending North Carolina NCAA Division I institutions*: Unpublished master's thesis. University of North Carolina at Chapel Hill.

Burnside, S. (2007). By traveling to London, Ducks, Kings taking one for the team. Retrieved November 30, 2007, from http://sports.espn.go.com/espn/print?id=3036914andtype=story.

Dillman, D. A. (2000). *Mail and internet surveys* (2nd ed.). New York: John Wiley and Sons. Inc.

George, D., and Mallery, P. (2000). *SPSS for windows step by step*: Allyn and Bacon. Massachusetts.

Greviskes, A. (2004, May 5). The evolution of college tennis. Daily Illini. (U. Illinois). Retrieved November 1, 2005 from http://www.cstv.com/sports/m-tennis.

Hollander, T. R. (1980). *A Geographic Analysis of Intercollegiate Foreign Track and Field Athletes in the United States.* Unpublished master's thesis. Eastern Michigan University.

National pastime takes on international flavor. (2007). Retrieved November 25, 2007, from http://sports.espn.go.com/mlb/news/story?id=2824295.

Mathes, S., and Gurney, G. (1985). Factors in Student Athletes. *Journal of College Student Personnel, 26(4)*, 327-333.

NBA Players from around the World. (2006). Retrieved November 30, 2007, from http://www.nba.com/players/international_player_directory.html.

National Collegiate Athletic Association (1996). 1996 NCAA study of international student-athletes.

NCAA Eyes Overseas Recruiting (2001). Retrieved Dec. 31, 2007 from http://www.ncaa.org/wps/portal/!ut/p/kcxml/04_Sj9SPykssy0xPLMnMz0vM0Y_QjzKLN4g3NPUESUGYHvqRaGLGphhCjggRX4_83FR9b_0A_YLc0NCIckdFACrZHxQ!/delta/base64xml/L3dJdyEvUUd3QndNQSEvN

ElVRS82XzBfMTVL?New_WCM_Context=/wps/wcm/connect/NCAA/
NCAA+News/NCAA+News+Online/2001/Association-
wide/NCAA+eyes+overseas+recruiting+-+7-2-01.

Nunnally, J. C., and Bernstein, I. H. (1994). *Psychometric Theory*. New York:
McGraw-Hill.

Ridinger, L. L. (1996). Recruiting foreign student-athletes: Creating
international awareness of American animosity? *Future Focus, 17(2)*, 20-
26.

Ridinger, L.L., and Pastore, D.L. (2000a). International student-athletes
adjustment to college: A preliminary analysis. *NACADA Journal, 20(1)*,
33-41.

Ridinger, L.L., and Pastore, D.L. (2000b). A proposed framework to identify
factors associated with international student-athlete adjustment to college.
International Journal of Sport Management, 1, 4-24.

Ridinger, L. L., and Pastore, D. L. (2001). Coaches Perceptions of Recruiting
International Student-Athletes. *Journal-of-the-International-Council-for-
Health,-Physical-Education,-Recreation,-Sport,-and-Dance-* 37(1), 18-25.

Siegel, S., and Castellan, N. J. (1988). *Nonparametric statistics: For the
behavioral sciences* (2nd). Boston, MA: McGraw-Hill, Inc.

Stidwell, H.F. (1984). Motives towards track and field competition of foreign
and domestic grant-in-aid student-athletes in NCAA Division 1 colleges
and universities. Unpublished doctoral dissertation. Oregon State
University.

Advances in Sports and Athletics. Volume 1   ISBN: 978-1-61122-824-3
Editor: James P. Waldorf   ©2012 Nova Science Publishers, Inc.

ATHLETIC ADMINISTRATORS PERCEPTIONS OF WORK-LIFE BALANCE POLICIES: A DIVISIONAL COMPARISON

*Nancy Lough[*1], Bonnie Tiell[2] and Barbara Osborne[3]*
[1]University of Nevada – Las Vegas, US
[2]Tiffin University, Ohio, US
[3]University of North Carolina, US

ABSTRACT

Intercollegiate athletics is recognized as a dynamic industry that places high demands on the time and energy of personnel regardless of the competitive division or size of the institution. Personal sacrifices in time and energy for the sake of the program are equated with contributing to high levels of work-life conflict. The purpose of this study was to analyze the perceptions towards work and life conflict among senior woman administrators and athletic directors at NCAA Division I, II, and III institutions regarding the work-life climate within the athletic department and the existence of workplace benefits offered at their institution. The impact of the presence of children on the perception of work-life climate within the athletic department was also examined. There were significant differences noted in the availability of benefits between DI and DII / DIII, but no significant differences in the perceptions of availability of benefits between ADs and SWAs.

[*] Address All Correspondence to: Dr. Nancy Lough, Associate Professor. University of Nevada Las Vegas, 4505 Maryland Parkway Box 453031, Las Vegas, NV 89154-3031. Phone: 702-895-5392. Fax: 702-895-5056. nancy.lough@unlv.edu

Keywords: Work-Life balance, climate, divisions, administrators, work-family conflict.

Intercollegiate athletics is recognized as a dynamic industry that places high demands on the time and energy of personnel regardless of the competitive division or size of the institution (Tiell, 2006). Collegiate coaches, athletic support staff, and administrators working in the twenty-first century are experiencing less and less "down" time due to factors such as increases in allowable off-season activities, overlapping sport seasons, and lengthened recruiting periods (Bruening and Dixon, 2007). Also contributing to a demanding work environment is the perceived role expectation of intercollegiate athletics employees in superceding personal needs to adhere to the needs of the department and/or athletes. Personal sacrifices in time and energy for the sake of the program are equated with contributing to high levels of work-life conflict. In addition, the culture of collegiate coaching and management is one that demands non-traditional work hours on nights and weekends thus further adding to work and life conflict (Dixon and Bruening, 2007).

As the largest and most recognizable national governing body for the majority of higher education institutions with athletics programs, the National Collegiate Athletic Association (NCAA) uses financial award structures, sport sponsorship minimums, and to an extent, stadium/arena capacities to sanction three divisions known as Division I, Division II, and Division III (NCAA, 2005). When considering media attention, revenue streams (especially television), and staffing, Division I athletic departments are highly distinctive from Division II and III athletic programs. DI schools are the major athletic powers, with larger budgets, more elaborate facilities, and higher numbers of athletic scholarships (Shulman and Bowen, 2001). Whereas, Division II programs often find student-athletes supplementing athletic scholarships with academic scholarships or part time jobs, demonstrating a reduced financial commitment on the part of the institution. Philosophically, Division III holds to a distinctly different set of values when compared to DI or DII; academics are given much higher priority and athletic scholarships are prohibited. Student-athletes are expected to focus the majority of their time on academic pursuits, with sport training serving as a release from the stress of academic rigor (Shulman and Bowen, 2001).

Regardless of division, each institution sponsoring athletics designates an "athletic director" (AD) as the department supervisor. This highest ranking position in the department is occupied predominantly by men (Acosta and

Carpenter, 2008). There is a NCAA constitutional bylaw (4.02.4) which further requires each institution to designate a senior woman administrator (SWA) who is "the highest ranking female involved with the management of an institution's intercollegiate athletics program" (NCAA Bylaws, 2006). Due to their status as the highest ranking administrators within the department organizational structure, the AD and SWA are likely candidates to have knowledge of the existence of institutional workplace benefits to potentially influence work-life conflict and have a sense of the general climate present in his or her department with regards to promoting work-life balance policies and benefits.

While the AD is recognized as the department head, the senior woman administrator reports to the AD except in the few instances when the AD also is designated as the institutional SWA. Research has noted differences between ADs and SWAs regarding their decision-making authority (Tiell, 2004, 2006; Lough and Grappendorf, 2007; Claussen and Lehr, 2002), but both groups are in positions to report their knowledge of work-life benefits offered by their institution and department, along with the perceived work climate.

In their 2008 study, Bruening, Dixon, Tiell, Osborne, Lough and Sweeney found that athletic administrators viewed work-life balance as an issue. Specifically, this study pointed to greater concern for women leaving and/or not entering the profession due to the inherent work-life conflict. One study that focused specifically on Division I administrators was found that addressed the question of whether ADs would report differences when compared with reports from SWAs relative to work climate and knowledge of work-life benefits offered (Dixon, Tiell, Lough, Osborne, Sweeney and Bruening, 2008). With both ADs and SWAs reporting the availability of most benefits, differences were found relating to the use of benefits based on the gender of the employees, and the climate effecting use. Still, this study examined strictly the high profile Division I programs, which represent only 119 of the total 1018 NCAA sanctioned athletic programs (NCAA.org). The stark difference in divisions beckons the question whether there are significant differences between the three divisions relative to the availability of work-life benefits and perceived climate. Finally, since research has noted that employees with significant dependent care responsibilities report higher levels of work-family conflict (Dixon and Bruening, 2005), the question remains whether the presence of children impacts the perception of administrators towards their knowledge of work-life benefits and the perceived department climate.

Thus, the purpose of the study was to analyze the perceptions towards work and life conflict among senior woman administrators and athletic directors at Division I, II and III institutions regarding the work-life climate within the athletic department and existence of work place benefits offered at their institution. The impact of the presence of children on the respondent's perception of the work-life climate within the athletic department was also examined.

Research Questions

The following three research questions further guided inquiry into the subject.

1. Is there a difference between the perceptions of the athletic director and senior woman administrator in NCAA division I, II and III programs regarding the existence of workplace benefits?
2. Is there a difference between the perceptions of these high ranking administrators in NCAA division I, II, and III programs regarding the work-life climate within the athletic department?
3. Is there a difference in the perceptions of work-life climate among ADs and SWAs based upon parental / non-parental status?

LITERATURE REVIEW

Characteristics of NCAA Membership Divisions

When considering media attention, revenue streams (especially television), and staffing, Division I (DI) athletic departments are highly distinctive from Division II and III athletic programs. Typically, DI schools are represented by the recognized athletic power programs with larger budgets more elaborate facilities and a significant number of students on full athletic scholarships (Shulman and Bowen, 2001). NCAA DII athletics programs try to find a balance between supporting highly competitive athletics teams by providing athletics related grant in aid, but also emphasizing student-athlete academic success and integration into the social fabric of the campus (DII Philosophy Statement, 2007). Finally, DIII athletics programs focus on the overall participation experience of the student-athlete with a greater emphasis on their academic experience (DIII Philosophy Statement, 2007).

The NCAA is federated into these three separate divisions with distinct philosophies and membership requirements. Division I schools offer athletic scholarships and sponsor at least seven sports for men and women, with contest and participant minimums for each sport. DI schools must play 100% of the minimum schedule against DI opponents. DI is further divided by sport and levels of scholarships. The Football Bowl Subdivision (formerly DIA) schools are those that the media focus on, the general public thinks of, and most academic research focuses on. At 119 schools, the Football Bowl Subdivision schools are actually just a little more than 10% of all NCAA intercollegiate athletic programs. The 118 Football Championship Subdivision (formerly D1AA) schools do not have minimum attendance requirements for football and have lower scholarship expectations, while the remaining 92 DI schools do not sponsor football teams. The smallest division is Division II, with 282 schools that sponsor at least five sports each for men and women. DII schools offer athletic scholarships and play at least 50% of their schedule in football and basketball against DII or DI opponents. The largest division is DIII with 422 members that sponsor at least five sports each for men and women but do not offer scholarships based on athletic ability (NCAA, 2007-2008).

From an administrative perspective, DI institutions generally have well funded programs with a fairly large administrative support structure and personnel working in positions that are delineated and unique. In contrast, DII and DIII programs have administrators and sometimes coaches that fill numerous positions (ie. marketing, rules compliance, sports information) while trying to accomplish similar goals with far fewer resources. The Athletic Director is typically the top administrator or manager within each of these intercollegiate athletics departments. In DI there may also be several additional upper level administrators (ie. Senior Associate Athletic Directors) who report to the AD, yet only a few additional athletic administrators in a DII or DIII organizational structure. Additionally, the NCAA requires that each institution designate a Senior Woman Administrator (SWA) who is the highest ranking female involved with the management of an institutions athletics program (NCAA Bylaw 4.02.4). Yet, it is important to mention that SWA is a designation or acronym and not a formal position, therefore the role that the SWA plays within each athletic department varies. Ideally, there is a strong relationship and good communication between the AD and SWA, regardless of divisional status.

"In theory, athletic administrators are expected to serve as liaisons between institutional policymakers and the employees who could potentially benefit from policies and programs related to work-life balance" (Bruening, et.al., 2008, P. 251). Therefore, these administrators serve as the conduit to both policy utilization and climate creation. Still the issue of work life balance has become more than an individual or even institutional issue. With implementation of a specific Work-Life Task Force, the issue has become one of concern for the entire NCAA membership and Association (NCAA Work-Life Task Force, 2007).

Work Life Conflict

There has been a significant body of research conducted on work-family conflict, which has evolved to work-life balance. The first studies sought to identify the phenomenon in the workplace and concluded that work-family conflict is bi-directional whereas work affects family and family affects work (Boles, et al, 2001; Greenhaus and Powell, 2003). The next wave of research looked at identifying the factors associated with work-life balance, and although both men and women experience work-life conflict, a majority of the studies concluded that women are more affected than men (Bruening, et.al., 2008; Hollenshead et al, 2005; Kossek, Colquitt and Noe, 2000). Within intercollegiate athletics, the notion that women coaches may be more affected by this issue than male coaches seems apparent from the consistent decline in the representation of women in college coaching. Dixon and Bruening (2007) examined the experiences of coaching mothers and found that personal "attitudes and behaviors reflected larger structural and social forces at work, and not simply individual choice" (p. 377). Thus, the relationship between the decline in the representation of women as collegiate coaches and work-life conflict appears to be validated.

The list of positive outcomes resulting from effective work-life supportive policies including increased job satisfaction (Eby, Caper, Lockwood, Bordeaux, and Brinley, 2005; Guest, 2002; Thomas and Ganster, 1995), increased productivity (Solomon, 1996), and decreased turnover (Eby, et al., 2005; Galinsky and Stein, 1990; Kingston, 1990), points to a win-win opportunity for organizations as well as employees. Yet, tradition rich cultures that dictate the work-life climate for employees can be slow to change. As Bruening, et al. (2008) found, most athletic administrators continue to believe that their environment is not one that can be conducive to work life balance.

Organizational Climate

In 2006, the NCAA implemented the "Life and Work Balance Inventory" using a tool similar to the instrument used in the current research and completed by over 4,000 athletics personnel. Of the responses received, 42% of the sample agreed that they were able to adequately balance their current life and athletics commitments effectively, while 40% of the sample disagreed (NCAA Digest, 2006). This study included both genders and multiple positions within an athletic department. When longitudinal data specific to women in college athletics collected by Acosta and Carpenter (2008) are considered, there is reason to believe that women may be leaving intercollegiate athletic positions, or not entering the field, due to the unique challenges placed on women in this profession. While men may also aspire to be parents, typically their work life balance is not as directly affected by parental status when compared to women. Kaufman-Rosen and Kalb (1995) noted that this conflict often led to job exit. They argued that women opted out of corporate jobs because they were unable to "reconcile the punishing schedule with family life" (p. 24).

Bruening and Dixon (2007), Dixon and Bruening (2007) and Dixon and Sagas (2007), have all looked at work-life balance issues in college athletics and retention of female coaches. Work-life conflict was found to be a contributing factor to women leaving the coaching profession. As women become mothers the demands of both professional and personal obligations lead to a decision to "opt out" of the profession. Contrastingly, research has found women coaches are no less committed to their careers than are men (Sweeney and Lough, 2005). For those who try to reconcile the two, the conflict may be felt most internally. Dixon and Bruening (2007) found family members tend to be more "forgiving" for work obligations, versus the opposite; creating family compromise and guilt for women coaches.

Research examining programs and policies that organizations provide to encourage or support work-life balance for their employees has been initiated to address the situation for both male and female employees who seek success in both realms (Dixon, et al. 2008). Still, the availability of policies alone does not ensure their use or their helpfulness toward work-life balance (Allen, 2001). While research suggests that such benefits as flexible scheduling and onsite childcare can reduce the stress associated with work-family conflict, in both corporate and university settings there is evidence that indicates such policies are not utilized (Allen, 2001; Clark, 2001; Hollenshead et al., 2005; Thompson, Beauvis, and Lyness, 1999; Williams, 2004). Similarly, research has shown that employees perceive the use of such policies as potentially harmful to their career advancement (Norton, 1994; Schneer and Reitman, 1990). Nonetheless, the best approach to remedy the problem of work life conflict is the initiation of programs and policies to support work life balance (Ferber and O'Farrell, 1991; Galensky, Bond and Friedman, 1993; Hollenshead, et al, 2005).

Clearly, the impact of the organizational culture is crucial to the viability of work life balance policies (Allen, 2001; Clark, 2001; Hollenshead et al., 2005; Williams, 2004). Due to the significant influence of both the availability of policies and the knowledge of such policies among direct supervisors in athletic departments, there is a need to assess the perceptions of athletic administrators. Because the SWA is female, while most ADs are male, both perspectives were considered beneficial to understanding work-life policies and cultures in athletics. Similarly, parental status may influence knowledge and /or use of related policies. Thus, parental status was included as a separate variable in the analysis. Lastly, the commonalities and differences inherent in the three competitive divisions of the NCAA provide a need for analysis of the issue to develop an understanding among all levels.

METHOD

Subjects

The population for the study consisted of athletic directors and senior woman administrators from the 1018 NCAA active Division I, II, and III schools during the 2005-2006 academic year. After deleting duplicate or non-entry data entries, the sample for the study consisted of 442 senior woman administrators (SWA) and 456 athletic directors (AD) for a respective response rate of 43% and 45%. Eight individuals in division II and 21 individuals in division III identified themselves as both the AD and SWA. The responses of these individuals were included in the AD data.

Instrument

The instrument utilized for the study was a partial replication of an instrument used in previous studies endorsed by the NCAA Division II Management Council and Division I and III Governance Staffs (Tiell, 2004).

The initial instrument used to research the perceptions of ADs and SWAs on the roles, tasks and career paths of the Senior Woman Administrator was modified with the addition of a series of questions adapted from the work-family conflict literature of Anderson, et al., (2002) and Allen (2001).

The content validity of the final instrument was determined by a panel of experts representative of all three divisions, both genders, and who were either employed in the field of athletic administration or who had published scholarly research on related subject matter (Ary et al., 1996). Revisions to the instrument were based on the recommendations of the expert panel consisting of academic professors, members of the NCAA headquarters staff, a DI conference administrator, a DI university president, athletic coaches, SWAs, and athletic directors.

Data Collection Procedure

Data collection procedures were identical despite occurring in two separate time periods approximately six months apart. Senior woman administrators and athletic directors from the 317 active NCAA Division I institutions were initially invited to complete the instrument followed by a separate data collection period involving the senior woman administrators and athletic directors from the 701 active NCAA Division II and III institutions. The deliberate lag in collecting data from the division II and III administrators was to create a significant time lapse between the current study and a previous study administered to the same population by one of the primary researchers. The two versions of the instrument administered over the six month period included identical sets of questions related to work-life interface.

The web-based survey was created using Perseus Survey Solutions XP Standard Edition software and was converted into an HTML electronic document. The NCAA was instrumental in supplying electronic mail addresses of the SWAs and ADs at a majority of the institutions; however, verification for personnel changes was made using the reference of institutional athletics department website directories.

The subjects were e-mailed the link for accessing the survey in addition to a brief explanation of the purpose of the study, a statement about the voluntary consent for participation, a confidentiality clause, a deadline for submission, and a statement regarding the support of NCAA President Myles Brand and endorsement from the NCAA Project Team on Life and Work Balance. Approximately two weeks after the initial electronic message was sent to a sample group, a reminder email was sent. In order for the survey to properly be submitted, the subject was required to check "yes" to a statement verifying their knowledge of the purpose of the research and their voluntary consent to participate. The statement also indicated that the subject had not waived any legal or human rights and that they could at any time contact the primary researcher or decline participation.

Data Analysis

Perseus Survey Solutions allowed for data to be easily transported into a database package then analyzed using SPSS. Frequencies and measures of central tendency were utilized to examine descriptive variables. An Analysis of Variance (ANOVA) was used as the statistical tool to describe the ordinal data indicating whether the subject groups generally agreed or disagreed with each statement describing the work-life climate of his or her department. Further post hoc (Scheffe's) tests of statistical significance were applied when the significance level was at .05 or less. Chi square analyses with an alpha level of .05 was used to determine whether sample groups agreed or disagreed on the perception of whether the institution offered workplace benefits to potentially address work-life conflict.

RESULTS

Demographic Characteristics

Athletic Directors: A majority of the 456 athletic directors in the sample were male (77.6%). Of the female ADs (22.1%) in the sample, the greatest percentage was reported in Division III (36.1%) followed by Division II (19.4%) and Division I (8.9%). A cumulative 90.5% of the ADs were White and 9.5% identified themselves as either Black, non-Hispanic; American Indian; Alaskan Native; Asian/Pacific Islander; Hispanic; or other. Seventy-seven percent of the AD sample was age 45 or over. Two individuals in Division II and one in Division III reported they were 29 years of age or younger. Most ADs (68%) reported their highest academic degree was at the Masters degree level. A Bachelors degree only was reported by 15.5% of ADs in Division I, 9.3% in Division II, and 7.8% in Division III. A majority of ADs (82%) reported having children and 45.3% reported having at least one dependent child residing at home. Twenty-five percent of the Division III sample did not have children, followed by 18.5% of Division II, and 10.1% of Division I.

Senior Women Administrators. There were 442 valid responses from SWAs. The respondents were female (99.1%), with the exception of one designated SWA in Division III who reported he was male. Eighty-nine percent of the respondents were White with Division III having the greatest percentage (95%) of white SWAs followed by Division II (89.8%) and Division I (82.9%). Compared to ADs, the SWAs were a much more diverse group in respect to age. Only 20.2% of SWAs were age 45 or older. SWAs between the ages of 30-39 were reported most frequently in Division II (42%), followed by Division III (36.8%), and Division I (only 25.7%). Eight individuals in Division I (4%), two in division II (1.9%), and one in Division III (.6%) were age 29 or younger. Most SWAs (70.7%) reported their highest academic degree was at the Masters level. Two SWAs in Division II (both females) reported having earned only a high school degree. Most likely this finding is representative of an administrative assistant being granted the SWA title, because she is the only female on the staff. Less than half of the SWAs (40.1%) reported having children and only 28.3% reported having at last one dependent child residing at home.

Benefits Available

Table 1 displays the reported availability of work-life benefits as indicated by both ADs and SWAs in all three divisions. Nearly all schools in Division I offered the majority of benefits. The opposite was true for division II and III where less than half of the institutional representatives reported the availability of work-life benefits. In comparing the responses of ADs and SWAs across all three divisions, there were no statistically significant differences in the responses of ADs and SWAs regarding any of the 17 benefit categories offered at the institution (p=0.00, p<.01). Table 1 shows that for all 17 categories, a greater percentage of the sample of ADs and SWAs in Division I reported the benefit was offered at his or her institution than in either of the other two divisions. In division I, the most frequently reported benefits available were Family Emergency Care Leave (AD = 89.9%, SWA = 94%), Tuition Reimbursement (AD = 83.9%, SWA = 88.9%), and Government Mandated Time off for dependent care (AD = 80.4%, SWA = 87.9%), In both division II and III, the most frequently reported benefits available were Phased or Partial

Retirement Plans (DII: AD = 37.0%, SWA = 50.0% / DIII: AD = 41.4%, SWA = 45.8%), and Programs for Family Problems - EAPs (DII: AD = 37.0%, SWA = 42.0% / DIII: AD = 41.1%, SWA = 45.8%). Paid paternity leave was regarded as the benefit with the greatest discrepancy between Division I and the other two divisions.

Table 1. Descriptive Results of ADs and SWAs for Availability of Work-Life Benefits

	D I		D II		D III	
	AD	SWA	AD	SWA	AD	SWA
Compensatory time off for required overtime	63.7%	62.8%	26.9%	30.7%	27.8%	23.9%
Flexible work time arrangements - job sharing	62.5%	54.3%	16.7%	14.8%	17.8%	24.5%
Compressed work week options	51.2%	47.7%	38.0%	39.8%	37.8%	33.5%
Tele-commuting options	50.0%	50.8%	15.7%	17.0%	22.2%	20.6%
Child care, resource finder / referral service	57.1%	50.3%	15.7%	12.5%	21.7%	19.4%
Family travel options for athletic events/activities	70.8%	66.8%	35.2%	37.5%	34.4%	38.7%
Wellness programs for employees	83.9%	75.9%	25.0%	30.7%	27.8%	29.7%
Family access to fitness and exercise opportunities	84.5%	76.4%	9.3%	14.8%	7.2%	9.0%
Referrals for resource provider for family-related problems	85.1%	78.4%	13.0%	13.6%	11.7%	9.0%
Programs for family problems (EAP)	79.8%	76.9%	37.0%	42.0%	40.0%	47.1%
Government mandated time off for dependent care	80.4%	87.9%	25.0%	29.5%	31.1%	29.7%
Paid paternity leave	82.1%	79,9%	4.6%	3.4%	10.0%	6.5%
Family Emergency care leave	89.9%	94.0%	11.1%	10.2%	7.5%	7.7%
Phased or partial retirement plans	81.0%	78.9%	37.0%	50.0%	41.1%	45.8%
Tuition reimbursement	83.9%	88.9%	25.0%	21.6%	31.1%	27.7%
Sabbaticals	47.0%	47.7%	3.7%	5.7%	4.4%	6.5%
Work-Life Task Force or Committee	56.0%	47.7%	13.0%	18.2%	19.4%	16.8%

In division I, the benefit was reported by 82.1% of ADs and 79.9% of SWAs, but was reported by only 4.6% and 10% of ADs in division II and III and by 3.4% and 6.5% of SWAs in division II and III. The second greatest discrepancy was reported for the benefit of Emergency Family Care Leave (AD: I = 89.9%, II = 11.1%, III = 7.5% / SWA: I = 94.0%, II = 10.2%, III =

7.7%). When combining the data from all three divisions and comparing the responses of administrators with children and administrators without children, a Chi square test reported statistically significant differences for all 17 work-life benefits (p < .05).

Work-Life Climate

Table 2. ANOVA Table for Work-Life Climate Statements based on Division

		Sum of Squares	df	Mean Square	F	Sig.
Family/Personal Needs Accommodated	Between Groups	6.633	2	3.316	3.914	.020
	Within Groups	758.366	895	.847		
	Total	764.999	897			
Employees Encouraged to strike life-work balance	Between Groups	34.514	2	17.257	15.150	.000
	Within Groups	1019.464	895	1.139		
	Total	1053.978	897			
Employees can easily balance work-life conflict	Between Groups	11.034	2	5.517	4.254	.014
	Within Groups	1160.721	895	1.297		
	Total	1171.755	897			
Work-life benefits are communicated to employees	Between Groups	38.151	2	19.075	15.679	.000
	Within Groups	1088.874	895	1.217		
	Total	1127.024	897			
Commitment to work-life balance publicized	Between Groups	30.956	2	15.478	14.342	.000
	Within Groups	965.908	895	1.079		
	Total	996.864	897			
There is interest in programs to reduce work-life conflict	Between Groups	7.674	2	3.837	3.704	.025
	Within Groups	927.183	895	1.036		
	Total	934.856	897			

Table 2 displays the ANOVA table for the six statements relating to the perceived climate of the athletic department based on divisions.

When analyzing the three divisions combined, there were no statistically significant differences reported between the sample of ADs and SWAs (p< 0.01) or between the sample of administrators with children and the administrators without children (p < 0.05) for any of the six statements referencing the perceived institutional and department climate for work-life balance.

In division I, there were no significant differences reported between the sample of ADs and SWAs (p<.01) for the six statements referencing the climate of the institution and department for work-life balance (p=0.00, P<0.01). In division II, a statistically significant difference was reported between the sample of ADs and SWAs (p=.920, p<0.05) on only one of the six statements, suggesting that the family and personal needs of employees are accommodated. In division III, a statistically significant difference was reported between the sample of ADs and SWAs for two of the six statements. The difference was reported for the statement that the family and personal needs of employees are accommodated (p=0.157, p<0.05) and the statement that employees can easily balance their personal/family life and work obligations (p=.839, p<0.05).

DISCUSSION AND IMPLICATIONS

A total of seventeen benefits were listed based on the previous research. Most noticeable was the high percentage of benefits available or offered according to both Division I administrators. The range for reported benefits available in Division I extended from a low of 47% to a high of 94% (see Table 1). In contrast, both DII and DIII administrators reported far fewer benefits available. The range in DII was between 3.4% and 50% while for DIII a low of 4.4% was reported along with a high of 47.1% for any single benefit. In essence, DI schools appear to provide the benefits that most effectively address work life balance. Given the budgets and high profile nature of these programs, this finding comes as no surprise. In contrast, DII and DIII either are not aware that many of the benefits are available at their institution, or they truly are not offered by their institution. In some cases, the lack of knowledge or awareness seems to be most likely, given the legal requirements all places of employment are held to.

ADs and SWAs provided similar responses, when examined by division. This was viewed as a positive in DI where both groups appear to have an established awareness of policies. However, agreement or similarity of responses in DII and DIII suggests reason for concern. If the administrators are unaware of benefits available at the institution, then the likelihood that coaches and other employees are aware or are encouraged to utilize the benefits that could in fact assist with work life balance appears limited. Additionally, some reports of fewer benefits offered may be reflective of the different environment DII and DIII athletic programs operate in. Many of these schools have far fewer or more restricted resources than those of many DI schools. Further concern is generated when the shared responsibility, or extended work load is considered in DII and DIII. When coaches and athletic administrators are required to fulfill multiple roles, there may be an even more pronounced need for work life balance policies. This result points to one of the key findings of our study, which is the evidence that DI athletic programs differ significantly from DII and DIII programs, and therefore merit research focusing specifically on DII and DIII issues and needs.

The rationale for an awareness of phased or partial retirement plans most likely is linked to the tenure of the administrators, and specifically the age of the Athletic Directors. The data supported the notion that knowledge of benefits was linked to the individual respondent's status. For example, the majority of ADs (77%) were over 45, when age categories were combined. Potentially, the closer the representative is to a career stage such as retirement, the more likely they are to have knowledge of that benefit. However, following the same line of thinking may be concerning for the next most offered benefit. Extended logic would indicate that knowledge of Employee Assistance Programs (EAP) was recognized due to the need for this benefit. Whether this need has arisen due to staff or personal needs, the fact that it stands out as one benefit these administrators are aware of, may also point to difficulty for those employees who are negotiating the work-life interface. Perhaps if the other benefits listed were available and utilized, the need for employee assistance programs would decrease. Finally, the discrepancy around paid paternity leave in DII and DIII indicates support for the social expectation of gender roles in which mothers are granted leave, yet new fathers are not always supported in this work environment.

When examining the perceived work life climate, six statements were utilized to measure agreement. No significant differences were found when the responses were analyzed based on parental status. Perhaps the explanation for this rests in the high percentage (82%) of ADs (men) who had children, and significant number (45%) of them who still had children living at home. Given this parental status, the male administrators may be more prone to creating a family friendly climate, which resembles a work-life balanced culture for all employees. Specifically at the DI level, there were no significant differences between responses by ADs and those from the SWAs on this item. The most interesting aspect of this lack of difference, rests in the fact that far fewer SWAs had children (40%) and even fewer had children living at home (28%). Yet previous researchers have suggested that women tend to be more aware and concerned with developing a family friendly climate (Bruening and Dixon, 2007). This statement appears to support the notion that even when women are not parents, they may still be as concerned with creating a family friendly climate as the men who actually are parents. Thus, the contribution that women make in regards to supporting work-life balance in an athletic environment should be recognized as positive.

CONCLUSION

A statistically significant difference between the perceptions of the athletic directors and senior woman administrators in division I, II and III programs regarding the existence of workplace benefits was not found. However, the congruence of responses between DII and DIII administrators reflected a shared lack of awareness or lack of policies. In contrast, the congruence among DI administrators reflected a shared knowledge and/or use of policies.

The potential influence that this awareness or lack of awareness has on the work-life conflict or climate at the institution merits further study. In reference to the difference between the perceptions of these high ranking administrators in division I, II, and III programs regarding the work-life climate within the athletic department, all reported a climate conducive to work-life balance. Division III administrators responded differently to two of the six measures, yet their overall impression remained that the climate was acceptable. Perhaps the next strategy to assess work life climate needs to delve qualitatively into the experiences of a variety of athletic department employees to compare their perceptions with the impressions of the administrators responsible for the perceived climate. Lastly, the difference in the perceptions of work-life climate among ADs and SWAs based upon parental / non-parental status remains an area that merits a deeper understanding.

The relationship between motherhood and work family conflict has been established, specifically for women coaches. However, fatherhood and work life conflict, or the direct influence of fathers as athletic administrators impacting the climate for other departmental employees requires additional inquiry. Similarly, the contribution that women make to a culture dominated by men warrants further study.

FUTURE RESEARCH

For future research examining work life balance in intercollegiate athletics, a focus on generational issues and/or values appears to be warranted. As younger generations fill the higher level positions, including coaches, a greater emphasis on work life balance is likely to be needed. Gen X, Gen Y and the millennial generation have all been described as unique from previous generations, with a greater interest in balancing their life with their work.

To prevent further decline of women in intercollegiate coaching and administration, the promotion of a work-life balanced climate or culture should be undertaken. When recruiting young coaches and administrators, this approach may allow one athletic program to secure a top talent, while a competitor struggles to understand how they failed to secure the employee. Increasingly this may be true for men as well as women, given that the generational attitudes are attributed to both genders. Future research is also needed that focuses specifically on issues confronting DII and DIII administrators.

To date, most studies that have included the lower divisions have done so as a comparison to DI. Given the philosophical differences and growing distinctions between the divisions, further study would be of value.

REFERENCES

Acosta, V. and Carpenter, L. (2008). *Women in intercollegiate sport. A longitudinal study – thirty year update – 1977-2008.* Unpublished Manuscript, Brooklyn College, Brooklyn, New York.

Allen, T. (2001). Family-supportive work environments: The role of organizational perceptions. *Journal of Vocational Behavior, 58,* 414–435.

American Council on Education. (2005). *An agenda for excellence: Creating flexibility in tenure track careers.* Washington DC: A.C.E. Office of Woman in Higher Education.

Anderson, D., Morgan, B., and Wilson, J. (2002). Perceptions of family-friendly policies: University versus corporate employees. *Journal of Family and Economic Issues*, 23, 73-92.

Ary, D., Jacobs, C. J., and Razavieh, A. (1996). Introduction to research in education (5th ed.). Fort Worth: Holt, Rinehart, and Winston.

Boles, J., Howard, W.G., Donofrio, H., (2001). An investigation into the inter-relationships of work-family conflict, family-work conflict, and work satisfaction. *Journal of Managerial Issues*, 13, 376-391.

Bruening, J. and Dixon, M. (2007). Work-family Conflict II: Managing Role Conflict. *Journal of Sport Management*, 21(4), 471-496.

Bruening, J., Dixon, M., and Pastore, D. (2005, February 2). Title IX moms: Gender, work and parenting in college athletics. Presentation at Bowling Green State University Symposium for Women and Sport: Before, During, and After Title IX.

Bruening, J., Dixon, M., Tiell, B., Osborne, B., Lough, N. and Sweeney, K. (2008). The role of the Supervisor in the Work-Life Culture of Collegiate Athletics. *International Journal of Sport Management, 9(3), 250-272.*

Clark, S.C. (2001). Work cultures and work/family balance. *Journal of Vocational Behavior*, 58, 348-365.

Claussen, C. and Lehr, C. (2002). Decision making authority of senior woman administrators. *International Journal of Sport Management*, 3, 215-228.

Dixon, M., and Bruening, J. (2005). Perspectives on work-family conflict: A review and integrative approach. *Sport Management Review*, 8, 227-254.

Dixon, M. and Bruening, J. (2007). Work-Family Conflict in Coaching I: A Top-Down Perspective. *Journal of Sport Management*, 21 (3), 377-406.

Dixon, M. and Sagas, M. (in press). The relationship between organizational support, work-family conflict, the culture of intercollegiate athletics and the job-life satisfaction of university coaches. *Research Quarterly for Exercise and Sport*.

Dixon, M., Tiell, B., Lough, N., Osborne, B., Sweeney, K. and Bruening, J. (in press). Exploration of Life and Work Interface in Intercollegiate Athletics: Perceptions of Division I Administrators Towards Policies, Programs, and Institutional Climate. *Journal for the Study of Sport and Athletes in Education*.

Drago, R.; Hennighausen, L; Rogers, J; Vescio, T. and Stauffer, K. (2005, August 19). Final Report for CAGE: The Coaching and Gender Equity Project.

Eby, L., Casper, W., Lockwood, A., Bordeaux, C. and Brinley, A. (2005). Work and family research in IO/OB: Content analysis and review of the literature (1980-2000). *Journal of Vocational Behavior,* 66, 124-197.

Galinsky, E. and Stein, P. (1990). The impact of human resource policies on employees. *Journal of Family Issues,* 11, 368-377.

Ferber M. and O'Farrell, B. (1991). Work and family: Policies for a changing work force. Washington, DC: National Academy Press.

Greenhaus, J.H. and Powell, G.N. (2003). When work and family collide: Deciding between competing role demands. *Organizational Behavior and Human Decision Processes*, 90, 291-303.

Guest, D. (2002). Human resource management, corporate performance, and employee well-being: Building the worker into HRM, *The Journal of Industrial Relations*, 44, 335-358.

Hollenshead, C. (2005). Work/family policies in higher education: Survey data and case studies of policy implementation. *New Directions for Higher Education*, 2005(130), 41-65.

Kaufman-Rosen, L., and Kalb, C. (1995, March 27). Holes in the glass ceiling theory. *Newsweek*, 24-25.

Kingston, P. (1990). Illusions and ignorance about the family responsible workplace. *Journal of Family Issues,* 11, 438-454.

Kossek, E.E., Colquitt, J.A., and Noe, R.A. (2001). Caregiving decisions, well being, and performance: The effects of place and provider as a function of dependent type and work-family climates. *Academy of Management Journal*, 44, 29-44.

Litan, R., Orszag, J., and Orszag, P. (2003, August). The empirical effects of collegiate athletics: An interim report. Sebago Associates.

Lough, N. and Grappendorf, H. (2007). Senior Woman Administrator's Perspectives on Professional Advancement. *International Journal of Sport Management*, 8(2), 193-209.

*NCAA. (2005). What's the difference between Divisions I, II and III? NCAA On-line Resource Center. Retrieved December 26, 2006 at http://www.ncaa.org/wps/portal/!ut/p/kcxml/04_Sj9SPykssy0xPLMnMz0 vM0Y_QjzKLN4j3CQXJgFjGpvqRqCKOcAFfj_zcVH1v_QD9gtzQiHJH RUUAc0tpTA!!/delta/base64xml/L3dJdyEvUUd3QndNQSEvNElVRS82 XzBfTFU!?CONTENT_URL=http://www.ncaa.org/about/div_criteria.ht ml

NCAA Bylaws (2006, July). Division II Manual 2006-2007: Constitution, Operating Bylaws, Administrative Bylaws. Published by NCAA Educational Services, Indianapolis, Indiana.

NCAA Digest. (2006, August 28). Life-work balance. Task force's first meeting focuses on recent research. NCAA News. Retrieved November 22, 2006 at http://www.ncaa.org/wps/portal/newsdetail?WCM_ GLOBAL_CONTEXT=/wps/wcm/connect/NCAA/NCAA+News/NCAA +News+Online/2006/News+Digest/NCAA+Digest+-+8-28- 06+NCAA+News.

Norton, S. (1994). Pregnancy, the family, and work: An historical review and update of legal regulations and organizational policies and practices in the United States. *Gender, Work and Organizations*, 1, 217-225.

Sagas, M., and Cunningham, G. (2005). Work-family conflict among college assistant coaches. *International Journal of Sport Management, 6*, 183-197.

Schneer, J.A. and Rutman, F. (1990). Effects of employment gaps on the careers of MBAs: More damaging for women than for men? *Academy of Management Journal*, 33, 391-406.

Shulman, J.L. and Bowen, W.G. (2001). The Game of Life: College Sports and Educational Values. Princeton University Press, Princeton, New Jersey.

Solomon, C.M. (1996). Flexibility comes out of flux. *Personnel Journal, 75*, 34-43.

Sweeney, K. and Lough, N. (2005, August). *Work-Life balance among college coaches of women's sport.* International Association of Physical Education and Sport for Girls and Women. Edmonton, Alberta, Canada.

Thomas, L.T., and Ganster, D.C. (1995). Impact of family-supportive work variables on work-family conflict and strain: A Control perspective. *Journal of Applied Psychology*, 80, 6-15.

Thompson, C., Beauvais, L.., and Lyness, K. (1999). When work–family benefits are not enough: The influence of work–family culture on benefit utilization, organizational attachment, and work–family conflict. *Journal of Vocational Behavior*, *54*, 392–415.

Tiell, B. (2006, January 7). Clarification of the designation of the senior woman administrator in intercollegiate athletics. Paper presented at the 2006 NCAA Convention. Indianapolis, Indiana.

Tiell, B., Dixon, M., Sweeney, K., Lough, N., Osborne, B., and Bruening, J. (2006). Progressive programs: Stopping the pull. *Athletic Management*, 18, 63-67.

Tiell, B. (2004). Roles, tasks, and career path of senior woman administrators in intercollegiate athletics. Unpublished dissertation.

Williams, J. (2004). Hitting the maternal wall. *Academe*, 90 (6), 16-20.

Advances in Sports and Athletics. Volume 1   ISBN: 978-1-61122-824-3
Editor: James P. Waldorf   ©2012 Nova Science Publishers, Inc.

THE IMPACT OF PLAYING POSITION ON PERCEPTIONS OF HORIZONTAL INTERPERSONAL POWER IN SPORT

Daniel L. Wann[*]
Murray State University, Kentucky, US

ABSTRACT

Interpersonal power involves the extent to which an individual has the ability to influence or change the attitudes and behaviors of others (Baron and Greenberg, 1990; Keys and Case, 1990). French and Raven (1959) suggested that there were five common forms of interpersonal power: reward, coercive, referent, legitimate, and expert. The current investigation examined the extent to which teammates possess differential levels of these five power bases. Based on the theoretical framework offered by Whetten and Cameron (1984), it was hypothesized that players occupying positions that were central, critical, flexible, visible, and relevant would be perceived as possessing greater levels of power than teammates playing positions that lacked these characteristics. To test this prediction, college intramural flag football players were asked to rate the power possessed by their team's best quarterback (a highly central, critical, flexible, visible, and relevant position) and best offensive lineman. The data indicated that the quarterbacks were viewed as

[*] This project was partially supported by a grant from the Murray State University Committee on Institutional Studies and Research (#2-12886). Portions of this paper were presented at the meeting of the Association for the Advancement of Applied Sport Psychology, Orlando, FL, October, 2001. The author thanks Al R. Rochelle for his assistance with the data collection. Address correspondence to Daniel L. Wann, Department of Psychology, Box 9, Murray State University, Murray, KY 42071 or to dan.wann@murraystate.edu via Internet (fax #270-809-2991).

possessing greater amounts of reward, expert, and legitimate power. Quarterbacks and offensive linemen were not perceived as possessing differential levels of coercive and referent power.

Keywords: power, centrality, leadership, athlete leadership.

Interpersonal power involves the extent to which an individual has the ability to influence or change the attitudes and behaviors of others (Baron and Greenberg, 1990; Keys and Case, 1990). Although research on interpersonal power is quite common in some areas of psychology (e.g., industrial and organizational, educational), sport psychologists have tended to neglect the important implications of power for sport organizations. Indeed, only a handful of sport scientists have written on this topic (e.g., Knoppers, Meyer, Ewing, and Forrest, 1990; Slack, 1997; Wann, 1997). This research and theoretical void is unfortunate because many persons in sport possess interpersonal power themselves and/or are influenced by the power of others. Such persons include coaches, players, owners, athletic directors, and even spectators.

In an attempt to initiate empirical research on interpersonal power in sport, Wann, Metcalf, Brewer, and Whiteside (2000) recently developed the Power in Sport Questionnaire (PQS). Based on the widely validated theoretical model of organization power presented by French and Raven (1959; see Podsakoff and Schriesheim, 1985), the PSQ was designed to assess five forms of interpersonal power: reward, coercive, referent, legitimate, and expert. Reward power involves the ability to change another individual's attitude or behavior because one controls access to desired rewards. Coercive power concerns the ability to change another individual's attitude or behavior because one controls access to one or more punishments. Referent power is the ability to change another person's attitude or behavior because one is liked and respected by the group members. Legitimate power involves the ability to change another individual's attitude or behavior because of one's position within the organization or group. And finally, expert power concerns the ability to change another individual's attitude or behavior because one is believed to be knowledgeable, skillful, or talented in a specific domain.

Wann and his colleagues validated two forms of the PSQ, the PSQ-O (i.e., other), which concerns an individual's perceptions of the power possessed by others, and the PSQ-S (i.e., self), which involves beliefs about one's own sources of power. Examinations of the reliability and validity of the PSQ were conducted on intercollegiate varsity and intramural coaches, athletes, and officials. This work supported the strong psychometric qualities of both versions of the PSQ. Thus, Wann et al. were able to draw several conclusions with respect to the influence of interpersonal power on sport participants. For instance, officials were viewed as having significantly lower levels of referent power than coaches, while head coaches were perceived of as having greater amounts of total power than assistant coaches. Further, intramural officials were viewed as having lower levels of power than varsity officials, with the exception of referent power for which the pattern was reversed.

The Wann et al. (2000) research laid important groundwork for both understanding and accurately assessing perceptions of interpersonal power in sport systems. However, Wann et al. limited their research to *vertical power*, that is, interpersonal power in which individuals occupy different levels in the organization's hierarchy (e.g., perceptions players have of the power of coaches and officials). A second and often equally important form of interpersonal power involves *horizontal power* (Whetten and Cameron, 1984; Yukl, 1994). Horizontal power concerns the influence of power among persons on the same hierarchical plane within an organization. Although previous research had examined factors leading to player leadership (e.g., Grusky, 1963; Kozub and Pease, 1991; Tropp and Landers, 1979), research on the horizontal power possessed by teammates had yet to be undertaken. In sport settings, horizontal power is most evident in the relationships among teammates. With respect to the sources of power described by French and Raven, teammates may possess horizontal power to the extent that they can influence the attitudes and behaviors of other players because they are viewed as an expert, possess access to certain rewards, and the like. The current investigation was designed to extend the Wann et al. research on vertical power in sport by investigating perceptions of horizontal power among teammates.

The theoretical model proposed by Whetten and Cameron (1984) was used to guide the predictions developed for the current study. Drawing on research in industrial/organizational psychology, Whetten and Cameron theorized that five characteristics of positions within an organizational system lead to increases in power among those occupying the positions. The five characteristics are centrality, criticality, flexibility, visibility, and relevance. Positions that are central within an organization or group are expected to possess more power than peripheral positions because persons occupying central positions have greater access to important information (Boje and Whetten, 1981; Hinings, Hickson, Pennings, and Schneck, 1974). Individuals in central positions can use this information to influence others in the system.

Research on athletes confirms the importance of central positions in the development of leadership (Glenn and Horn, 1993; Grusky, 1963; Kozub and Pease, 1991; Loy, Curtis, and Sage, 1979; Melnick and Loy, 1996).

Similar to centrality, critically concerns the extent to which positions within the organization or group are responsible for the most critical tasks. According to Whetten and Cameron, a position is critical to the extent that its function is "unique" and because of "its location in the work flow" (p. 251). Thus, individuals occupying positions that a) are not redundant with other positions and b) control the flow of work (i.e., assignments) have the potential to greatly influence others. The importance of criticality has also been demonstrated in sport settings. For instance, in their work with field hockey teams, Tropp and Landers (1979) found that the independent tasks executed by goalies (e.g., blocking shots, clearing) led to the high level of leadership ascribed to these players (see also Chelladurai and Carron, 1977; Loy et al., 1979).

The third characteristic in Whetten and Cameron's (1984) theoretical model, flexibility, involves an individual's ability "to improvise, to innovate, to demonstrate initiative" (p. 254). Flexibility is most often associated with positions that involve variety and novelty, as well as the use of one's own judgement (Hickson, Hinings, Lee, Schneck, and Pennings, 1971). Persons will have the potential for greater power when they occupy positions that often allow them to make decisions without first gaining the approval of others. Such latitude and authority allow these individuals to exert considerable horizontal influence over their co-workers and associates.

Visibility is the fourth important position characteristic described by Whetten and Cameron (1984). The relationship between visibility and horizontal power is relatively straightforward. Simply put, persons occupying positions that render their task performance more visible (i.e., their actions are viewed by larger numbers of individuals) will have the potential for greater levels of power than those occupying positions in which their efforts are "unseen" by others in the organization (Korda, 1975; Mechanic, 1962). In sport settings, Chelladurai and Carron's (1977) model of player leadership suggests that visibility (i.e., propinquity) will be an important determinant of leadership potential (see also Lee, Coburn, and Partridge, 1983).

The fifth and final position characteristic, relevance, concerns the extent to which persons occupy positions that "are generally associated with activities that are directly related to central objectives and issues" (Whetten and Cameron, 1984, p. 258; see also Perrow, 1970; Salancik and Pfeffer, 1977). Positions within an organizational hierarchy that most impact the organization's goals will be perceived as most relevant (Hellriegel, Slocom, and Woodman, 1992). Consequently, persons occupying such positions will likely have greater levels of horizontal power than individuals in positions that are perceived as less relevant.

Thus, according to Whetten and Cameron's (1984) theoretical framework, persons occupying positions that are central, critical, flexible, visible, and relevant should have greater amounts of horizontal power than associates in positions that are peripheral, redundant, routine, unseen, and irrelevant. As noted, this conceptualization was used to guide predictions of horizontal power in sport teams. It was hypothesized that persons occupying central, critical, flexible, visible, and relevant positions on a sport team would be perceived by teammates as being more powerful than players occupying positions that lacked these qualities. This prediction was tested using collegiate intramural flag football teams. It was expected that players would perceive their team's best quarterback as possessing greater amounts of power than their team's best offensive lineman. This prediction is consistent with Whetten and Cameron's theory because, relative to offensive linemen, the position of quarterback is more central and critical (information typically flows through the quarterback, e.g., plays are sent in to the quarterback who then relays this information and the corresponding work assignment to teammates). Further, the position of quarterback is more flexible. For instance, quarterbacks typically have the authority to change the play at the line of scrimmage and are able to be innovative during a play (e.g., scrambling). In addition, because research indicates that individuals tend to focus on the player in possession of the ball (Steele and Wann, 1999; Wann, Brewer, and Carlson, 1998; Wann, and Steele, 1998), offensive linemen should be less visible than quarterbacks. And finally, quarterbacks may be more relevant than offensive lineman. Although, each position in football is vital to the success of a team, quarterbacks may be especially important because they handle the ball on almost every offensive play and a poor performance by these persons seriously damages the team's chances for success. Anecdotally, it is often believed by coaches that it is extremely difficult to win without a quality quarterback, a perception that also suggests the heightened relevance of this position.

Two additional points warrant mention about the positions selected for study. First, perceptions of the team's *best* quarterback and offensive lineman were examined so as not to confound the relative talent required to play each position. In addition, this eliminated the possibility that some participants may have targeted their team's best quarterback but worst offensive lineman and vice versa. Second, both quarterbacks and offensive linemen play on offense, thus eliminating the potential confound that could result from comparing offensive and defensive positions.

Because the position of quarterback is more central, critical, flexible, visible, and relevant than the position of offensive lineman, a team's best quarterback was expected to be viewed as possessing greater amounts of power than the team's best offensive lineman. However, the aforementioned research by Wann et al. (2000) indicates that there is often an interaction between sport target and the various forms of interpersonal power. It was believed that a similar interaction would occur here. It was hypothesized that, although quarterbacks would be viewed as possessing greater amounts of power than offensive linemen, this finding would be limited to certain forms of interpersonal power. Specifically, quarterbacks would be viewed as possessing greater amounts of legitimate and expert power but that players occupying the two positions would be viewed as possessing equal amounts of referent power.

With respect to legitimate power, one's position of authority within an organizational system is a strong determinant of this power base. Because flexibility is predicted to lead to increased perceptions of authority (Whetten and Cameron, 1984), it was expected that quarterbacks (a highly flexible position) would have greater legitimate power potential. As for expert power, the position of quarterback is high in criticality. Consequently, those occupying this position should be viewed as an expert, both because they are playing a highly specialized position (e.g., it is not redundant with other positions as there is only one player in this position on the field at a time), and because they possess special talents that let them control the flow of work assignments. Quarterbacks and offensive linemen were not expected to possess differential levels of referent power because research indicates that possession of a leadership position in sport does not guarantee increased perceptions of referent power. For instance, Wann et al. (2000) found that although players report that their head coaches possess greater amounts of coercive, legitimate, and expert power than assistant coaches, the two levels of coaches were not viewed as possessing differential levels of referent power.

In summary, persons occupying the position of quarterback were expected to possess greater amounts of legitimate and expert power than those playing offensive lineman. Perceptions of the referent power of persons in the two positions were not expected to differ. Predictions about perceptions of the reward and coercive power of the players were less obvious. Neither theory (e.g., French and Raven, 1959; Whetten and Cameron, 1984) nor research (e.g., Wann et al., 2000) led to suggestions with respect to the relationship between player position and perceptions of reward and coercive power. Consequently, potential differences with respect to these forms of power were investigated with the framework of a research question and no hypotheses were tested.

METHOD

Participants

Participants were 99 college students participating on one of 12 different intramural flag football teams. The respondents received $5.00 in exchange for their participation. Twenty-three of the subjects were removed from the sample for various reasons (see below), resulting in a final sample of 76 persons (35 males, 41 females). The participants had a mean age of 20.03 years (SD = 1.81, range = 18 to 27). They reported playing flag football for an average of 2.17 years (SD = 1.68, range = 0 to 10) and for their current team for an average of 1.51 years (SD = 0.84, range = 0 to 4). Their class standings were: 18 percent freshmen, 41 percent sophomore, 16 junior, 24 percent senior, and 1 percent graduate.

Procedure and Materials

Intramural flag football coaches were contacted prior to a scheduled contest involving their team. The coaches were told that a researcher in the Department of Psychology was conducting research on athletes' perceptions of their teammates. The coaches were further informed that, prior to their team's next game, a research assistant would be stationed at the flag football field. The coaches were informed that all participants who completed the 15-minute survey would receive $5.00. Coaches were asked to relay this information to their players. At the field, the research assistant was located under a pavilion with a large sign reading "Psychology Study on Perceptions of Teammates -- Earn $5.00 for Your Participation". When players arrived at the pavilion, they were handed a clipboard containing a questionnaire packet and a pencil. The players were instructed to have a seat under the pavilion to complete the packet.

The questionnaire packet contained four sections. The first section contained general demographic items assessing age, gender, and year in school. The second section contained items assessing the participant's experience with flag football and his or her team. The first two items in this section asked subjects to indicate the number of years that they had played flag football in general and, specifically, with their current team. Next, the respondents indicated how much they expected to play "this season" by circling one of the following responses "I expect to play only about 1 of the team's games," "I expect to play about half of the team's games," "I expect to play most of the team's games," or "I expect to play all of the team's games." The players then indicated if they were usually a starter or substitute on offense and a starter or substitute on defense. They then reported the offensive and defensive positions they expected to play most frequently. Finally, they were to indicate if they were the coach for their flag football team.

The third and fourth sections of the packet contained two versions of the Power in Sport Questionnaire - Other (PSQ-O; Wann et al., 2000). As noted earlier, the 15-item PSQ-O is a reliable and valid instrument for assessing perceptions of the power possessed by others. Five sources of power are included in the PSQ-O: reward, coercion, referent, legitimate, and expert. Each of the five subscales contains three Likert-scale items. Response options to each item range from 1 (*this is very untrue*) to 9 (*this is very true*). Thus, higher numbers on the PSQ-O indicate beliefs that the target person possesses greater levels of power. In the first version of the PSQ-O, the respondents were asked to name their team's best quarterback and to indicate if this person was the head coach for the team. Subjects then completed the PSQ-O for the individual they perceived to be the team's best quarterback. The second version asked subjects to repeat the process for the individual they believed to be their team's best offensive lineman. Subjects read that if they believed they were their team's best quarterback or offensive lineman, they were to leave the items on the corresponding PSQ-O blank.

After completing the questionnaire packet (approximately 15 minutes), the participants were asked to return the clipboard, questionnaire packet, and pencil. They then signed a receipt and were given $5.00. They were then handed a debriefing statement explaining the hypotheses of the research. The statement also contained contact information if they wished to receive a copy of the final research report. The participants were then excused from the testing session.

RESULTS

As noted above, 23 of the original 99 participants had to be removed from the sample. Four of the questionnaire packets were incomplete. Nine of the participants reported that they were their team's best quarterback while four individuals indicated that they were their team's best offensive lineman. Consequently, these 13 participants were not included in the analysis (for these persons perceptions of the best quarterback or offensive lineman would have been self-perceptions, not perceptions of the power held by a teammate). One person believed that her team's best quarterback and best offensive lineman was the same individual. This person was not included in the analyses because it would not have been possible to compare perceptions of the team's best quarterback and offensive lineman. Finally, four subjects listed a best quarterback who was also the team's head coach while one participant's best offensive lineman was also the coach. Because the position (i.e., quarterback or offensive lineman) was confounded with coaching status for these five targets, these subjects were also removed from the sample. The result was a final sample of 76 persons who had complete packets, did not view themselves as either their team's best quarterback or offensive lineman, felt that their team's best quarterback and offensive lineman were separate individuals, and did not list a team's head coach as its best quarterback or offensive lineman. Cronbach's reliability analyses of the final sample indicated that the PSQ-O subscales and total scale were reliable (subscale alphas ranged from .62 to .86; total scale alphas = .87 and .89 for perceptions of the power of the best quarterback and offensive lineman, respectively).

Relationship between Perceptions of Power and Subject Variables

To insure that PSQ-O scores were not confounded by the participants' gender, level of involvement with the team (i.e., amount they expected to play), starting/substituting status, primary offensive and defensive position, or involvement as a coach, correlations or ANOVAs were computed involving these subject variables and PSQ-O subscale and total scale scores. Because of the large number of correlations computed (i.e., 12 per subject variable), the alpha level was set at a more conservative .01. With respect to gender, no significant relationships emerged involving this variable and the PSQ-O subscales and total scales (rs ranged from -.26 to .17). Indeed, 75 percent of the coefficients ranged from -.15 to .15. Thus, consistent with past research (Wann et al., 2000), gender was not related to perceptions of power in sport and, consequently, subsequent analyses were conducted across this variable.

With respect to involvement level, 1 percent of the sample expected to play only about 1 game, 7 percent expected to play about half the games, 24 percent expected to play most of the games, and 68 percent expected to play all of the games. A correlation analysis failed to reveal any significant relations between playing expectations and PSQ-O scores (rs ranged from -.16 to .18, 83 percent ranged from -.15 to .15). Thus, future analyses were conducted across this variable.

As for starting/substituting status, 63 percent of the participants expected to start on offense (37 percent expected to substitute) and 58 percent expected to start of defense (42 percent expected to substitute). Correlational analyses with PSQ-O scores failed to yield significant relationships for both offensive starting status (rs ranged from -.18 to .13, 83 percent ranged from -.15 to .15) and defensive starting status (rs ranged from -.07 to .22, 83 percent ranged from -.15 to .15).

With respect to the subjects' primary playing positions, on offense, 47 percent of the participants listed wide receiver, 33 percent listed offensive lineman, 4 percent quarterback, and 15 percent running back (1 percent did not list an offensive position). On defense, 14 percent listed linebacker, 43 percent defensive back, and 40 percent defensive lineman (3 percent failed to list a defensive position). The relationships between playing position and perceptions of power were analyzed using a pair of within-subjects ANOVAs. The 2 (Target: best quarterback and best offensive lineman) x 5 (PSQ-O Subscale) by 4 (Primary Offensive Position: wide receiver, offensive lineman, quarterback, or running back) offensive position ANOVA failed to indicate any significant main or interaction effects involving offensive playing position. Similarly, the 2 (Target) x 5 (PSQ-O Subscale) x 3 (Primary Defensive Position: linebacker, defensive back, or defensive lineman) defensive position ANOVA failed to indicate any significant main or interaction effects involving defensive playing position. Consequently, all subsequent analyses were conducted across this variable.

Finally, the impact of the participants' involvement as their team's coach was examined by correlating responses to this item with the PSQ-O scores. Eight percent of the sample indicated that they were their team's coach (92 percent were not their team's coach). Correlational analyses failed to indicate any significant relationships between coaching status and perceptions of power (rs ranged from -.13 to .09). Therefore, all analyses were conducted across coaching status.

Perceptions of Power as a Function of Playing Position

The hypothesis that persons occupying a central, critical, flexible, visible, and relevant position on a sport team would be perceived by teammates as possessing greater amounts of power than persons occupying a position lacking these characteristics was tested through a 2 (Target: best quarterback and best offensive lineman) x 5 (PSQ-O Subscale) within-subjects ANOVA. Means and standard deviations for this analysis appear in Table 1. The analysis yielded a significant main effect for target, $F(1, 75) = 19.61, p < .001$. As expected, the team's best quarterback was perceived of as possessing greater amounts of power than the team's best offensive lineman. The PSQ-O subscale main effect was also significant, $F(4, 300) = 65.51, p < .001$, indicating that the targets were viewed as possessing differential levels of the five forms of power. The main effects were qualified by a significant two-way interaction, $F(4, 300) = 7.10, p < .001$. As revealed in Table 1, consistent with expectations, the team's best quarterback was viewed as possessing greater levels of legitimate and expert power than the team's best offensive lineman while persons occupying the two position types were not perceived as possessing differential levels of referent power. Quarterbacks were also viewed as possessing greater levels of reward power. Quarterbacks and offensive linemen were not viewed as possessing differential levels of coercive power.

Table 1. Means and Standard Deviations for Perceptions of Power for the Team's Best Quarterback and Offensive Lineman

	Quarterback		Offensive Lineman	
Power	M	SD	M	SD
Reward*	16.30	6.83	13.86	7.13
Coercive	10.61	6.56	9.80	6.60
Referent	19.29	5.65	19.18	6.41
Legitimate*	17.42	5.97	13.20	6.61
Expert*	19.91	5.49	17.45	7.25
Total power	83.68	23.32	73.49	26.06

DISCUSSION

The results presented above extend past research on player leadership in sport (e.g., Chelladurai and Carron, 1977; Grusky, 1963; Kozub and Pease, 1991; Tropp and Landers, 1979) by providing strong support for the hypothesized pattern of effects. The data also indicate that Whetten and Cameron's (1984) theoretical model of horizontal power is a useful framework for understanding player-to-player influence on sport teams. As expected, players occupying central, critical, flexible, visible, and relevant positions were viewed as possessing greater levels of power than players not occupying such a position. However, also as expected, the power attributed to these persons was limited to specific forms of power, namely, expert and legitimate. Also as predicted, players occupying the two position types were not viewed as possessing differential levels of referent power.

The data also revealed that persons occupying the "key" position were viewed as possessing greater amounts of reward power than persons playing a less key position. This finding suggests that individuals view persons in key positions as having more direct access to and control of desired rewards. This does seem logical, particularly if one considers the sport targeted in the current investigation (North American football). Because a quarterback tends to function as a team's on-field decision maker (they are often referred to as "field generals"), other players may perceive of the quarterback as possessing . the ability to make decisions that are favorable to them. For instance, a wide receiver may view the quarterback as a powerful figure because he/she could throw often to the receiver. Because the quarterback controls access to this desired reward (i.e., play selection and pass execution), he or she is able to change the attitude and/or behavior of the receiver.

With respect to coercion, no differences in perceptions of this form of power were found between central, critical, flexible, visible, and relevant positions and positions lacking these qualities. At first glance, this finding may seem puzzling, particularly in light of the fact that persons occupying key positions were perceived of as possessing greater levels of reward power. For instance, to return to the example above, one may be tempted to argue that the receiver should also be concerned that the quarterback will not throw to him or her. Consequently, he or she will view the quarterback as an individual possessing large amounts of referent power. However, such logic is invalid and reflects the common confusion between punishments (i.e., coercion) and response cost (see Wann, 1997, for an in-depth discussion of the sport implications of these two strategies for changing behavior). Coercion and punishment involve the application of a negative stimulus to decrease unwanted behavior. An obvious sport example would be a football coach requiring her receivers to run laps each time they dropped a pass. Conversely, response cost involves the removal or withholding of a positive stimulus to decrease behavior. Thus, response cost, rather than punishment or coercion, is being employed when a quarterback refuses to throw to a particular receiver or call a play for a specific player. Rather than applying a negative stimulus, the quarterback is withholding a positive consequence. In all likelihood, punishment and coercion are only initiated by the head coach of a team. Other members of the coaching staff and even prominent players such as team captains are more likely to utilize response cost as a method of reducing unwanted behaviors. The work by Wann and his colleagues (2000) substantiates this line of reasoning as they found that head coaches were perceived as possessing significantly greater amounts of coercive power than assistant coaches.

There are a number of important implications to the findings detailed above, for both coaches and sport psychologists alike. With respect to coaches, it would be in a coach's best interest to locate players who are viewed by teammates as most powerful. Most likely, these will be the players who are able to most effectively exert influence on other players, including the desires of the coaches. Coaches are often better able to encourage compliance with team rules and regulations when powerful players exert force toward the same end. Players would seemingly be less likely to challenge a coach's directives if powerful players push for the same directives. Thus, coaches are wise to get key players to adopt their position and help in influencing the remainder of the team (in fact, this is often viewed as one of the responsibilities of a team captain). The data presented above, coupled with the theoretical framework offered by Whetten and Cameron (1984), provide coaches with valuable information on whom these powerful players will be. That is, coaches should look to align themselves with players occupying central, critical, flexible, visible, and relevant positions. Alliances between coaches and players occupying powerful positions may be particularly valuable during certain times. For instance, the initial days of training camp are an important time in teaching team norms to new players. A unified front involving powerful players and coaches would be highly effective in facilitating the socialization process for new players. Similarly, coaches could use the support of powerful players during crises, such as during a long losing streak or when there is desention among teammates.

With respect to sport psychologists, these applied professionals could also benefit from aligning themselves with powerful players. One of the most difficult tasks facing performance enhancement professionals is getting all players on a team to commit to a psychological skills program. In many instances, although some teammates readily endorse such programs, other players are quite hesitant and skeptical.

By gaining the endorsement of key players, that is, those players viewed as powerful, the sport psychologist may get a larger proportion of the team to accept the program. Again, the current study and the model it tested offers concrete and (now) empirically supported predictions of who these players will be.

Finally, because this was the first sport-specific test of Whetten and Cameron's (1984) model, additional research is warranted. Such research should focus on different sports and positions within those sports (e.g., pitchers in baseball and point guards in basketball) and with other levels of competition (e.g., scholastic, recreational, professional/elite). Another important step in this research would involve testing the self-perceptions of players occupying the key positions. Wann et al. (2000) found a great deal of similarity between self-perceptions of power and how one is viewed by others. For instance, head coaches felt that they possessed high levels of legitimate power and players did in fact view these individuals as possessing high levels of this form of power. Based on Wann's findings, one would expect that players occupying central, critical, flexible, visible, and relevant positions to view themselves as possessing greater amounts of power (particularly expert, legitimate, and, perhaps, reward power) than persons playing other positions.

REFERENCES

Baron, R. A., and Greenberg, J. (1990). *Behavior in organizations: Understanding and managing the human side of work* (3rd ed.). Needham Heights, MA: Allyn and Bacon.

Boje, D. M., and Whetten, D. A. (1981). Effects of organizational strategies and contextual constraints on centrality and attributions of influence in interorganizational networks. *Administrative Science Quarterly, 26,* 378-395.

Celladurai, P., and Carron, A. V. (1977). A reanalysis of formal structure in sport. *Canadian Journal of Applied Sport Sciences, 2,* 9-14.

French, J. R. P., and Raven, B. (1959). The bases of social power. In D. Cartwright (Ed.), *Studies in social power* (pp. 150-167). Ann Arbor, MI: Institute for Social Research.

Glenn, S. D., and Horn, T. S. (1993). Psychological and personal predictors of leadership behavior in female soccer athletes. *Journal of Applied Sport Psychology, 5,* 17-34.

Grusky, O. (1963). The effects of formal structure on managerial recruitment: A study of baseball organization. *Sociometry, 26,* 345-353.

Hellriegel, D., Slocum, J. W. Jr., and Woodman, R. W. (1992). *Organizational behavior* (6th ed.). West: New York.

Hickson, D. J., Hinings, C. R., Lee, C. A., Schneck, R. E., and Pennings, J. M. (1971). Strategic contingencies theory of intraorganizational power. *Administrative Science Quarterly, 16,* 216-229.

Hinings, C. R., Hickson, D. J., Pennings, J. M., and Schneck, R. E. (1974). Structural conditions of intraorganizational power. *Administrative Science Quarterly, 21,* 22-44.

Keys, B., and Case, T. (1990). How to become an influential manager. *Academy of Management Executive, 4,* 38-51.

Knoppers, A., Meyer, B. B., Ewing, M., and Forrest, L. (1990). Dimensions of power: A question of sport or gender? *Sociology of Sport Journal, 7,* 369-377.

Korda, M. (1975). *Power: How to get it, how to use it.* New York: Ballantine.

Kozub, S. A., and Pease, D. G. (2001). Coach and player leadership in high school basketball. *Journal of Sport Pedagogy, 7,* 1-15.

Lee, M. J., Partridge, R., and Coburn, T. (1983). The influence of team structure in determining leadership function in Association Football. *Journal of Sport Behavior, 4,* 170-183.

Loy, J. W., Curtis, J. E., and Sage, J. N. (1979). Relative centrality of playing position and leadership recruitment in team sports. In R. S. Hutton (Ed.), *Exercise and sport science reviews* (Vol. 6). Santa Barbara: Journal Publishing Affiliates.

Mechanic, D. (1962). Sources of power of lower participants in complex organizations. *Administrative Science Quarterly, 7,* 349-364.

Melnick, M. J., and Loy, J. W. (1996). The effects of formal structure on leadership recruitment: An analysis of team captaincy among New Zealand Provincial rugby teams. *International Review of the Sociology of Sport, 31,* 91-105.

Perrow, C. (1970). Departmental power and perspectives in industrial firms. In
    M. N. Zold (Ed.), *Power in organizations*. Nashville: Vanderbilt
    University Press.

Podsakoff, P. M., and Schriesheim, C. A. (1985). Field studies of French and
    Raven's bases of power: Critique, reanalysis, and suggestions for future
    research. *Psychological Bulletin, 97,* 387-411.

Salancik, G. R., and Pfeffer, J. (1977). Who gets power—and how they hold
    on to it: A strategic-contingency model of power. *Organizational
    Dynamics, 5,* 3-21.

Slack, T. (1997). *Understanding sport organizations: The application of
    organization theory.* Champaign, IL: Human Kinetics.

Steele, N. L., and Wann, D. L. (1999). Type of play, temporal position,
    salience, and attentional focus of sport spectators. *Psi Chi Journal of
    Undergraduate Research, 4,* 113-118.

Stodgill, R. M. (1963). *Manual for the Leader Behavior Description
    Questionnaire--Form XII.* Columbus, OH: Ohio State University Bureau
    of Business Research.

Tropp, K. J., and Landers, D. M. (1979). Team interaction and the emergence
    of leadership and interpersonal attraction in field hockey. *Journal of Sport
    Psychology, 1,* 228-240.

Wann, D. L. (1997). *Sport psychology.* Upper Saddle River, NJ: Prentice Hall.

Wann, D. L., Brewer, K. R., and Carlson, J. D. (1998). Focus of attention and
    sport spectators: Beliefs about caUStion. *Perceptual and Motor Skills, 87,*
    35-41.

Wann, D. L., Metcalf, L. A., Brewer, K. R., and Whiteside, H. D. (2000).
    Development of the Power in Sport Questionnaire. *Journal of Sport
    Behavior, 4,* 423-443.

Wann, D. L., and Steele, N. L. (1998). Attentional focus of sport spectators.
    Perceptual and Motor Skills, 86, 1163-1167.

Whetten, D. A., and Cameron, K. S. (1984). *Developing managerial skills.*
    Glenview, IL: Scott Foresman.

Yukl, G. (1994). *Leadership in organizations* (3rd ed.). Upper Saddle River,
    NJ: Prentice Hall.

INDEX

T

U

V

W